Undone, Unafraid

Evolving Through Trauma, Betrayal, Femininity & Faith

Becky Moller

Undone, Unafraid

Copyright © 2025 by Becky Moller

Inspired Legacy Publishing is a division of (DBA) Inspired Legacy, LIC
PO Box 900816
Sandy UT 84090-0816.

This book is not intended as a substitute for the medical advice of physicians. The reader should regularly consult a physician in matters relating to his/her health and particularly with respect to any symptoms that may require diagnosis or medical attention.

The excerpt from Alcoholics Anonymous is reprinted with permission of Alcoholics Anonymous World Services, Inc. ("A.A.W.S."). Permission to reprint this excerpt does not mean that A.A.W.S. has reviewed or approved the contents of this publication, or that A.A.W.S. necessarily agrees with the views expressed herein. A.A. is a program of recovery from alcoholism only – use of this excerpt in connection with programs and activities which are patterned after A.A., but which address other problems, or in any other non-A.A. context, does not imply otherwise.

This book is a memoir based on true events from the author's life. While every effort has been made to accurately recount experiences, some names and identifying details have been changed to protect the privacy of individuals.

Paperback: 979-8-9935147-0-3
Hardcover: 979-8-9935147-1-0

Printed in the United States of America.

What People Are Saying

"If you have ever felt betrayed, you know the deep prison of darkness, shame, rage, and hurt that it evokes. In this raw and beautifully written memoir, Becky Moller offers a pathway out of this darkness, one that brings healing to our hearts and reclaims the luminosity of our spirit."
—**Tara Brach,** Ph.D., spiritual teacher, psychologist and author of *Radical Compassion* and *Radical Acceptance*

"This memoir is a beautiful blend of emotion, authenticity, and encouragement, which will be a mirror both welcome and uncomfortable; a portal to growth, serving as an un-earthing of previously unexamined shadow, while also filled with beautiful, emotionally moving encouragements to continue on and find the magic in it all. Chills filled me every inch for countless portions of my reading."
—**Alaina Jo,** LCSW, www.resolutiontherapyutah.com

"Becky shares her shock, pain, confusion, and traumatic experiences following discovery of sexual betrayal in her marriage in an honest way that mirrors the experiences of those who are betrayed in their primary relationships… If you've been betrayed, you will see yourself in Becky's story. And you'll be encouraged."
—**Barbara Steffens,** PhD., Board Certified Coach, Founding president of APSATS (Association for Partners of Sex Addicts Trauma Specialists), Board member emeritus, Co-Author of *Your Sexually Addicted Spouse: How Partners Can Cope and Heal* (Steffens & Means, 2009; 2021)

"Becky's book is a guide for anyone who is navigating trauma in their lives. Her story provides a template for confronting the narratives that keep us from moving forward through the pain of trauma. I highly recommend this book!"
—**John Wollenzien,** faith-transitioner

"This book unfolds with honesty and self-awareness. It's beautiful and self-reflective to follow the un-doing and re-building of a life, to see it change from fragmented awareness to full, embodied presence. A journey worth reading."
—**Ashley Mae Hoiland,** artist, mother, and author of *One Hundred Birds Taught Me to Fly*

"This book feels sacred on so many levels. I marvel and bow to the courage and strength of Becky to do the hardest work there is—the true inner work of undoing, unraveling, and healing in a raw, real, go-for-the-throat sort of way. No excuses, no justifications, no coping strategies—just the relentless pursuit of truth and freedom."
—**Nesha Woodhouse,** Truth-seeker, Co-founder of Lifehouse Body & Soul, Owner of Lifehouse Performing Arts Academy

"Becky's book is a must-read for anyone who's ever had the rug pulled out from under them and feels angry, hurt, confused, and/or completely lost. It's a roadmap to maneuvering through heartbreak with clarity, love, and compassion."
—**Brielle Wollenzien,** mother of a beautiful human struggling with drug addiction, mixed-faith marriage navigator

"Moller's story is vulnerable and raw, but she tells it with great courage and authenticity. Her compelling narrative offers solace, validation, and empathy for the human experience, holding space for both herself and for her audience."
—**Melissa Davis,** esteemed English professor, critical thinker, and avid reader

"*Undone, Unafraid* wrecked me in the best way. It's not just a story about betrayal—it's about what it means to lose everything you thought was safe and still choose to love, still choose to trust. Becky's words are sacred. I found pieces of myself in her grief and her fire."
—**Max Acalde,** spiritual seeker, Death & Rebirth Guide

"This book is a powerful testament to the resilience of the human spirit. Through the lens of betrayal trauma, Becky takes us on a raw and honest journey of awakening. After reading, I have a deeper sense of clarity and renewed commitment to mind-body-spirit integration in my own life."
—**Ali Springer,** MFT, pineviewtherapyclinic.com

"A breathtaking journey through the terrain of pain, courage, and the quiet magic of rising again. This book is for anyone who has shattered, grieved, and dared to gather their pieces with trembling hands. It doesn't offer perfection—it offers truth. A luminous reminder that healing is not linear, and resilience is not loud. It is steady, sacred, and beautifully human."
—**Robyn Maria,** Author of *From Surviving to Creating: A Journey to Abundance* and Founder of Unboxed Hearts: A Charity for Foster Children

To the most broken and pitiful version of me…and all of us…
To the one who was scared, small, and shattered,
Who thought life was over and wished to either die or disappear:
Thank you for your willingness and courage
To show up and do the hard things,
To face yourself and let it all fall apart.
It is you who brought me here, one day at a time.
I love you.

—BECKY MOLLER

My Dear Reader,

Before you proceed, I'd like to offer a heads-up. This story contains a raw retelling of betrayal disclosures, trauma responses, and the subsequent growth, which often appears as a falling apart.

If you've personally experienced betrayal, please take extra care with yourself—particularly in Part One. If you feel flooded or overwhelmed at any time, consider stepping away for a moment: You have my full support to put down the book, skip chapters or whole sections, tend to yourself with loving awareness, or reach out for help—even to me personally (I mean this sincerely).

Because of the sensitive subject matter, you may find your worldview challenged, your triggers poked, or your own shadows lurking in various ways. I encourage you to pay attention to these discomforts with loving curiosity. Despite being painful, they can help you uncover what still needs healing in your life: beliefs to be reconciled or released, parts of yourself asking to be acknowledged and expressed, or safety that still needs to be established.

If you have the bandwidth, helpful questions to reflect on in such moments might include, "Why is this part of the story bothering me so much? Is there a part of my ego or identity it's poking at? Is it asking me to consider something I'd rather not look at? Is this an opportunity to clarify why I feel the way I do? Do I simply need to slow down and offer myself some love and space?"

My intention in sharing is healing, not harming. And healing is wholeness; the ability to hold all things in love with no need to push away, justify, prove, or shut down.

Inner freedom is the ability to meet life exactly as it is with an open heart. This story is the difficult path that taught me how to do just that and is filled with secret breadcrumbs that could guide you on your journey to find the same, as you're open to finding them.

Know that your path is your own, and that mine is mine. There's no one right way to move through trauma, loss, or change.

Trust your timing and only push yourself to hold what you feel capable of.

May this book help you feel the permission to be a messy human, just like me, to find and own the authentic path that truly serves you according to your own inner guide.

May seeing me in my weakness allow you to love yourself in yours. It is all as it should be, and there is room for every single part.

Don't worry—it's going to be a beautiful story.

Love,

Becky

ACKNOWLEDGEMENT

As I finish this book—an indescribable peak on this decade adventure—I've never been more aware of the shoulders I stand on. I cannot adequately express the *Namaste* I feel for so many.

Thank you to *Nate.* You've been my life partner in every sense of the word. You keep showing up, *every* time, and for that I will be forever grateful. Your patience, honesty, willingness, playfulness, and humility have created a space that would never have been possible otherwise. It is my honor to evolve alongside you through this lifelong journey. I love you with the depth of my whole soul.

Thank you to my children, *Caleb, Madi, Chloe, Jayden, and Tyson.* You have held me in love and forgiveness every step of this uncomfortable way. You have been open and flexible, full of integrity and courage, as life has rearranged me underneath you. Each one of you is a perfect expression of Light and Love, passion and messiness, a magnificent mix of both the hardest and most beautiful parts of your parents, and also each so uniquely your own. You are my greatest joys in life by far. I cannot wait to watch you continue to unfold into all that you are.

Thank you to *my Holly*: your Light has always been so bright. It awakened me, in so many ways, to my own—and once I knew this Light in me, I couldn't not spend my life helping others uncover the same for themselves. So much of what I teach, still today, comes from being a dedicated student of all that I see in you. I can never repay what you have been in my life. You will always be my mentor, my Light, my angel, and my dear friend.

Thank you to *Nesha*: our partnership was such a fun adventure and an unexpected gift. You've inspired me with your vision, integrity, and creativity as long as I've known you. Your trust and belief in me have been an irreplaceable factor in where I am today.

Thank you to my editor and publishers. *Marissa,* my book doula who dropped out of the sky, you were the missing link I waited for over five long years, and I am still in awe of the way this work blossomed under your wise, caring, and intuitive presence. Though we didn't end up where we thought we would, I will always hold sacred the mystical creation space we shared for a season. *Rebecca* and *Bridget,* birthing this book into existence with you has been a supremely magical growth experience. I will be forever grateful for your guidance and support.

Thank you to *Steven & Rhyll Croshaw* and *SA Lifeline Foundation:* our 12-step family and dear friends. Nate and I would never have found our way without you. Thank you for your years of sacrifice, for your tireless commitment to sharing the message of hope and healing, and for laying your lives down for the Greater Good. We will always hold you in love and can never adequately thank you for all you've meant to us. We honor you as the recovery pioneers you are.

Thank you to *my family:* my parents, who have always been a refuge of love and light, of safety and stability, and unconditional love. My siblings and their spouses, each of whom I respect as fabulous humans and true friends. My grandparents and cousins, a tribe that has always filled my life with a sense of being part of something very special. Each of you is such a part of me.

Thank you to every single person with whom I've had the privilege to journey on a deep soul-level: through *the LDS church, 12-Step, MMTCP, Lifehouse Body & Soul,* or *Undone Academy.* I have been so fed by our sacred fellowship and the transcendent moments in mentoring sessions when willingness, courage, honesty, and Love create soul-level growth and healing. I see the magic in each one of you, and I will forever be grateful that our paths have crossed. Your wholeness has deepened mine.

Thank you to *Dr. Barbara Steffens, Ashmae Hoiland, Tara Brach, Mel, Alaina, Lynda, Brielle, John, Max, Robyn, Janet, Lisa,* and *Ali* for your time, feedback, encouragement, and questions. Your honest engagement was a powerful and needed step to get this book and my own soul to where it needed to be to move forward. I will be forever grateful for each one of you in this.

Thank you to the *artists, spiritual teachers,* and *creatives* whose passion continues to inspire me to find my own voice. Lin-Manuel Miranda—seeing Hamilton was a distinct moment that urged me forward. *"Why do you write like you're running out of time?"* ...*"I'm past patiently waitin', I'm passionately smashin' every expectation, Every action's an act of creation."* I feel so deeply the magic in you and honor the courage and commitment it takes to create the unfiltered space within yourself to let your light and truth shine so clear and bright. *Namaste.*

Thank you to *the Universe* for loving me so deeply, so well. Thank you to my green Wisconsin trees and my snow-capped Utah mountains. Thank you for roots, deep and strong. Thank you to the open sky, the seeming well-spring of this creative flow, and the magic I've found in floating there. The empty space seems to be where all the Good ideas come from. Thank you to my safe and sheltered Door County beach, and the countless ways you have held me through the years. And to the Pacific Coast, the wild horizon that welcomed me to a bigger, broader life than I ever imagined and continually invites me to rub off so many rough edges. I am always learning to surrender to the Waves and ride with joy, lightness, and ease. And thank you to the Fire, that heat and passion and intensity I once hated in myself but now see as so needed and so useful. It burns bright inside me, whether I like it or not, and as I learn to use it skillfully, who knows? It could help warm the whole Earth.

Thank *you*, dear reader, for picking up this book, for opening your heart to me and my story. May the time you spend here serve your awakening, and our collective journey toward peace, expansion, and inner freedom in the world we're creating together.

May you have all you stand in need of. May you be at peace.

TABLE OF CONTENTS

PART THREE LARGER HORIZONS

LAKE POWELL
BECKY MOLLER, JUNE 2016

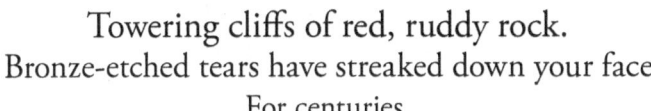

Towering cliffs of red, ruddy rock.
Bronze-etched tears have streaked down your face
For centuries.
Until over time, you learned
To let go and trust.

Allowing yourself to be chipped away,
Sandy chunks at a time,
Chiseled by the living water of
A Master Sculptor.

How many centuries did it take before you trusted
Yourself to His care?
How many eons did you grieve
Your formerly impressive stature?
How much envy and shame did you feel as you
Eyed other granite castles,
And wished for their height and breadth?

Did your collapsing foundation
Fuel the desperate fear that
You were disappearing?
Never knowing that the water whittling away
Your very nature was changing you into something
More beautiful
More holy
More…
Than anything you could have conceived in your
Strength and comfort?

I sense the bowels of your sorrow,
I feel the depth of your peace,
the wisdom in your beauty.
I look at you and see
The face of God.
How I long to submit myself to such a Creator
And come to know the humility that has made you

Breathtaking.

FOREWORD

From the moment I met Becky as a junior at BYU, I always knew there was something special about her. The first thing I asked her when we first met was, "How tall are you, like 4'10"?" to which she responded with a punch to my gut. I deserved it then, and it was indicative of how our relationship has evolved and grown: me doing and saying thoughtless and stupid things—and Becky learning to call me out...but loving me anyway.

To me, we're the perfect Yin/Yang combination.

Back then, and even now, I had no idea the level of depth, thoughtfulness, compassion, and empathy she could show another person. I've been lucky enough to be the recipient of that. And as she's dedicated her life to sharing this message of hope and healing, I've witnessed what it's done for so many others to help them heal and become empowered.

I'll be honest, however: I've been scared to death to endorse this book, which is such a vulnerable thing for both me and Becky. Every time I sat down to write this Foreword, I found myself avoiding the task. *Isn't there a Yankees game to watch?* Part of it was, I knew that nothing I wrote could do justice to all Becky and I have been through over the last ten years. It's like trying to explain the beauty of a sunset: the combination of the darkness and the light working together to create something beautiful.

A person can't really explain what recovery from addiction and betrayal trauma takes, unless they've been in it. Whenever I hear stories about how a wife's gone crazy or she is off her rocker, now I'm able to pause and think, *Do they really know what she may be going through?* because I've seen it first-hand. I've also caused that level of crazy in my own wife because of my own thoughtless choices.

People who've read this book often seem to be interested in my perspective. What was I feeling? And I have to say, when I first revealed my rock bottom to Becky, I couldn't feel much. I was so used to numbing any painful feelings. But I'll never forget the night of that first disclosure. I'd never seen her face look like that before—so full of terror and anguish. She was completely broken, like a little girl who was so scared, so lost. I had no idea I could wreak that sort of havoc on another human being.

And... I had no clue what to do next.

Every day, I could see the battle inside my wife. Part of her wanted me to keep her safe and warm, and part of her knew she couldn't trust me to do that. And I knew I couldn't trust myself to do that, either. It was hard for me to even believe I'd gotten us there. So much of that time, I felt frozen.

All I could mutter to myself was, "How can I fix this fast? How can we just get back to 'normal'?"

The problem was, I was still emotionally immature. Addiction does that. I was thinking mostly about myself:

What was going to happen to our life?

Would I be abandoned? Would I be disowned?

Would my life with my best friend and the family we'd built together be over?

Would my selfish choices be the cause of losing everything most precious to me?

My whole life, I'd told myself I wasn't hurting anybody but me. Suddenly, I had to face the fact that I was truly hurting others. I was the one who had gotten us both lost in what felt like a dark, lonely cave, and I knew that Becky had no reason to trust me. This was probably the first time in my life I had to face real feelings without any way to opt out of them or numb them out. It meant huge growth on my part, which is still in progress. I have to take daily accountability.

Still, this book isn't about me.

Although I have played a part in the story, it's not my story.

This book is about how someone took a terrible experience and turned it into something magical, something mystical, and something that can help serve and heal so many others.

It's hard for me to even comprehend the work and dedication Becky has brought to this healing journey. My choices took her life in a completely different direction, and she jumped in with both feet and stood by me, even when she had every right to leave.

Becky did nothing to deserve all the pain that I put her through. I brought a lot of baggage with me into our relationship, most of which I didn't even know I was carrying until it was too heavy for either one of us to bear.

That's what this book is really about. I've read it multiple times now, in many of its varying renditions, and I support every word that's been written.

It's our experience. It's Becky's experience.

And I am so amazed at how she can express her feelings and emotions on paper in such an eloquent way.

For many, this book won't be easy to read. Some may disagree with the content. But what I've learned from my own experience is that when I talk in the "I," there isn't much argument. My experience is my experience. My feelings are **mine**. They may not be right or completely worked out, but they are how I see the world at that time. And that's what this book is: it's Becky, speaking from her own experience; it's Becky, sharing what she's learned and what she's gone through, and how she's processed the pain and the trauma and the hurt and turned it into a whole new way of being.

The purpose of this book is so much bigger than our story. It is to provide hope for anyone who has experienced trauma, whether it's relationship trauma or betrayal trauma or religious trauma or all the other types of traumas that are out there. There is hope.

It's not easy. It doesn't happen overnight.

Also, it doesn't happen as quickly as you might wish, but it can happen and it does happen. I'm so grateful for what I'm learning about what emotional health looks like and feels like. This book has helped me do that. My experience with Becky has helped me do that. It's an ongoing and evolving path, and I couldn't be more grateful for having a partner to do that with, one day at a time. I love her with all my heart—more today than I could ever even explain.

I hope this book will help you, if you are looking for healing.

I hope this book can be a valuable asset in your recovery process.

I hope this book will help you let down your guard and recognize the vital importance of your feelings and emotions.

This book is a deep dive. It's an evolution. And I'm so proud to be a part of it.

Enjoy the journey. One day at a time.

—*Nate Moller,*

Becky's husband

PROLOGUE

I am lying in the dark and the world is spinning, my eyes glazed as I stare at the sticky-back, glow-in-the-dark stars just a foot above my face. Cheap, tacky stars stuck to the bottom of a child's bunk bed, a rudimentary taunt to the black hole of nothingness I long to sink into. But I can't sink into nothing. I am inescapably here, lying in the bottom bunk with my heart pounding out of my chest and my 9-year-old son huddled against me.

His body is stiff and tight, and I am trying to calm him, but my voice sounds hollow and unfamiliar, like an echo from a cave far away. The tones sound strange and soft, an almost eerie calm that cuts through the deafening pounding in my ears. I clutch my son to my body with an instinctive knowing, a fierce knowing that comes from generations of mothers lifting cars and jumping buildings, that somehow I must pretend to be steady for him. Somehow, I must keep him safe in the midst of my own agony.

"Shhhh, it's going to be alright. I'm here. I'm right here. I am never going to leave you."

More a battle cry than a solace; I'm trying to somehow devise words that feel true yet offer comfort. This is all I can come up with. This is all I know for sure: "I'm here. And I am never going to leave you."

And that *is* all I know, because just moments ago, my world came crashing down. Just moments ago, a 2x4 smacked me across the face in the form of unimaginable words tumbling from my husband's mouth, and now my world is spinning, spinning, spinning: my heart is hammering in my chest and the thunder vibrates through my eardrums and skull and there is a strange sensation that I am floating in black empty space and there is nothing, nothing, nothing to tether me.

I am floating alone in utter darkness.

Just a few, short, casual words, so carefully placed mid-conversation—like a delinquent child tiptoeing to class, hoping to slip in without a head-turn from the teacher—unleashing an incomprehensible rewrite to my past and future and leaving me groundless and alone. Words that were out of my realm of reality. Words I had never before considered:

"So, you know… I had an inappropriate relationship last summer."

Something about his words felt like walking straight into one of those sliding glass patio doors. You know the ones…where you don't even realize it's there until you walk at full speed into the thick pane of glass, completely unprepared for impact. That's how those words felt as they dropped like lead in my chest and landed like icy toothpicks on my face and shoulders.

Does. Not. Compute.

"Excuse me? I'm sorry…wh-what did you say?"

I am baffled. Just moments ago, we were connecting. It was a Sunday night, and we'd finally reached that blessed hour of bedtime when our four kids were settled behind closed doors and we could at last take a moment to breathe.

Nate and I had been married almost thirteen years before this moment. We'd had four children and just barely moved into a new home and neighborhood. We were in the thick of it all, still making our way, still feeling the pressure of unsteady careers and unstable identities, wondering if we could really afford our new mortgage and meet the sense of completion and confidence our early thirties seemed to demand.

Things had been tense, fragile between us for a while, and piecing together real conversations that didn't somehow unravel into arguments felt tenuous and rare. This Sunday night had started as a glimmer of hope. We'd spontaneously settled into the stools around our kitchen island and were talking, *really* talking, about the Sunday School lesson at church. I loved engaging in meaningful conversations and had felt starved of it with my husband for the past while—quite a *long* while.

So when he starts breaking down the lesson and offering thoughts, I am an eager participant. *This is so cool,* like the old days when we could talk for hours. I can tell he is thinking, really engaging, and it lights me up inside. Amidst it all, the topic of dreams comes up. Spiritual dreams, scriptural dreams, like when biblical Joseph wakes up and knows he is supposed to marry Mary, the mother of Jesus.

I'm nodding and encouraging, "Yes, I'm with you. I hear what you're saying. Yep, please continue," I just want to keep this part of him here, *with me.* This part that is thinking about things and sharing things and letting me in.

"So, yeah, dreams. It got me thinking. It got me thinking about last summer, when you had a dream. Do you remember when you had a dream? You woke me up in the middle of the night and told me you had a dream that I was having an affair online—that I was messing around with someone online."

I'm still nodding, trying to follow. "Yep, mmmhmmm, sure. Yeah, I think I remember that."

"So, you know…that was actually happening. I mean, I had an inappropriate relationship with someone last summer."

There it is: the sliding glass pane. And I sit there, completely disoriented, and I don't understand.

"Excuse me? I'm sorry…wh-what did you say?"

And then the fumbling begins. The pin-drop stillness of utter shock has passed, and suddenly everything is moving. Even in the energy between us, a momentum starts swirling. His body steps back, and his hands come up before I've moved a muscle. He starts speaking quickly, sloppily, spitting out words; I keep hearing gibberish mixed in with, "…inappropriate relationship… inappropriate relationship…"

My eyes widen, and something inside me takes over that I have never felt before, and suddenly a cup is flying out of my hands and bouncing around on the tile floor of the kitchen. I don't even realize that I am yelling until I turn around with horror to the small but unmistakable sounds of my 9-year-old son sobbing in the hallway, his shaking frame a dark silhouette against the harsh glow of the hall light behind him.

This is when my mother-bear instincts kick in and save me from actually harming my husband. I immediately whisk myself around and run straight to my child. *How much has he heard? What did he see?* My mind is racing desperately to figure out the best way to protect him, the best way to keep him safe from the monster thrashing in the kitchen.

"Everything's fine, let's go back to bed. It's fine, it's fine," I snap the hallway light off and walk him straight to his room, my arms wrapping around him, my steps quick and desperate. "Look, see, it's fine, I'm going to lie right here with you."

We crawl into his bed together, the bottom bed with an empty top bunk above it, and as we lie, his sobs slow under the weight of my hushing reassurances. I stroke his hair and hold him tight.

Even though I lie here with a heart pounding out of my chest and a racing mind, I am grateful for the escape. Hushing my son becomes my lifeline to reality; it gives me purpose and grounding that steadies my panic. A part of me is floating in outer space as I lie here holding him while another part is flipping frantically through card after card in the *How Did This Happen?* File box of my mind, piecing together snippets of information that were meaningless before but that now seem to form a fuzzy constellation.

Part of me wants to rip off my husband's face, part of me wants to throw myself on the floor and beg him not to leave me, part of me is melting into a puddle of helpless despair, and part of me is glaring down at myself, disgusted, arms folded across my chest. *Well, this was bound to happen to you sooner or later...*

There is so much intensity I can hardly bear it, but I hush my son and run my fingers through his hair.

"It's going to be alright. I'm here. I'm never going to leave you."

Even as I comfort my son, my words accuse my husband. *I will never leave you. I would never do something like that. Never. Never. Never.*

As his sobs eventually quiet and his breathing steadies, I keep repeating these words. I don't know anymore if I am talking to my son or myself. But I need the words. The words keep me alive. As long as I whisper these words, I am able to bear the horrible aching pain growing inside me that threatens to swallow me whole. *What does he mean by 'inappropriate'?*

I lie there a long time, spinning in the darkness, only anchored by my son's breath, staring at the glow-in-the-dark stars pasted on the bunk bed while my heart beats out of my shirt. I am lost, wishing for oblivion...somewhere far away where I don't have to somehow figure out how to move forward, how to walk outside and look at the stranger who used to be my best friend; where I don't have to face the reality of who I am and how I have disappointed everyone that matters. I lie there disappearing as long as I possibly can until the compulsive need for information pulls me back to reality: *What exactly does he mean by 'inappropriate'?*

I hate the word already: it sounds so neat and formal, so detached and tidied up. *What the hell does he mean by 'inappropriate'?* I must know. I don't want to know. But I must know. I take a deep breath and gingerly unpeel myself from my son's sleeping frame, resolved to handle this like a respectable adult.

My heart pounds and I am trembling as I pad through the dark hallway back to the living room, where my husband is now lying on the couch. I want so badly to be calm, but at the mere sight of him, my whole body lurches into violence.

"So, are you going to tell me what the *fuck* has been going on?" My 5'2" frame towers over him with hands on my hips, but I am shaking so badly, my knees won't even hold me up. I am the paradoxical picture of wobbly rage.

My husband has never heard me use this word. "Let's wait on this, Beck. Please, can we wait on this? Let's call a counselor, let's call someone, I don't think we should do this without a therapist here," he begs.

I point at the door to the back patio and hiss, "Like there are therapists just sitting around at two in the morning waiting to rescue assholes who cheat on their wives? What the hell are you talking about?!" I can't find enough swear words to do justice to the rage coursing through me. I point to the back patio and thus begins the exhaustive interrogation.

The story slips out in disjointed pieces as I literally chase him around the deck, whisper-screaming at times to get him to speak. In all honesty, the night is only loosely held together now by snippets of memory, just vague images of dark shadows, me getting in his face, me moving as far from him as I can get, like some kind of crazy magnetic dance. Then, I seethe and breathe and pull my hair and sob and collapse and heave…until a new thought moves in, a new question, a new intolerable obsession, and I stalk back over to demand another piece of the puzzle between expletives and insults.

In my memory, there are very few words; more just crazy images: my disfigured face and his small, defeated yet defiant posture trying to stave me off. Mostly, it's the overall sense of being totally overwhelmed by pain, completely overloaded, neural synapses snapping, burning, firing on a mental switchboard that is trying to make sense of my unraveling life, and a swirling sense of powerlessness, of sinking deep into a black hole of self-hatred and despair.

His face is a hard, empty mask of defiance. His answers are short and justifying. The nothing I feel from him at first infuriates me and eventually defeats me. *How is it that my entire world is shattering, and my husband feels nothing?*

The night ends, browbeaten, with us back inside the house; an unspoken, shared agreement of no more screaming. We are lying on separate couches staring across at each other in the early morning dusk of sunrise. An image enters my mind, dreamlike: of us, fifteen years ago, on our first date in our college apartment complex, lying just as we are now, on separate couches, talking about the secrets of our hearts, talking like we could talk forever. In the memory, he looks deep into my eyes and smiles at me; a sweet, innocent smile that seems to reach into my soul and ask me to trust him. I flash back to the present: *How could this be the same sweet Idaho farm boy? How on earth did we get here?*

No Tears for Me
Becky Moller, March 2014

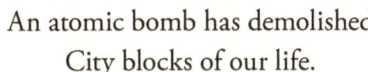

An atomic bomb has demolished
City blocks of our life.

Every day I wake up with a gasp
From short hours of fitful rest,
Dreading that first moment of consciousness
When my too-mortal brain remembers
What it can't believe is true.

And I feel it fresh,
For the first time again.

The pain consumes my body,
My chest, like ice chips, numb and cold,
My stomach, a knotted fist,
Empty eyes stare blank,
As the darkness overflows
Down my stinging cheeks.

My feet are heavy,
My steps, slow,
How did I walk so quickly before?

Flesh on fire, my heart collapses,
And I look to him.
He sees me burn, watches me writhe in pain,
He knows he is the cause.
Yet his eyes show nothing.
Vacant pools
Of unrequited love.

I sit stupefied, struggling to understand,
For tears have fallen
From his eyes in nights
Of passionate confessions.
But tears of fear fall different
Than tears of true remorse.

His façade only mourns its own casualties:

Tears for a true friend who shows compassion,
Tears for a sister whose hero must fall,
Tears for parents, whose perfect son must disappoint,
Even tears for the woman who caused it all.

For these victims of his selfish deluge,
True sadness and regret fill his face,
Bringing me relief that
This stranger is at least capable of feeling.

But when he watches me,
Quivering on the couch,
Crippled by corpses of dreams,
His face goes blank.

He tries to configure an appropriate weight,
His features attempting to portray
An emotion he simply does not feel.
There are no tears for me in there.

There are no tears for me.

PART ONE

THE
CARVING
OUT

CHAPTER ONE

ROCK BOTTOM

*R*ock bottom.

The night it all came crashing down, I lay in the dark of our house, sleepless and spinning, the dried salt crunchy on my cheeks as I floated away into a disassociated void. Somewhere in the house, Nate shuts a door, and the sound reverberates through my very core, chaining me back to the quicksand of fear in my stomach. *Oh shit, I'm still here.*

Up to this moment, Nate and I had a "normal marriage" in all the ways I knew to measure: we were solid, successful, and religious. We went on weekly dates and had sex three to four times per week. We had four beautiful children.

We'd been living the dream, juggling the balls, and checking the boxes. So, how in the span of a few short hours could my whole world come crashing down?

In the 12-step recovery world, they call this moment rock bottom. When I first heard that term, it conjured up images of blown-out debris, a toppled tower, a life stripped to bedrock. That's what the entire year of 2014 would become. It started in dramatic fashion on that spring Sunday night.

On Monday morning, I find myself somehow ushering kids into school-day clothes and brushing teeth, not even tired despite not sleeping. In the aftermath of last night's explosions, everything feels slow-motion with a murky haze. My husband slinks to his home office and shuts the door. The night's dramatic edge is over, and the unwelcome discomfort of a shifted reality settles over the house.

I drive the kids to school and call my mom as soon as they pile out the door of our minivan. I sit right there in the elementary school carpool lane as I give her the stark and simplified story. At this point, I still don't have many details. But even the essentials stand naked and jarring in the spotlight of an empty stage.

My mom is supportive and kind, steadier than I thought she'd be. Part of me wonders if I am overreacting; if really this isn't that big a deal and I am blowing things out of proportion. But when my dad gets on the phone, he asks, "Are you going to stay with him? We'll support you whatever you decide to do."

I feel the weight of his question, and the floor sinks out from under me again. I'm grateful for my dad's immediate support, but at this point, it still hasn't occurred to me that leaving is an option—that I'm in a situation where leaving is something that someone might do. Panic returns to my stomach and my breath shallows. My mind skips straight to money: I've just barely received a promotion at my part-time work, from a paid-hourly fitness instructor at two local universities to the BYU Intramural Aerobics Coordinator, adding a modest salary to my hourly teaching wages.

Perhaps God is in the timing, I think, adding numbers in my head, *Could I make it on my own if I had to?*

But even as I do the math and consider selling the house, I know the answer is "no." *No,* I don't want to leave. I want to stay. I want our marriage to last. I want the forever family I was promised when I married my husband in the Mormon temple, for time and all eternity. I am in this for the long haul.

So, I go home and I rush past the enemy in his home office and I lock my bedroom door. I pull my sheets up over my head and I cry and swear and scream and try to escape to sleep. And before long, I am worrying and obsessing and feverishly praying that I will do this the right way. That I will do this God's way. Suddenly, it all feels like a test that I've already failed.

I set up an appointment with my bishop—my religious leader. He will meet with me tonight at the church. I open the scriptures and pore through them, desperately looking for some sort of answer to grasp onto. I cancel the fitness class I'm supposed to teach at BYU this evening—something I've never done before without lining up a sub. I cannot pull myself together. I cannot stop crying. I cannot get out of bed.

Something has clicked inside me, and I know somehow that I am never going back to "normal." Our "normal" is exactly what got us here, and I won't feel safe until I understand it. My mind starts festering with the relentless obsession that will drive it for the next three years:

How could this possibly have happened? How did we get to Rock Bottom?

When I meet with my bishop, I am utterly helpless. Throughout my life, I have more or less always been in the "good girl" chair in bishops' offices, being praised for all the ways I'm meeting the expectations. Today, I come humiliated, broken, and pleading. I can feel my bishop poking around for reasons why Nate would do what he did: "Do you pay enough attention to him? How often are you intimate? Are you having regular dates?"

I am raking my own soul with the same kinds of questions, but as deep as I look, I can't genuinely find a reason that makes any sense. We have sex basically every other day, and I've always planned and scheduled weekly dates for the two of us, even with our young family. "I don't know, Bishop. I just don't know. All I can say is that in my gut, I feel like it's not humanly possible for anyone to give Nate the amount of attention he seems to need. There's a hole there that I can't possibly fill, no matter how I show up. And I'm so scared, because I don't know how to do better. I don't know if I can possibly fill that hole and keep him here."

I leave the office with instructions from my bishop to go on more walks with Nate, and I feel grateful for his time and feedback. I want nothing more than to get back into the "good girl" seat, to be patted on the head and told that I'm doing more than anyone could ask for. That I'm exceeding any reasonable expectation. In this case, I suppose that means to forgive, and I plead with God to help me do it.

It's funny how even that first day, I am already cornering forgiveness, backing it against a wall, begging for it. I cannot bear to sit with the horrible ugly rage and hate, self-pity, and despair battling inside me. I am desperate to be able to say I forgive my husband so I can be at peace with myself. I am desperate to land safely in the good person box.

By the end of the day, I am already regrouping, moving toward solutions, my wheels already spinning. I am going to figure this out.

How did we get here? This question becomes my logical mind's lifeline. Not only will it secure the solution to prevent this humiliation from repeating

5

itself…it will give resolution to the terrifying whispers that have clawed at me every second since the bomb dropped the night before. It will allow me to banish whatever unspeakable darkness in myself caused my husband to hate me, to stop loving me, to abandon and betray me—perhaps the same darkness writhing within me right now—the shadow I have always hated in myself, deep down.

The darkness that makes me so fundamentally unlovable, whispers my swirling shame.

How did we get here? It feels as though everything depends upon my figuring this out.

TRUTH
BECKY MOLLER, MARCH 2014

I've long known that he doesn't love me,
I remember well the day,
That I realized in all his foolishness,
He was pushing my love away.

I saw from above with clarity,
The fractured fallout from this choice,
I saw how he chose to shut me out,
I warned him with my voice.

You are choosing not to love me.
You are choosing it every day.
When there is so much here to hold onto,
You are purposely pushing away.

You are seeking out my imperfections,
You are holding them, white-knuckled grip,
You are gluing them onto your eyeballs,
You are pasting them onto your lips.

You take glory in my imperfections,
You are hungry to find them and see,
That you're justified in all your anger,
And the blame must reside with me.

Don't you see that love just can't abide this?
Love's a miracle which soon will fade,
When you see only my imperfections,
Then it's hate that your heart will invade.

And I've watched every day how you chose it,
With stubbornness, selfishness, pride,
How you grasped onto my imperfections,
And shut out all the love I supplied.

And so now you have no way to see me,
It's so clear it's not there, though you try.
There is nothing you feel, though you offer,
Your "I love you" just feels like a lie.

To you, I am just imperfections,
They've been pounded through time in your brain,
They have freed you from guilt, pain, and sorrow,
Through your wanderings, day after day.

It's hard to think how you could hide it,
And look in my eyes just the same,
But you only saw my imperfections,
So you looked and you simply saw blame.

And it breaks my heart now as I see you,
And I love you with all my soul,
How you want to feel sad for your sweetheart,
But you don't, your heart's just a big hole.

It's been buried beneath imperfections,
It was carefully covered with pride,
It is gone and you simply can't fake it,

You don't love me.

I'll take it in stride.

CHAPTER TWO
How Did We Get Here?

O ver the years, I've learned that rock bottom (in whatever form it takes) places us squarely in front of two distinct doors. One is a siren call back to "the way it was"; a desperate resistance to the pain of all that's been lost. The other is the door to the unknown: a surrender to what is, exactly as it is, a door that potentially opens to a new way of being. Walking through that door may be the bravest thing any of us will ever do, in my opinion. As J.K. Rowling, author of the Harry Potter books, aptly stated, "Rock bottom became the solid foundation on which I rebuilt my life." Ten years down the road, I can echo her sentiment.

Clearing space for something new to be born is exactly what I believe rock bottom is meant to do, in the divine scheme of things, though when I was face-down, choking on the dust, I certainly wasn't ready to see my un-wanted reality as an opportunity. Even from those first frenzied moments, my husband's disclosures ripped me from the hypnotic flow of my daily existence and forced me to see the frayed edges of the unresolved wounds that I'd always been running from.

The funny thing is, I'd never before thought of myself as "wounded." My earliest memories are vague and fuzzy: golden images of my small self in an imaginary world with make-believe friends. As a little girl, I would author songs and choreograph dances, play out relationship dramas, all in the company of my own fantasies, with sunlight pouring through the windows and my little soul, hungry to understand this big mysterious world safely from the confines of my own bedroom.

As a child, I often preferred to be alone; I never seemed to land on quite the right note for playtime. When we visited family, my siblings would jet down to the basement to play with cousins, and I would snuggle into my dad's armpit on the couch, spying with great interest on the meaningful intricacies of grown-up conversation. When the neighbors would collect my sister and me to play Barbies, my game always ended with someone dying or getting divorced, a bit heavy for plastic dolls on a summer afternoon. It seems I've always been serious about figuring out the big stuff in life.

And I was so lucky to have plenty of wide-open space to feel its bigness. I grew up in a sprawling house perched atop rolling Wisconsin hills. Our front window gazed out over dairy farms, and the smell of fresh manure would waft up to us on summer days. My backyard was a wild, wooded wonderland where I liked to trek down and search for trilliums, alone with my imagination, feeling perfectly cocooned and harbored by friendly, arching trees.

I was the oldest daughter in a large Mormon family, with three brothers and two sisters to be exact. My dad had a stable and successful job. My mom was a devoted homemaker. Our faith was unusual in Wisconsin and core to our identity, giving us community, purpose, and clear direction. It also gave us a very busy schedule. So much of who I was in my youth was an outgrowth of my faith and family.

Being Mormon in Wisconsin made me feel special and safe. My dad served as a bishop of our local congregation (or ward) for years and this "ward family" was truly that for me. I can easily name a dozen leaders who were like second parents, mentoring me through adolescence and devoting countless hours to serve me on Sundays, weeknight activities, and summer camps. Walking into a church service, whether in a chapel with burlap walls and blue carpet or the funeral home we met in when establishing a new congregation in my hometown, always felt like coming home. The beloved hymns, the familiar prayers, the steady, structured pace of the service, the smiles and hugs from lifelong friends…this was belonging.

For as long as I can remember, I understood that my faith made us unique, chosen even, and this was an exhilarating weight I felt even as a young child. We were the one and only true church on the planet, and how lucky was I to be born into it? My little brain internalized the responsibility both as a Mormon and as the oldest daughter to be an example, to show others the way, to do something extraordinary with my mortal life. "Where much is given, much is required" was a scriptural verse that rang in my head often. It encapsulated how blessed I felt for all I'd been gifted, and how deeply I hoped to live up to my privilege.

But these underlying mindsets were overshadowed by the more obvious markers of Mormonism in the "mission field" of Wisconsin. By the time I was in Junior High, the most notable traits that differentiated me from my peers came from my religious observance. These were the black and white lines etched deep in my psyche as the definition of safety and success as an adolescent Mormon: I didn't drink. I didn't smoke. I was not going to have sex or do any sexual touching before marriage. I attended church services each Sunday, weekly church activities, and weeklong church summer camps and conferences. I read scriptures nightly and devoted myself wholeheartedly to church leadership roles and service opportunities. I was kind to those who needed kindness. And it all brought me joy. I wanted nothing more than to make God, my parents, and my church leaders proud of me, to exemplify what it meant to be a disciple of Jesus Christ.

And of course, I always knew I would be married to another person who had also lived such a morally clean life. We would be sealed together for time and all eternity in a Mormon temple and create our own eternal family, which was often called "the plan of happiness" at church. The love and commitment to family life I witnessed in my own parents' marriage certainly created a happy childhood for me. I knew in my heart that the sacred covenant of temple marriage would be the most important thing I would ever do, the pinnacle of any disciple's journey, and it was always in my mind's eye as I grew into adulthood, navigating first kisses and Homecoming dances.

But like everything, my high ideals had a shadow side, often bleeding over into perfectionism. Whether from Mormonism or my family placement, the expectation of standing out was a tangible presence in my air, and I sucked it up like a sponge. In first grade, I declared that I would be the first female president. In second, I won a grade-wide debate and secured the fate of the stegosaurus as the most popular dinosaur. By third grade, I had self-studied my way into finishing the sixth-grade math book. By fifth grade, I was leading my *Odyssey of the Mind* team to a World Competition in Boulder, Colorado.

By eighth grade, I had been awarded by the Midwest Talent Search for scoring a 28 on the ACT at the age of thirteen.

Because I got so much validation for my achievements, I felt both an innate joy and a fear-driven pressure in doing everything possible to keep producing. Achieving excellence made me feel safe, and yet the never-ending pursuit meant that insecurity was always chasing me from behind. I knew I was smart, but I also recognized I was unattractive and intense. As adolescence loomed, I ping-ponged between arrogance and self-loathing.

I compulsively chewed my fingernails down to bloody stubs. I hid my soft belly behind baggy clothing. I struggled with the urge to abrasively overshare my strong opinions and also with the almost desperate desire to fit in and not be a loser. Approaching Junior High as a weirdly smart Mormon kid with little athletic ability and bad acne, this desire felt almost unattainable.

So, by eighth grade, I swore like a sailor to normalize the fact that I wasn't going to drink, do drugs, or mess around with boys. I hosted parties at my house and allowed friends to sneak in alcohol even though I wouldn't drink any myself. I even took my brother's car for a midnight joyride once with my pack of fourteen-year-old besties, savoring the feeling of freedom and power and a little rebellion, too. (It's funny how I had no moral issue with stealing my brother's car and driving underage, but I would sooner die than take a sip of alcohol.) When my friend took a sharp turn too quickly and the car ended up in a cornfield, we pushed it back onto the road in a panic and crept slowly back to my family's country home on the hill. Somehow, I managed to hose out enough corn stalks from the undercarriage to keep from getting caught.

All in all, despite my token adventures, I think I was a pretty normal product of the nineties, prone to perfectionism and highly attuned to the high school popularity game. By the time I graduated in the Top 10 of my 650-person graduating class, I had been voted both "Most Likely to Succeed" *and* "Best Listener." I had mastered the game: I was ready to take on the world.

So, you'll understand my surprise when, years down the road, after the implosion of my marriage and worldview, when my deep desire for healing forced me to peel apart how I ended up where I did, I realized it had all started right here, in my earliest memories. In my very beginnings, my idyllic childhood.

And it wasn't anyone's fault. You see, almost from the moment I could read my parents' facial expressions, I began hustling for my worth, formulating a self-made, self-protective, ever-striving identity: my own, unique ego. And this didn't happen because anybody did anything wrong. It happened because I am human.

Just like all humans, I wanted to be loved. Just like all humans, I began to have life experiences, and with each experience, I constructed a meaning—without even realizing it. With each experience, I drew a conclusion: what was good, what wasn't. Even as a tiny towhead, I was unconsciously mapping what made people love me and what didn't. And just like every human, I wanted to be safe. I wanted to belong.

So, when we start to look at my infamous Sunday night or your irretrievable Tuesday afternoon or whatever the snapshot day and time was when everything fell apart and we ask, *"How did we get here?"* we have to realize we're not looking at the past few weeks, months, or even years. We have to open our eyes to more than just the love story and the sex life and the career moves, personality clashes and struggles. We're looking at the way we've made meaning about who we are and who we're supposed to be. We're looking back at our entire lives. Because we bring all of it into these intimate relationships and traumatic moments. If we want to understand how we got here, we've got to peel it all the way back to the seed: to the way we see the world, to the way we see God—to the way we see ourselves.

If we really want to understand how we got to rock bottom, we've got to deconstruct it all.

"There is a necessary suffering that cannot be avoided, which Jesus calls 'losing our very life' or losing what I and others call the 'false self.' Your false self is your role, title, and personal image that is largely a creation of your own mind and attachments. It will and must die in exact correlation to how much you want the Real. 'How much false self are you willing to shed to find your True Self?' is the lasting question. Such necessary suffering will always feel like dying, which is what good spiritual teachers will tell you about very honestly."

—RICHARD ROHR, *FALLING UPWARD*

CHAPTER THREE

How Did *He* Get Here?

From the moment of Nate's confession, I am baffled; his behaviors seem so far from the person I thought I knew. I try desperately to respond like I would to any other problem: educate myself. Search the scriptures for answers. Make lists and resolves. Within the week, I'm proactively building strategies in my journal.

WEEK 1: What I Have Learned This Week

Answers from God:

- *Sin brings misery. Forgiveness brings peace.*
- *I need to forgive.*
- *The Atonement is Real and has the power to change us.*
- *I need to be careful of my mental health. I need to try to get more sleep.*
- *I cannot allow myself to wallow for more than two weeks.*

Answers I feel like I am receiving, but I am not sure if they are from me or God:

- *The root of Nate's addiction, affair, and much of our marital discord is selfishness.*
- *We both need to work every day to choose to stay in love.*
- *I can do more to show my love and make our marriage my top priority.*

Nate is making similar proactive strides. One night, as I gingerly pull back the covers on my side of our shared bed, Nate clears his throat across from me. His darting eyes tell me he's afraid to start the emotional mudslide that's become our new nightly ritual, but I can tell he's anxious to share.

"Hey, Beck, I found a cool article today about a scripture story from the Book of Mormon. It's about the Anti-Nephi-Lehies, a bloodthirsty people, who become converted to the Lord. As part of their covenant, they bury their weapons, a sign of their total commitment to a new way of life. I want to create my own covenant. I want to figure out my weapons and I want to bury them, for good." His eyes are pleading, proud, and hopeful, and they search my face. I can't keep myself from the longing to believe that it could all be okay again.

"That's great, Nate," I say, cautious but encouraging. Within the week, Nate has formulated his own boundaries around his acting-out behaviors: no more Facebook, or any social media, for that matter. No more texting or private meetings with any woman. No more staying up late at night. And no more porn. He calls this "Burying his Weapons of War." I follow suit, applying the story to myself and creating my own list:

BURYING MY WEAPONS OF WAR:

MY WEAPONS:

- *Trying to analyze Nate's behaviors for him.*
- *Criticizing or correcting in any way when Nate or the kids try to help out.*
- *Trying to force Nate into the intimacy I need (talking, emotional closeness, introspection).*
- *Pushing myself and all of us so hard.*
- *Telling instead of asking.*
- *Thinking that I am better than him.*

MY RESOLUTIONS:

- *Move more slowly.*
- *Think less. Talk less.*
- *Ask more. Listen more.*

- *Try to think positively.*
- *Try to get some sleep.*

By WEEK 2, my list affirms that I'm sure I love Nate with all my soul, professes that honoring my covenants will keep me safe, and vows that faith in Jesus Christ is the only sure foundation.

WEEK 3 has me admonishing myself to be filled with gratitude to have someone in my life who's willing to try and love me. My WEEK 4 journal entry states, "The time to grieve is passing."

Oh, honey, I think when I read that now.

Along with my weekly resolutions, I survive the first month by piecing together our past and finding all my mistakes. I start at the beginning.

The first time my husband told me about his porn use, we'd only been married two years. From my rock-bottom vantage point, I clearly didn't take it seriously enough. *If I had been more concerned, perhaps we wouldn't be here.*

At the time, our firstborn was scarcely two months old. Nate was struggling to sell printers, his first job post-college, and it wasn't going well. He would come home in the middle of the day and lie face-down, spread-eagled on the floor of our apartment, apparently having lost the will to move, eat, talk, or certainly cold-call office buildings to sell printers.

When he came to me anxiously admitting his draw to pornography, I was unruffled. I encouraged him to go talk to our bishop. When Nate told me that he was worried he might be an addict, I affectionately rolled my eyes.

This squeaky-clean Idaho boy I married? He was not the jock, not the bodybuilder, not the kind of guy I knew better than to date. Nate was a safe bet. Sweet. Innocent. Religious. *He is surely exaggerating.*

I grew up with a dad who loved to playfully pinch my mom's behind and three brothers who gravitated to girlfriends at a young age. Guys enjoy sex—there's nothing newsworthy in that. I'd heard all my life that men think about sex more than women. A little porn didn't seem like that big of a deal. I wasn't worried.

He talks to our bishop—smooths it out. Takes his slap on the wrist. But unbeknownst to me, Nate's been confessing about porn and masturbation to bishops for over a decade. Perhaps this is why he seems so worried. Confessing has never actually resolved his concerns.

As for me, I am confused and mildly upset for a day but forgive him the next. I feel like such a good wife, thinking, *What a big person I am to understand this.*

Life moves on. We hardly miss a beat.

* * *

Two years later, we've got two kids, and I've begun to feel that our marriage is a roller coaster. There are times when we're so connected and close, everything seems to be firing on all cylinders. We are peas and carrots—truly best friends—his playfulness the perfect complement to my more serious and responsible nature. And then, for some inexplicable reason, everything I do or say either irritates or offends him, and we are on the downward trajectory again. There never seems to be any rhyme or reason to whether we are going up or down. I suppose it's normal. *I guess this is what marriage is.*

But there is so much anger in him. And when it's here, we are like two north-pole magnets, almost obsessively trying to connect but never able to actually make contact. I mean real contact—emotional, mental, spiritual connection. Intimacy: into-me-you-see.

Sex has never been the problem. We are on a strict every-other-day regimen regulated by Nate's pouting and isolation and my need to please. It feels like we are always having sex, and it is never enough.

* * *

The next pornography confession comes three years later. He comes to me this time with a sense of desperation, of being out of control. This confession feels bigger, more serious, and I begin to feel the shame and fear in the pit of my stomach. *What is wrong with me? Why does he need to look at other women? Why aren't I enough?*

I confide in one friend, the President of the Women's Relief Society at church. It's the first time I've ever told anyone about this, and it feels like a betrayal to Nate. But I don't know what to do with the pain and confusion and helplessness that's accumulating inside of me.

I fly home to my family in Wisconsin for two weeks, leaving Nate with a threat I have no idea how to back up: "You better do something about this…or else!"

When I return, my husband has attended his first 12-step meeting and confessed to another bishop. Both his addiction recovery program and our religious requirements encourage complete abstinence from porn, just as a person would completely abstain from alcohol or drugs, and Nate seems fully committed to the challenge. His anger, which is the more problematic issue for me, seems to magically disappear. We start talking for hours each night instead of flipping through channels while he gropes me on the couch. The tension settles. Life falls back into rhythm. We breathe a big sigh of relief. That was a close one; we both feel that.

Let's move on.

* * *

Four years later. We have four kids. He's starting his own web development business from home. The day he quit his job, I made steak for supper, a celebratory gesture to convey my full support for his entrepreneurial dreams. I'm our bookkeeper, and each month, it's my job to add up our budget and let him know how much money we'll need to survive. It's his job to figure out how to make it. So far, we haven't missed a single bill.

I have big responsibilities at church; I'm the President of the Young Women's organization. He helps with the kids while I'm off running youth nights and summer camps for our ward. To my relief, he has long since stopped going to 12-step meetings and sobriety is assumed, a now-irrelevant problem from the past. I think, *Thank goodness—we have another night of our life back.*

Life is moving so fast now, and on the outside, it looks successful, but inside, we are imploding. Every time I try to talk to him, he is mad. Hard eyes filled with darkness. A defiant and impenetrable mask on his face.

"Where are you?" I keep asking. "Maybe this is the problem…" I lecture. I am trying so hard to figure it out.

"Why would I ever want to talk to you?" he says. "You just think you're better than me." Mostly, he says nothing.

I beg him, plead with him to talk to me, to come to bed with me. He sits silent with a stone face. "Okay, I guess I am going to bed then," I say, climbing the stairs by myself again.

I guess it's normal. Everybody has stress. Four kids, starting his own business… That's stressful, right? I need to support him. I will plan a special date for us next weekend. This is normal, right? My parents don't always go to bed at the same time...

One summer night, I wake up sobbing, terrified, and heart-pounding. I have woken him and he asks if I am alright. "I had a dream, a dream that you had a girlfriend online. That you were having an affair," I am crying and shaking, but now he is holding me and I quickly calm down. Such a thought never entered my mind, before or after. We both go back to sleep, back to the treadmill of anger and blame and misery. He even seems to be losing interest in sex, though I am careful to make myself available. For the first time in our marriage, there are times when he cannot perform sexually.

* * *

One year later, and I am so tired. Tired of my resentment, of his rage and blame. Tired of trying to figure out what I can do better. Tired of fighting the deep gnawing at the back of my head that I am beginning to hate my husband. *How can I be a better wife? What am I doing wrong?* Praying to God, *Please, tell me, God... How can I be a better wife?*

One Friday, we meet after work for a date at the temple, the holiest house of worship in the Mormon faith. As I sit in the stillness with a prayerful and pleading heart, God finally whispers, "Ask him if he's on porn." This is something that has not occurred to me in the slightest.

Later, we head to our favorite sushi restaurant. Sitting across the table, my heart is pounding. I ask: "Are you back on porn?"

He answers with no words but with the face of a deer caught in headlights.

I'm thrown off guard by the overpowering emotion that bursts up from the pit of my gut into my throat and my face. My mind is silently putting together pieces of the past year—synapses flashing as I relive each accusation he has thrown at me, each silent treatment he has given me, each time he has demanded quiet in the house because he is "working in his office," each time I am shushing the kids because we can't bother Daddy, each time I am apologizing, and trying to be more sexual and flirting and planning dates and apologizing and listening and asking and talking and putting my whole self out there and getting nothing...nothing...NOTHING...and being told it is me...it is me...it is ME...and trying so hard to be good, to be better, to be enough…and all this time, all this time, all this time…it is the PORN. THE PORN. *THE PORN.*

I've been playing myself so small, into such a corner for his comforts, taking the blame to be good enough for someone who, this entire time, was hiding part of himself—a very impactful piece of our relational problems—from me, and actively telling me that I was the problem.

In a split second, I go from clueless to knowing, deeply knowing, that no matter what he has done that I have never seen him do, this doing is affecting every single aspect of our lives. Before I know what is happening, I am throwing my glass of water in his face and walking out of the restaurant—I guess throwing water is some kind of gut-level thing for me—I am walking down the sidewalk of Riverwoods outdoor mall, hanging lights twinkling above my head, couples arm in arm floating in my peripheral vision. I am hearing a horrible sound, a guttural moaning, like an animal dying, and it takes me a good thirty seconds to realize it is me. I am shaking, moaning, I am dying. *What is this pain? What is happening to me?*

I get in my car and begin to drive. Now, it is raining, water pelting my windshield. I can't see where I am going, and part of me hopes I run into something. I dial my mom, forgetting that it is close to midnight where she is. The alarm in her voice as she hears my own does not even faze me. "Mom. He's back on porn. He's back on porn, and I don't know what to do." This is the first time it really registers that, as we say in Step One of the Twelve Steps, I am chasing a snowball down a hill.

An hour later, he opens the door after dropping off the babysitter, and the house is dark. I am lying in the dark with a stinging face, clinging so far to the edge of our bed it is remarkable I have not fallen off. I listen with dread to the sounds of the garage door closing, him hanging the car keys, opening kitchen cabinets, and the creak of his footsteps nearing our bedroom door. My heart is still racing, but my body and brain are so tired. I am sinking into a black hole, and everything is beginning to feel so slow, so empty, so dark.

"I'm going to go back to the Bishop," he says as he climbs into bed, turns his back to me, and seeps into his pillow.

It is my turn to say nothing. I have no words.

I slowly sink into a sandpit of darkness; alone, isolated, afraid, and not believing for a second that his talk with our church leader or his return to

12-step meetings will make any difference. He is still angry and defiant. I am still not enough. And there is nothing I can do about it.

* * *

Two months later is the spring Sunday night when we discuss the Sunday School lesson and he off-handedly mentions his online affair.

That Sunday marks the beginning of six months of ongoing disclosures, where every few days, weeks, months, another discovery leaves me reeling, eyes open to different aspects and lengths of his acting out that I'd never even considered, trying to wrap my mind around a whole next level of reality to accept.

Eventually, my neatly packaged weekly resolves disappear from my journal. A stupefied emptiness seems to take their place. It appears I will be grieving longer than planned.

Down the Rabbit Hole

Becky Moller, May 2014

Deep inside the rabbit hole,
Panting, sweating, gasping for air.
Trying to claw his way out
Of the pit he so gradually chose to explore.
One slippery step at a time, loose gravel skidding under each carefully
placed paw,
Willfully making his way down, glancing behind him…
No one is watching…

But now it's clear
There is no traction.
His feet flail wildly.
It's a slippery slope, a gaping hole,
It will claim him, body and soul, if he doesn't turn around now.

RIGHT NOW! CLIMB!! GET OUT!!
His paws claw frantically at the smooth, wet soil,
His only chance at escape. His heart begins to pound.
How had he felt so comfortable coming down this far?
His eyes dart around in the dark, his breath, shallow and quick,
His instincts have finally returned and he realizes he may be trapped.

NO NO NO!! HOW DID I GET HERE?
He desperately clings to the falling rocks and scattering pebbles
That rain in his frenetic attempt to escape.
He makes headway, lunges, starts, stops, clings to a few loose roots.
Hurls himself forward, white-knuckled grip, scraping himself towards
the light.

Suddenly, I hear him. I know where he is.
I see the struggle to live or die.
I breathe into the deep pain in my chest,
I feel the full impact of the situation,
Realizing every step he had to take to get so deep into this pit.

This is not the first time he's been here. How could he have forgotten its treachery?
How could he have forgotten how difficult it was to get out before?
How could he? How could he?
How could he?

But as I hear the quivering body,
Buried in the dark,
I am moved with compassion.
A gift from God.
And I throw myself on the ground and reach out my arm.

Immediately, I find him, his flailing paws that end in sharp claws.
The points cut deep into my flesh; the pain almost more than I can bear.
I grit my teeth and grasp firmly onto his shaking limbs.
He grabs onto my flesh and squeezes desperately. *Don't leave me!*
Not even realizing that the scratches he inflicts leave deep, red wounds.
Even now, they fester and sting.

In my pain, I writhe around,
Sending more mud down the hole.
He is trying to find the light, but the darkness rains down upon him,
A fallout from my pain
Threatens to bury him, pushes him further down the hole.
Now, he is sliding, losing traction,
And I lie thrashing in misery myself, my arm shoved into the earth,
Barely holding on, my heart, breaking.
I am in so much pain, but I cannot lose him.

When suddenly, strong arms appear to pick me up with surety.
They wrap around my struggling shoulders and whisper,
"This is too deep for you."
Gently, they set me at my Savior's feet,
His hand so reassuringly stroking my head.

He reaches into the pit with calm strength.
So effortlessly, He grasps onto shaking, sliding paws,
With one fell swoop He lifts him up to the Light.
He holds him tenderly for a moment.

My husband's small, frail body shakes from the effort,
Blinking clumps of dirt from eyelids as he slowly comes back to himself,
From the terror of the dark,
From the very near reality that he had almost gone too far,
Too far to scrape his way out of that hole.

Loving arms stroke his battered, matted fur, and
Knowing eyes gaze into his soul with compassion.
The Savior loves him. He wants him back.

He pleads with him to stay away from the hole.
Never to go sniffing around there again.
Never to test the edge with his paw like that.
Never to come wandering back anywhere near this spot of ground.

He releases him to my waiting arms,
And relief floods my chest.
I feel his body and spirit return to me from their long absence,
Gratitude for the rescue overflows my heart.

But as I look down at the tattered flesh of my own arm,
Scraped into oblivion from the effort of reclamation,
I know I cannot survive this again.

I know He will be there next time, to pull him out with strong and
steady arms,
If he chooses to come.
But my beleaguered body and spirit cannot endure it again.
This is the last time I will reclaim what chose to be lost.
Fear settles deep into my heart, the pit of my stomach, the marrow of
my bones,
As we run away, bodies pressed together.
Backs turned to the awful pit,
The thief of our happiness and the source of our pain.

Will he be able to stay away?
We cannot possibly build enough fences.

CHAPTER FOUR

I Can Fix That!

At this point, Sundays might be my hardest days of the week: the day I feel and see most clearly that I no longer belong where I once did. It's the day I'm forever trying to stitch back together the sureties that have been blown apart. One such Sunday, I come home from church and journal my newest insight:

God has felt so distant lately...and it occurs to me that it may be a sign... that God may be trying to restore the patriarchal order in our home. For a long time, I have been rowing this boat of our marriage and family. I was strong, I was confident, I was independent, I was frustrated that my husband, for a reason I could not identify or explain, was not rowing it. So, I just took the oars and started rowing.

But Heavenly Father's plan is not to have me row our family's boat. That is Nate's job. And if God continues to give me the answers, it will be too easy to go back to rowing it. I think maybe I need to be compelled to rely on Nate for spiritual guidance, and he needs to feel the stewardship of his role as head of our home and family. This answer was confirmed for me today at church as the speaker spoke about personal revelation and worthiness. I am so grateful to see the bigger picture and recognize that God is not leaving me, He is realigning me with His plan.

It breaks my heart to look back at passages like these and see how hard I am trying to humble myself, take responsibility, and receive the counsel. I am so quick to assume that I am the problem. Staying in line, making sure

I keep myself smaller than "the man," "being nice" is how I instinctively believe I will regain my safety. This is my framework.

And it's the lens I view our situation through as I spend most of my waking hours piecing together the ugly puzzle inside my head, between diaper changes, dishes, fitness classes, and good-night kisses. The obsession grows more feverish because new information keeps trickling out, and I know in my gut we haven't gotten even close to the bottom of understanding any of it. Just when I feel like I have some sort of handle on what's happening, a new detail pulls the chair from under me again. I begin to feel too afraid to try to sit down anymore.

For more than three years, Nate has been attending our church's version of the renowned 12-step addiction recovery program to address his pornography problem. So, our automatic assumption is that sexual addiction is the culprit that got us here. And within the first month, this is the church-focused lens we both turn to for help.

My first 12-step meeting is a massive train wreck. Just over a week after our *Sunday Night Disclosure,* Nate and I had walked hand in hand into a church building for this unwelcome first. Before he headed toward the packed classroom for pornography addicts, he patted my shoulder, a paltry encouragement for the feat I was facing: my official initiation into a club I never wanted to join.

When I bravely opened the door, I was met with two elderly female name-tagged missionaries, sitting in a room of empty desks and chairs. Their faces lit up when they saw me, and I immediately got the unfortunate sense that they were both delighted and surprised that someone had shown up.

Over the next ninety minutes, I learned that they were both well-worn alcoholics volunteering at the pornography-addiction spouse-support group. Neither one had ever experienced betrayal, and I proved to be the lone participant all night. I cried uncontrollably through the whole meeting and left with one tragic thought: *Am I the only one in this entire city wretched enough to be cheated on?*

But I am committed to following the rules of recovery, so I keep trying. Eventually, Nate and I find a well-attended 12-step group at another church building twenty minutes from our house. We diligently drive the distance weekly and settle into our groups. These meetings give me a place to hear others' experiences and release the pressure of secret-keeping each week.

I buy half a dozen books and throw myself into understanding a completely new world: the world of addiction, compulsive sexual behavior, and betrayal. I read and journal hundreds of pages. We both find therapists. Recovery is now a full-time job. I live every second of every day desperately looking for the answer. If I can figure out the root of the problem, then I can control it.

We need more sex? *Great! I can do that!*

I need to be less driven? *Totally doable! I no longer care about anything other than saving our marriage.*

Nate's an addict? *Right-o! We've got a solid prescription of Twelve Steps and therapy.*

Check, check, and double-check!

These surface solutions give me a sort of footing through the chaos of the first-year post-disclosure. But such fear-based motives also keep me in the realm of reactive decisions that eventually only add to my pain and self-blame.

Sometimes, what I really want is the safety of being blameless. In some ways, when I ask, "How did we get here?" what I'm really asking is: "Is this Nate's fault? Or is it mine?" If it's Nate's, then *whew...let's make sure everyone realizes I'm innocent.* There's some safety in that.

But not really. There's a relentless voice in my head insisting I must have done something to deserve this, and I find a strange safety in that line of thinking, too. After all, if I caused the problem, then I can fix it.

I know I am lucky to have a husband who is willingly disclosing the truth. For the first time in our marriage, we are playing with a full deck. For the first time, all the information is out on the table. No more missing pieces. No more hidden secrets. No more unconscious shame erupting inexplicably as rage at me or my kids. Night after night, we put the kids to bed and then spend hours peeling his sex addiction apart.

Why and when does he act out?

First, we wonder if maybe the problem is all those babies. At a glance, his acting-out cycles seem to coincide with my pregnancies. *I can fix that.* We make a quick and rash decision for Nate to undergo a vasectomy. Even though I always wanted five children, I'm not willing to risk another pregnancy if it means getting cheated on again. We make an appointment and buy a jockstrap and bags of frozen peas. *Check.*

Connection is another theory we come up with together. I've been reading about pornography's exploitative pull for false connection, and Nate acknowledges that he often feels lonely. *I can fix that.* So, I take on another responsibility: to make sure Nate never feels disconnected. I will make sure I am always here, always available. *Check.*

Nate's therapist suggests the problem has more to do with Nate's inability to deal with difficult emotions than it has to do with me. After all, the problem was here long before Nate and I even met each other. *I can still help fix that.* I commit myself to never reacting to Nate's attacks. Instead, I will recognize his angry outbursts as signs that he is struggling. I must stay calm and help him connect with his emotions. *Check. At least, theoretical check.*

Day by day, as Nate finds the courage to honestly share his secrets and I find the courage to hear them, we piece together the emerging narrative that seems to answer our imperative: *This* is how we got here, this pattern that cycles through every few years: from stress to anger and isolation, to acting out and hiding, to pushing away and gaslighting, to confession and remorse, to honeymoon periods of calm and abstinence...until inevitably a new stress comes along and triggers the same insanity all over again. It's the classic addict cycle: shame/pain to pre-occupation, pre-occupation to ritualizing, ritualizing to acting out, acting out to more shame and pain. Round and round it goes.

As we're given the addiction framework, it seems to make sense of our entire marriage, and Nate readily proclaims, "I am a sex addict." There's a seeming relief as he recognizes the cycle in himself and acknowledges that it has *always* been at play; his long periods of seeming sobriety are more aptly a disguised repression—a pseudo-healing that amounted to nothing more than white-knuckling.

His "addict" declaration, rather than making him feel ashamed, seems to free him, offering words, reasons, and brotherhood to share in what previously must have felt like a supremely lonely struggle. The hole he so often feels inside of himself now has a name: "God-hunger," as the 12-steppers say. Suddenly, he is not so alone in his pain.

MIND
SELF-ABSORBED CHATTER

BODY
DISCONNECTION

SHAME creates SEPARATION & SUFFERING

HARM is CAUSED, SUBSEQUENT SHAME

INABILITY to COPE with NEGATIVE EMOTIONS

ESCAPE PAIN by ACTING OUT in ADDICTION

BUILD a CASE for VICTIM IDENTITY & JUSTIFIED HARM

FIXATION & FANTASY

SPIRIT
ISOLATION

ADDICTION CYCLE

"Unconscious Insanity—driven by fear & judgment."

beckymoller.com

But as Nate's burden lightens, mine deepens. Day in and day out, I obsessively scrutinize our past through the addiction model. It brings sense to much of the chaos: it explains the personality shifts that spew out during Nate's long periods of self-betrayal, and his almost-giddy carefree highs at the top of the peaks. It calls out the vast difference between "not using" and actual healing and seems to unlock the mystery of the Dr. Jekyll and Mr. Hyde I've lived with these twelve years.

There's an undeniable comfort in seeing our chaos drawn out on paper, of seeing the science behind the patterns and knowing we are neither alone nor crazy. But right alongside this comfort, I feel my sinking smallness against it: this powerful tide I have no hope of controlling. Clarity isn't coming fast enough. Everything feels murky and senseless, our progress feels so up and down. This pattern, this compulsion, this history and baggage and weight… it all feels so much bigger than me. We are in so far over our heads.

What I want is solid ground, something logical and concrete that secures a future where we won't repeat these insane cycles of suffering. So, I cling to resolutions, and I pile on promises to perfectly support Nate's recovery, to be long-suffering, patient, attentive, and always available. But even as I do, a debilitating weight settles onto my shoulders like a heavy chain. The sense of inevitable failure sinks deep in my stomach.

How long can I keep this up?

JUST SHUT UP
BECKY MOLLER, MAY 2014

Please, shut my mouth and open my ears,
How I've loved the sound of my voice.

Trying so desperately to understand how we got here,
I tried to force you to see we were in free fall.
When you refused to open your mouth,
I opened mine for you.
Telling you why you were so angry,
Telling you why you were stonewalling.
How I had everything all figured out.
You didn't seem to be thinking about it.
So I thought for you.

But it wasn't fair to put words in your mouth. To put thoughts in
your head.
In my desperation to understand, I played the role of omniscient,
And assigned you motive and method.
How right I was is not the point.
The point is that I had no right.

Would things be different if I had only asked?
Just asked the question? Again and again?
Darling, what is wrong?
Just patiently waited when you stared into my eyes, face laden with hate,
teeth clenched, jaw set,
If I could have seen past your hostility and silence,
And seen your pain, your weakness, the sin you wanted to hide for shame,
And had the mercy and patience to wait another day and ask again,
My love, my love, what is wrong?

Would things have been different?
How many times would I have had to ask?
Fewer times than I lectured, my heart whispers.
Unkind words spewed in frustration wouldn't have left me with so
much regret.
May have coaxed you, ever so gently, to say,
Here I am. Help me.

CHAPTER FIVE
How Did *I* Get Here?

When your partner betrays you, it's easy to fixate on their behavior, their past, their childhood trauma. But over time, it becomes clear that no matter how hard you try, you can't change, fix, or control any of that. So eventually, my framework changed. I realized that if I really wanted to *heal,* I had to start asking how we got here without an agenda. I had to ask it to *understand,* not to fix or blame or control. And I had to love myself and trust myself enough not to be afraid of the answer.

This took time—years really. Because with time, it became more and more apparent: no matter how sober Nate got, no matter how informed or submissive I became, no matter how many fences we built around his hurtful behaviors or how many apologies he made, my pain was still there. My fear was still there.

Eventually, I started asking: *What is my part? How did I get here...so lost and scared and desperate?*

Thus began a deconstruction of my little self—my ego—the unraveling of the stories and identities I'd been living through my whole life, completely unaware. This deconstruction didn't actually start until much later—three years later, to be exact—when I was finally out of the physiological trauma haze and I had the bandwidth for it.

And, dear reader, that timeline is crucial. After any rock bottom, your solid prescription is self-care, support, and space for grief. For me, the grieving stage hung around for one to three years after Nate's *Sunday Night Disclosure,* a hearty length of time I often resisted, kicking and screaming. But my temper tantrums were pointless: the grief would take as long as it would take, and there was little I could do except surrender to it.

From a physiological perspective, I was stabilizing my nervous system, learning to recognize my triggers and ground myself through embodied trauma responses. From a spiritual perspective, I was clearing space: emptying the clutter of my strong opinions, my clear definitions of success, my narrow hopes for my life journey, and my limiting beliefs.

Over the years, I created enough safety inside myself to look inward with trust—in my own Self and a Higher Power who has my back. As meditation allowed me to look deeper, what I found surprised me. Snippets of memories began to weave an awakening—a slight shift from my previously idealized life narrative. I learned to follow the river of my pain to its source. I learned to sit with it and allow it to teach me:

Where in my body do I feel this pain the most?

What is the quality and texture of the sensation in my body?

Have I ever felt this before?

What do I need right now, if anything?

With practice, I learned how to investigate through my body instead of my mind. I learned to find an open space of awareness inside of me, with no agenda. Just an open cloud of loving curiosity.

Darling, I'm here. Darling, I want to see you. Darling, I want to understand.

Memories began to float from my subconscious, painting a new picture on the canvas of my personal history. The therapeutic exercise of a Trauma Egg gave me my first concrete way to collect these memories on the page. I looked inside and allowed any impression that still held a negative charge to surface. Without judging or arguing with it, I sketched it on a page: stick figures with snippets of words and phrases. I filled a large egg shape on a blank posterboard with such small bubbles of memory, what yogis refer to as Samskaras: experiences that for one reason or another leave an impression on our internal system and get stuck.

The picture they created opened my eyes to a new story, a story just as real as my idealized narrative. A picture of a little girl who desperately wanted to be loved, who was always striving so hard to belong. A picture of a little girl who pushed herself to the brink, who became sure that perfection was the only way to secure her safety, bringing pressure and insecurity into every interaction, killing herself to be enough, and resenting when others overlooked the overwhelming price she was paying for their love. A picture of a little girl who had always carried the pain I was feeling in one way or another.

Healing began with seeing this little girl inside of me…and recognizing that brick by brick, one experience at a time, she had created a way of being in the world that was unsustainable: driven by fear, resting on unrealistic expectations (her own and others'), and void of self-compassion. Her well-intended confusion about who she was had so much to do with how I got here.

* * *

I am a little girl, seven or eight, and I'm lucky enough to be in the high school production of *The Sound of Music* with my brother and sister. I play Marta, and although I'm not as cute as my little sister, who plays Gretl, I feel special to be with high school kids on a big stage under bright lights.

Today, the makeup artist is demonstrating stage makeup, and she picks me to come up and be her assistant. When she lifts my straight, flat bangs, a ripple of giggles and sidelong glances skitters across the teenagers. I feel my face flush hot with embarrassment and remember the hundreds of tiny pink pimples that cover my forehead, hidden underneath my bangs. I know they are laughing at me. But I sit frozen under their scrutiny in the glaring lights of the dressing room until the end of the demonstration, all the while cementing what I feel in that shameful moment: *I am a freak. I am exposed. I am disgusting.*

* * *

I am in seventh grade but sit in the back row of the only extra-advanced eighth-grade math class at the Junior High. This class has the most popular eighth graders and the most beautiful boy I've ever seen. Of course, none of the cool people talk to me. I am one of only three seventh graders in the class, including a boy who wears matching sweatsuits every day and another who never brushes his teeth or his hair. We're the "smart freaks."

I finish the last question on the test and know intuitively that I've scored 100% again. Our teacher posts the grades each week according to our student ID number, but everyone has figured out mine. I have the highest grade in class, and whenever a new grade sheet is posted, the most popular girl sneers at me and rolls her eyes at her friends, who erupt into giggles and whispers. I pretend I can't hear them, but I do.

Today, I turn my pencil upside down and erase two of my answers, changing them to different, wrong numbers. Maybe this will go over better. It's important to be good, but not too good. I hand in my paper and congratulate myself for finding a way to keep myself small enough to be loved. Or at least not hated.

I may be only in seventh grade, but I'm already mapping the rules of engagement. I'd rather be accepted than shining, and it's becoming clear I have to choose.

* * *

I am in ninth grade and have my most serious crush yet. At our last regional church dance, musky, wonderful Joshua grabbed my waist and swept me away for at least three slow dances, smelling of the most delicious cologne. It feels like a miracle that he is paying attention to me...*to ME!* I'm usually the friend, the confidante, short and unimpressive, the little sister with acne and a dreamy big brother. My brother is sparkly and funny, bright and shiny. He steals the stage wherever we go and I am genuinely proud of him from my corner.

After that weekend, a group of us, my brother included, decide to drive to another weeklong church camp in a different state, and Joshua wants to come. He calls every day. We talk and laugh, and I can't wait. On the drive down to camp, my whole body tingles every time his arm brushes mine. The tension is palpable in our playful banter and any time our pinkies inadvertently touch. I breathe in his heavy *Cool Waters* aroma, in heaven, all six hours of the ride.

But when the camp starts, we are organized into different groups, and before I know it, he has found a bright and shiny girl of his own; tall, skinny as a rail, with full pink lips and a curvy chest to boot. Out of my league—it's a no-brainer. By the end of the week's festivities, every girl at the camp is smitten as usual with my brother and his friend, who've reigned supreme as the bright-and-shinies-of-the-week.

Joshua has spent most of the week making out with Tall Skinny Blonde With Lush Lips. When the six of us drive home in the packed car, there is zero electricity and supreme awkwardness. I lean so far against the door that I could pop out of it. I am not mad. I am more…resigned. Accepting defeat: *It's okay. This is just who I am. Can't blame him. When you could have bright and shiny, why would anyone pick me?*

* * *

I am seventeen years old and am inexplicably being pursued by the most eligible bachelor in my church region: Ryan. He is everything I have never trusted: flirtatious, good-looking, popular, charismatic, and the quarterback for his high school football team. It seems unreal that his gaze settled upon me at one of last summer's regional church activities. From the moment he stumbled up a steep set of stairs to ask me on a date and I teased him mercilessly for it, the game was on. We've been dating on and off for the past six months, and things are getting serious.

I believe deep down that he shouldn't be interested in me. I know he is out of my league, but I am enjoying the newfound euphoria of being chased by someone I'm actually interested in. I am playfully coy and cautious, safely aloof, and I keep the nagging feeling of imminent abandonment primarily at bay. As spring warms the air and heats up our relationship, I stop eating because I've decided I am too fat. After all, a guy like him deserves more than me. He deserves someone bright and shiny.

Almost overnight, my life begins to mold around my new objective. I avoid my friends at lunch hour and find some reason to be busy for family dinner. I walk daily on my parents' treadmill, something I have never done before. Within a month, I have dropped over fifteen pounds, and my unathletic-but-not-really-overweight figure has slimmed down to a waif-like form. I am enchanted and enthralled; this newfound power brings fresh purpose to my daily existence.

Everything else in my life fades to the background as I zero in on the scale: the uncertainty of the future, my impending high school graduation, the inevitable termination of this whirlwind romance.

But this number on the scale, this is something I seem to have total control over.

It's like a drug to my system to watch how magically I can make the scale drop. Day after day, I shock myself with my ability to eat less and less.

My mind is more powerful than my body, and this makes me feel invincible. When hunger and weakness threaten to override my willpower, I lace up my walking shoes and motivate myself with cruel self-talk: *You are fat! You are fat! You are fat!* I chant to myself with each footstep. *You are ugly! You are ugly! You are ugly!* It keeps me moving on another stretch of highway. *You need to look like the kind of girl he deserves. Or he is going to leave you.* It helps me push the hunger away for another hour.

What I don't realize is that each time I cut myself off from my body, each time I punish my reflection in the mirror, I fragment off another piece of my heart. I am trading the temporary euphoria of total control for joy. I am trading the unique expression of my own soul for the security of matching myself to airbrushed images. Each time I shut my ears to the pleading requests of my own body, the divine thread that connects me back to Source grows a little thinner. And I don't even know I am doing it. With a bright and shiny smile on my face and a hard, triumphant heart, I'm trading my birthright for a mess of pottage.

* * *

I'm eighteen years old and I want so badly to make my senior year of high school perfect, to do amazing things, to leave my mark on this place. I am the Senior Class Treasurer, an officer in the Environmental Club, and head of the madrigal singers. I am the lead in the high school musical, and I single-handedly choreographed the end-of-year madrigal dinner show. I am taking Advanced College Calculus II home-study because they don't offer any math classes I haven't taken at the high school. I am acing all of the weighted classes I could possibly register for. In a class of 650, I am currently ranked #4 with a perfect 4.0. I am in the Kiwanis Club and am composing an original choral piece to be sung by the madrigals at graduation. I am the president of my age group at church. I am designing huge art panels to decorate the gym for prom with my art class. I am still somehow inexplicably dating the most fabulous, cute, quarterback-popular guy in my church region. I feel totally in control of my world.

Until I don't. Until it's all too much, all of a sudden. Until I realize that I don't have time for my friends because I am too afraid they will want to go eat somewhere, and I don't do that anymore. Until I realize I am snippy and demanding towards everyone in my family because they are all just obstacles in the way of me adding another bullet point to my resume. Until I realize I cannot separate the way my body is disappearing from the way my soul is disappearing, and I'm not willing to let go. Suddenly, I am lost and weak and fragile and brittle and numb. I cannot even fathom the joyful and confident person I appeared to be once upon a time, just months ago.

How did I get here?

And then one day, in the midst of a million end-of-year deadlines, I pull an all-nighter on my final paper for Advanced World History. I find myself walking in late to school, totally uncharacteristic of me. My choir teacher, usually my buddy-old-pal, sees me in the hall and asks where I'm headed. "Oh, I'm late today. Can I get a note from you?"

He pats my shoulder and gives a knowing shake of his head. "Oh no, no, no…you seniors think you own this place! Let's get you to the office for a tardy slip." At first, I think he's joking, but then suddenly I'm shaking, and tears are leaking out of my eyes.

All the balls. All the balls I am juggling. I can't flinch. I can't pause. I can't breathe. I can't stop. I will drop the balls. The balls are dropping. Everything is closing in. I can feel my buddy-old-pal getting stiffer and more uncomfortable as we make our way to the office, and I am falling apart, and he virtually shoves me through the door and hightails it away.

My art teacher buddy-old-pal is in there and sees immediately that I am not okay. She slowly sits me down on a chair as I crumble before her eyes. I cannot speak. She has the office call my mother, who takes me home, where I retreat into sleep. I wake up hours later and realize I never turned in my paper. I have missed the deadline. I freak out, hysterically berating my mom, stomping through the house, blaming her and everybody at the school for this life-ending disaster. I am a crazy woman. The balls are flying. This is the first sign that something inside of me has broken. I have snapped under the pressure. And nobody but me is putting it there.

* * *

I am eighteen at college. There's this guy—now that I'm twenty pounds lighter, there are lots of them. I am bright and shiny now, and I like it. A lot. This guy, however, is different than the rest. See, Jared knew me before I was skinny. He is five years older than me, and his little sister and I have been best friends for years. There has always been this unspoken thing between us, a flirtation, an expectation. But he was twenty-one and I was sixteen when his family moved to our ward and we began spending his summers home from college in perfect teenage tension.

But as I got older, this playful fantasy became an all-too-heavy reality. When I graduated high school, I reluctantly kissed my puppy-love high school quarterback goodbye for the last time. He was off to BYU and would leave on his mission (Mormon men often serve a two-year proselytizing mission at the age of nineteen) in a few months. And Jared was waiting impatiently in the wings.

As I drink in the giddy joy of belonging at BYU (the first place it's ever NOT been weird for me to be a Mormon), my frequent dates are peppered with awkward excursions with Jared. But after the sweeping and unexpected romance of my senior year, our outings feel sterile and uncomfortable. We've never even held hands, and the idea of kissing him makes me almost burst out laughing.

One late afternoon in downtown Provo, we sit at a table at an outdoor café, and he lays it to me straight: "Here's the thing," he says. "I've been waiting around for you a long time. But the Becky I knew before was different. You were curvy and fun and funny and smart. Now you've got this eating thing. You've lost all this weight, and people are saying you're anorexic. And I've looked into this...and if you've got this eating thing, it might affect your ability to have kids...and I've got to think about my future. I mean, before, I thought you were perfect. But you're not."

His words hang heavy in the air, and I begin to feel removed from my body, like I'm floating ten feet above this conversation. There is a part of me that is hard and brittle and caustic, that's almost laughing inside as he speaks.

You're not perfect. So I don't want you.

The words that have unconsciously been my very worst fear for my entire life have just materialized in front of my face. *So, this is what this feels like*, I think. *To be totally rejected.*

Well, it's a good thing you figured it out now. That I'm not perfect. I would've hated to disappoint you once it was too late.

* * *

I am twenty years old and am so afraid for my heart. There is this guy, Nate. For the first time since Ryan in high school, I am on a roller coaster where I'm not entirely in control. I'm twisting and turning with emotions, confused and afraid that I'm going to get this all wrong. After a year of casual dates, prank wars, food fights, ice-cream runs, and midnight chats, Nate and I are dating. Quite seriously. And at BYU, it often goes from first date to the altar, often almost overnight—*crazy, right?!*

This is one reason I haven't even held a guy's hand since I came here. I've gone on scores of dates; almost every weekend, I've been out with someone different. But nobody has even piqued my interest. My heart still belongs to my Ryan, my first love, my high school quarterback. He returns home from his two-year mission in a few short months. I've just started my junior year of college, and it seems that everything is setting up to work out perfectly, which is why I want to kick myself for deciding to date Nate over the fall.

Nate has been like a little brother to me for the past year and a half. He lives down the hall and our friendship started when he and his roommates filled my entire car with wadded-up newspaper as a joke. My roommates and I responded by nailing them with an entire bucket of water from a second-story window. *I would say we won the prank-war, wouldn't you?*

Our first unofficial date was last year: a Halloween party where I just happened to dress like a cheesehead and he just happened to dress like a cow. Since then, we became each other's easy pick for last-minute dates or group outings. We seemed to go together like, well…cows and cheeseheads.

Except for when we don't, that is. Many days, I simply have way too much fun being bright and shiny to pair off with anyone. And although Nate and I are peanut butter and jelly when it's just the two of us, in groups we are oil and water. He is clingy and weird. I feel suffocated and smothered. Even as we come out as an official couple, there are times when I dread coming home to my apartment, knowing he is going to be sitting there waiting for me. The pit in my stomach tells me I'm not sure how I feel about our growing relationship.

So, when Ryan returns home from his mission, I am caught in a vortex of confusion and fear. *What am I going to do?* I come home from a date with Nate, and Ryan calls me on the telephone. I'm not hiding anything from either of them, but I feel a mounting guilt and pressure. Someone is going to be very disappointed. Someone is going to get hurt. And it is going to be my fault.

I decide to cut it off with Nate. When I do, he calls and asks me to come to his apartment. He plays a song on his guitar that he's written for me. The words are simple and perfect:

"Just want you to know you're my very best friend,
I could be with you 'til the very end
Of each and every day, it's just the way
I feel inside, no I can't deny..."

He asks if he can hold me one more time, and we dance to the radio in his room, clinging to each other with tears running down our cheeks. Eventually, I peel myself away and run down the hall to my apartment. I slam the door, hyperventilating. *What am I doing?* I call home. My dad answers the phone. "I don't know what to do, Dad. I don't know what to do. He just loves me so much," I say. I am terrified of making the wrong choice.

Weeks pass, and I avoid Nate like the plague. I fly home for Thanksgiving. I see Ryan, and although things are different after a two-year absence, I feel fairly confident that this is still the path I want to take. I ask my parents what they think. My dad says, "You already know what to do." This annoys me because I have never known less what to do. *What is that supposed to mean?* In my mind, I make a firm resolve. Ryan will start as a student at BYU in January, and so I'll just wait for him. My only goal is to avoid all boys until then.

I fly back to school, and Nate offers to pick me up from the airport, which is weird because we haven't spoken for weeks. For some inconceivable reason, I accept his offer. As soon as I settle into the front seat, Nate's infectious teasing pulls me in, and there's not a moment of silence all the way home. It just feels so easy with him. Before I set foot back in my apartment, Nate and I are dating again. *What?! How did this happen?!*

I just need to make sure. I just need to give this one more try, so I will know for sure, I tell myself. This time, our whirlwind romance picks up another notch. My heart outwits my head, and I'm falling faster than I can track. Even though my mind keeps coming up with reasons it won't work, I cannot deny that every time I'm with Nate, I feel so safe. I feel so seen. I have never met anyone who seems so interested in really, truly knowing me—and not just the bright and shiny me I've learned to project to the world. The *real* me—warts and all. His playful laugh, his mischievous grin, his unabashed arrogance. It's all so irritating and endearing. *Why is he so sure I will pick him in the end?*

But in the end, I do. I fly back home for Christmas and spend much of the week with Ryan, but it is too late. Every moment I'm with him, all I can feel is what's missing: the safety, closeness, and easy connection I feel with Nate. It's over. I am gone. I leave Ryan's house on a dark, snowy Wisconsin night, hop in my parents' minivan and feel my stomach flip as I fire up the engine. *I think I am getting married!* I think in my head.

"I think I am getting married!" I say out loud.

"Oh my gosh—I am getting married!" I shriek into the silence of my parents' minivan. I am giddy and joyful and for just this moment, oh so sure of myself. I call Nate when I get home and tell him the good news. I have made up my mind: It's him I want.

And before I know it, six months have passed, and I've worn the dress and made the vows. I've made my decision and followed it fully through. There are still moments when I feel unsure, when I feel trapped or suffocated, like I am trying to hold up something heavier than I can bear. But this is marriage, and I truly believe that mine will be one of the happiest. After all, Nate is my best friend.

I've also been told that marriage means saying yes to sex. Every time. And so, I do. Even on our wedding night, I've learned that much. And as we fly off to our honeymoon, I don't think twice about the never-ending treadmill I am stepping onto. I have already learned the artful skill of shutting down any bodily protests. That's how I lost almost twenty pounds in one month.

So, sex is just a natural progression, just another aspect of the many ways I am expected to give of myself without a thought for how it feels inside. This is what it means to be a woman, especially a woman of faith. To give selflessly. To put everyone else's needs above my own. I don't resent this. It is simply the way it is. It's what God wants from me. This is how you win at the game, and if there is anything I'm good at, it's reading the game and winning approval. This game of marriage, this is what it has all been about all along. This is the ultimate destination, the final countdown, the World Series. Of course, I am going to do whatever it takes to win here.

In the words of Mormon prophet David O. McKay, "No success can compensate for failure in the home."

* * *

I am thirty-three years old, and it's the pivotal Sunday night of our twelve-year marriage. My husband has just told me about the "inappropriate relationship" he was involved in a year prior. I have thrown a cup full of water, screamed hysterically, and lain in bed hushing my nine-year-old son to sleep.

All the balls. All the balls I am juggling. I can't flinch, I can't pause, I can't breathe, I can't stop. I will drop the balls—a lifetime supply of balls is dropping all around me. Everything is closing in. I have wandered aimlessly around the house, lain down, gotten up, chased my husband around, throwing jabs and questions and "How could you's" and now I am lying on the couch, defeated. I can't carry the balls anymore. For the first time in my life, I must let them fall. As I lie here, I am shocked that this is even possible. And yet, it is.

I am, in this moment, no longer the flame. I am the pitiful pile of ash. It is somewhere close to morning. My husband is lying on the other couch. We stare at each other as if for the first time. He is completely foreign to me.

"How could you do this to me?" I whisper, this time soft and broken, without accusation. This time, it's a pleading, to understand, to make sense of it.

He looks right at me, with the cold, hard, empty mask of a stranger, and says the only words that still ring crystal clear from that horrific night: "I haven't felt you loved me in three years."

Of all the screaming, rage, and wild despair I felt that night, this quiet moment in the eerie stillness of the morning is the moment that truly breaks me. All the chaos swirling in the pieced-together fragments of my shattered mind closes in. Time stands still.

Every failure, every moment I forgot to thank him for helping with a household task, every late night I spent at the church, every time I was too distracted to welcome him home with a hug, every night I was too exhausted to make love with the energy he wanted, every answer I gave him with too sharp a tone, every time I rolled my eyes at him, every failing and frustration of four young kids and a struggling marriage comes crashing down on my barely-hanging-on heart and spirit, and my psyche shatters.

This is your fault. You are a failure. An ugly, fat bitch and a failure. Nobody could ever love you. And deep down inside, you've known it all along. You've always known it. This was always coming for you.

Of all the words he says to me that night and the nights that would follow, these are the words I cannot forget: "I haven't felt you loved me in three years." This is the moment where I willingly take responsibility for it all. This is where all my deepest fears become my chosen identity.

I shrink to a lone atom floating in an infinite universe of dark and empty space. Imploding. The balls are all floating around me in the vastness, floating beyond my fingertips, like clouds of stardust telling how wide the light-years are between myself and everything I thought I knew. I cannot reach them. And for the first time in my life, I do not care. *So, this is what this feels like,* I think. *To be utterly rejected. To fail so completely.*

This is what I have been running from my whole life. Now, here I am.

Looking in the Mirror
Becky Moller, September 2014

My reflection is not my friend today.
Today I only see,
The holes within my character
Of which I'm longing to be free.

Today I see the impossibleness
Of loving my pimpled face.
How everyone must wonder,
"How can he stand to be in her space?"

I think too much, I talk too much,
I'm so sure my eyes see clear.
It's taken betrayal to realize,
I see nothing now but fear.

Everything's so confusing
Nothing I feel makes sense.
How did I think I knew so much?
I'm such a revolting mess.

CHAPTER SIX

THE GLACIER

Home, for me, will always be the rolling hills and cow pastures of rural Wisconsin, where everything is green and lush, damp and always growing. Leafy canopies swallow up entire towns; occasional peeking steeples are the only clue that communities are living, breathing, laughing, and dying amidst the carpet of green. To the casual observer, the landscape is picturesque and straightforward: cornfields, barns, and endless deciduous forests.

But everyone who grew up in this area—known to locals and geologists as the Kettle Moraine—knows there is more to the story. What appears today as a tranquil and overgrown woods was once buried under sheets of ice, sometimes two miles thick. The Ice Age was not a gentle sculptor; frozen panels became powerful swords, slicing through seemingly impenetrable walls of stone, dumping debris in their wake. In short, they made a colossal mess.

But in another way, the Ice Age created a standout topography, uniquely beautiful and complex. In fact, Wisconsin is the best place to witness many of the distinctive landforms created by continental glaciers. Once you become aware of this, you can hardly drive down the highway without some reference to an Ice Age visitor center or hiking trail hitting you in the face.

It seems very important to the people of Wisconsin to honor the history of the land we love: to remember that once, everything that is now so green and vibrant seemed cold and dead. The seemingly stable world was literally flipped upside down. The Ice Age laid the foundation for every breath we take, every footstep we make. It's what shaped the way we see...well, everything.

Glaciers have been described as keystones of life on Earth: they support the planet's ecosystems and transport essential nutrients as they move matter and bear massive reservoirs of freshwater. Yet for all the life-giving nourishment they provide, they are also inherently destructive: gathering gravel, knocking out trees, even displacing mountains. To a family of saber-toothed tigers whose cozy home has just been turned upside down, the impact of glacial upheaval might range from serious inconvenience to utter devastation—even *traumatic*. Standing in the middle of the carving out usually isn't pretty.

But if we zoom out to consider the evolutionary nature of this ball of rock that's sustained life for 3.5 billion years, we recognize that when the Universe seems to be dumping debris on our heads, it's not the end. Instead, we are at the beginning. We are in the creative process of something new, potentially life-giving, drastically different, and potentially closer to our essence.

Mountain ranges soar only after tectonic plates collide. Breathtaking canyons display their otherworldly beauty only after eons of wind and water corrode them to their rugged essence. Many of the most fertile and life-giving places on the planet are often traumatized by tropical storms. Catastrophe, even an Ice Age lasting a few thousand years, can eventually become something beautiful—with a unique and authentic capacity to sustain and nourish—just like the Kettle Moraine.

When we have eyes to see, Mother Earth points to divine patterns everywhere, manifesting the mystery of all that is. In every creation, she whispers, "Look. See. Let me show you how it is." If we lived closer to Her, we might not be so surprised to find that we cannot reach our greatest heights without similar tectonic-scale collisions; that our own breathtaking essence is often revealed through weather that wears our smooth façades away. Rock bottoms, or *traumas*, can operate just like those filthy sheets of ice. And, like saber-toothed tigers, humans have animal instinct, spiritual intuition, and time-tested tools available to navigate the damage, adapt, and even thrive in uncertainty.

Those first stumbling, shaky truths that spring Sunday night were such an upheaval for my husband and me: a new beginning of tenuous truths rather than lies, denial, and unconscious striving. But oh, did it feel like an end. At that moment, *I ended*. Who I was, what I believed about myself, the way

I saw the world—it all ended. For a while, this ending was all I could see. But over time, and with lots of care and tending, it became something new.

Betrayal was the beginning of my unraveling, the glacier that would carve new terrain into my soul for the rest of my life. But it could have been anything. It could have been a financial reversal, a chronic illness, the loss of a child or loved one, an accident, a disability, the list goes on. Any experience that shatters your previous identity has the potential to become such a tectonic-scale collision.

Eventually, this collision cut through the fog, exposing my illusions and leading me intuitively to the Real: that which is universal and indestructible. With support and resources, I have seen trauma become the ugly impetus to a rich bed of empathy, wisdom, and inner strength in myself and many others. Whether trauma becomes our jumping-off point, or the cliff we jump off of, depends on how consciously we move through it.

This movement has a shape and pacing that is a little different for everybody, but it starts with the simple and clear decision to stop resisting and surrender to the natural flow of life. But when life has handed us such a bitter pill, how do we trust it again? This is a profound question that each person must discover for themselves.

Mindfulness, the simple practice of compassionate curiosity, has been the key to this process for me. As I've learned to pause and really observe, I've found it the way of all living things to intuitively grow and reach for the light. This has been true of my houseplants, my children, and my heart.

I've found that when we accept what is and learn to trust the process, we are in line with Nature, with God. From there, trauma-healing becomes an intimate dance with your Deepest Self; a moment-by-moment art form that unfolds through willingness, community, self-awareness, compassion, and aligning ourselves over and over again with the evolutionary laws of Life itself. No matter how long this process takes us, we can trust that with a willing heart, gut-level honesty, and wise action, we are on a healing path.

In contrast, the world around us offers unrelenting strategies to skip past or simply avoid our pain—mental, emotional, physical, or spiritual. We are virtually swimming in a sea of alluring and empty promises of titles, obsessions, sensations, or diversions to keep us comfortably floating along the surface of life.

We can pretend we don't care. We can immerse ourselves in victim narratives and surround ourselves with possessions and people who validate our stories. We can make ourselves so busy we don't have time to think about or feel anything other than what's next on our calendar. We can compare ourselves to others and tell ourselves to suck it up. We can look toward a heavenly reward and say we simply need to endure to the end, all the while bypassing the internal dissonance we feel on a daily basis. We can binge on Netflix or Facebook, drink or drug ourselves into painless oblivion. We can get degrees, plastic surgery, or a promotion and redouble our efforts to secure validation and prove our worth. The ways we might cope are endless, and in light of the legitimate pain we're trying to avoid, they're often understandable.

But none of the coping will free us from the underlying fear or pain that drives our behavior. None of the distractions will transform us from internal bondage to spiritual strength. None of these things will answer our soul's yearnings to be free.

To create a rich and vibrant Kettle Moraine, we first must accept the mess. We must relinquish our resistance to discomfort and allow life to be as it is. We must stop blaming others, casting ourselves as victims, and expecting somebody else to rescue us. We must create space for all of our emotions, pull up a chair, and listen to what they have to teach us. We must pick ourselves up, educate ourselves about what is happening inside, and play the hand we have been dealt. Only then can pain become a pathway to progress.

Making the choice to play our hand rather than wish our circumstances away is difficult. It may take weeks, months, or even years. Believe me, in the face of my husband's betrayals, I spent well over a year spiritually kicking and screaming. But when I finally made the choice to let go and deeply accept my reality, it changed my trajectory. There's been no greater accelerator of divine grace in my life than to submit to exactly what is and become a willing student of the mess.

We also must understand trauma. The American Psychological Association (APA) defines trauma as "the emotional response to a terrible event." But Kirk Voss with EmotionAlly Podcast defines it more colorfully, that: "Trauma is what happens when our individual capacity for coping with something is exceeded or over-run." As in, we hit our own personal ceiling for what we can emotionally process. I like this definition because "over-run" is exactly how trauma felt for me; or rather, *run-over* by a large semi-truck—that my husband was driving. I was flattened, and I simply did not have the tools to navigate or face my new reality. I felt powerless, and in many ways, I was.

And that powerlessness is an important qualifying factor. While we all experience a wide range of stressors, it was helpful to learn that it is the feeling that we were *robbed of our agency* that can tip us from "stressed" to "traumatized," clinically speaking. This is why offering choice is an essential factor in any trauma-informed care. For me, my safest and most primary attachment—my husband—was obliterated overnight. In my mind, his betrayals rewrote the context of our entire relationship. The feeling that I didn't really get to *choose* this person I married—because I didn't really *know* this person I married—created as much trauma as the specific betrayal behaviors themselves. The lack of consent and sense of powerlessness had my limbic system running for the hills.

The loss of primary attachment is another reason why relational trauma is such a doozy, creating layers of complexity to a person's healing process. When people experience a general trauma, their safe and stable attachments typically provide the needed stability for healing. Their limbic survival system is able to settle and calm as they are supported by "their person."

But in Betrayal Trauma, a person's safe and stable attachments are often the very source of their pain. In other words, you're telling your body to relax and drift off to sleep when the dangerous monster who hurt you is lying next to you in bed. Betrayed partners tend to swing on a crazy pendulum of pushing and pulling: desperate for comfort but terrified to put themselves at risk of being hurt again. This was certainly the case for me.

Books like *The Body Keeps the Score* by Bessel van der Kolk and *Your Sexually Addicted Spouse* by Dr. Barbara Steffens gave me the crucial information to better understand my experience and how to work with it. If you're looking to educate yourself on trauma, these are great places to start. What I know and understand about trauma today comes from a decade of educating myself through reading, conferences, and certifications, but most importantly, from my own lived experience and witnessing the experience of others through 12-step fellowship, teaching embodiment classes, running mindfulness groups, and mentoring individuals toward their own mindful awareness.

I have come to passionately believe that widening the lens of what we think of as trauma can help us all to access better tools with more self-love and insight as we work with our emotional baggage. We don't have to be an "expert" to learn wisdom from this very embodied experience, and having the framework of trauma can lead us to a more compassionate, holistic approach. Without it, we can miss the fact that it usually makes perfect sense to be feeling exactly what we are.

In the past decade, I've often reflected on how tragic it is that trauma reactions were likely the very things that shipped people off to asylums in earlier days, and yet they are perfectly understandable evolutionary survival responses. These frightening symptoms spin most people upside down and can appear to outsiders as a wicked tornado ripping the person they knew to shreds. But, in another way, the trauma response is the body's version of tectonic plates colliding, a wise, intuitive message that something inside needs shifting... The world will never be the same...*nor should it.*

And this is where the empowering shift is possible: Pain does not need to be pathologized. Pain can become the teacher, the guide, the Mother, the friend.

What if, when we felt emotional discomfort, we released our dread that something must be deeply wrong, and instead trusted that something in our soul is deeply right...and it won't quiet down until we find a way to heal what's still wounded? What if we were slower to medicate our pain and more committed to following it to the false beliefs and self-betrayals that might be causing it? What if, when we were able, we trusted the Universe enough to let the chaos of trauma carve out a new landscape in our lives, perfectly engineered by a Power greater than ourselves?

This possibility is called post-traumatic growth, and it's exactly what this book is about.

AMBUSH

BECKY MOLLER, MAY 2014

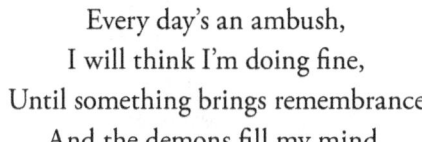

Every day's an ambush,
I will think I'm doing fine,
Until something brings remembrance
And the demons fill my mind.

Something like a cell phone,
So innocent you'd think,
It makes my head start whirling
Into darkness black as ink.

And then the "what-ifs" start up,
And fill my weary head,
I keep living in those moments,
Remembering, instead.

Of looking to this moment,
With hope for fresh new starts.
I keep questioning what happened;
Every time, it breaks my heart.

But I can feel beneath the heartache,
And the emptiness inside,
That each day he shows he loves me,
And there's nothing left to hide,

It will make the burden lighter,
'Til it's just a distant dream,
Though we never can erase it,
We can start this new day clean.

It takes courage to keep trying
To put my heart at risk again
When it's been so badly battered
By my very dearest friend.

But I think it will be worth it,
Cause I think he wants to change,
And I know that I can make it,
Even though it feels so strange.

To think of life without him,
I must live so I can be,
Happy with him or without him,
My happiness resides in me.

So, I'll try again tomorrow,
Though an ambush may await,
These memories may not leave me,
But they won't destroy my fate.

CHAPTER SEVEN

LIVING IN HELL

The entirety of my 2014 can be chalked up to the immersive experience of trauma boot camp. Amidst ongoing disclosures, my body settles into extended high alert, always bracing for the next shoe to drop. I've learned over time that the first year post-betrayal is often tortuous, littered with anniversaries of things-you-didn't-know-about, and in 2014, I relive each one as though it were fresh. It's like slowly peeling off a Band-Aid, hairs popping, skin ripping, feeling the full impact of each millimeter tug. During this year, I become intimately acquainted with the general insanity of the human mind.

I swing from deep depression to crazy rage. The emotions are so intense that I become desperate for any way to escape. More than once, I drive late at night and try to get the nerve to swerve off the empty highway. There's a sober comfort in the idea that killing myself would conclusively cease my pain and do everyone else the favor of being rid of me. I sometimes think I am legitimately going crazy, and this thought only deepens my hopelessness, self-loathing, and despair.

I can't count on myself to hold it together at work or during social events like kids' soccer games, church meetings, or group dates with friends. Most of my energy in social settings is spent bracing against the possibility of a humiliating tailspin in front of witnesses. I engage with others like a tight-faced, armored zombie, behind a careful wall that most likely leaves old friends feeling confused at my strange detachment. I never know if tomorrow will be a day where I'll be able to follow through on assignments and meet commitments, or if it will be a day where I crumble into bed and barely scrape myself off the floor by the time the kids arrive home from school.

The internal pain of this period is impossible to describe. Neil Gaiman names it well when he says, "I think hell is something you carry around with you. Not somewhere you go." I'm in the thick of the carving out, tectonic plates colliding within me, just trying to hold on and survive through the shifting chaos, and there is very little I can do about it.

Every day, it's the same struggle: The morning light filters through my curtains and eyelids, and I drift towards consciousness. There's a transient moment where I exist blissfully beyond my story with lightness and ease. Then *WHAM!* My reality whaps me over the head, and off I go, kicking and screaming in involuntary tantrums again. The stories of all that is happening and has happened and might happen cascade over my mind-body like a mudslide. My heart beats faster, pounding louder in my chest, clamoring for escape.

No, no, no, nonononoNONONONONONO! My brain screams. *This is not my life! This is not my reality! This cannot be happening to me!*

Each morning, the latest details flood in fresh, and I go through the entire grief process on fast-forward: Shock. Denial. Anger. Bargaining. Depression. Depression is usually where I hang out—although, some days I set up camp at anger.

All of this before I even get out of bed. Then, I start the daily rituals. I pull my covers over my head. Maybe I cry, maybe I just lie there and pray for a different life. Eventually, I drag my heavy feet over the edge of my bed and somehow make my way to my littles' bedrooms. I barely hold it together as I mechanically pull school clothes off hangers, pluck wrappers and yesterday's art projects off the floor. Before my two oldest leave for school, I make sure we share a scripture or a "Mormon Message": short videos that offer an uplifting thought. I've never been more desperate to bind us all to God, and they can feel it in each morning's heartfelt and often tearful devotional.

Nate sits beside me, fully supportive of my efforts to somehow process this all in a way that will help our family. And then he's off to work, behind the closed door of his home office. I'm often baffled at how persistently cheerful and optimistic he is, a fact that both irritates and relieves me. It feels like we've done a massive pendulum swing: when I was confident, stable, and thriving, he was insecure, moody, and unstable. Now that I'm destroyed and vulnerable, he's never been better. He often tries to lighten the mood and cheer me up with his boyish teasing, and I actually appreciate the new role he's taken on. Heaven knows I can't pull myself together. His energy of "It's all going to be fine, Beck" feels like a life raft I desperately need.

Some days, I am slow and lethargic. Other times, I am so triggered and anxious I can barely stay in my skin, finding brief moments to sneak away and fall apart again with sobs and shakes in the privacy behind my closed bedroom door. My mind is a voracious animal; it cannot pull itself away from the carcass of disjointed facts that splay open and fresh with each new detail that comes forward. I pull past phone records and feel my stomach in my throat as I highlight dozens of calls and texts over months of time. *What were they talking about for so many minutes? How could I have never noticed? Why wasn't he talking to me?*

I am a lion feeding, picking through the rot, trying to make connections. *Does this make sense here? Did that happen there?* I am forever piecing together the reality I've perceived against the reality going on under my nose and out of my awareness. The pace of the piecing is breakneck speed, and no matter how many pieces I pick up, it only seems to add to the pieces still scattered on the floor. I study old pictures of us together and try to match the dual realities. Every single memory of our life together feels tainted. I stare at our wedding pictures and wonder, *Who was he looking at over my shoulder that day?*

Mundane tasks like folding laundry are my anchors. They offer the sweet relief of my knowing exactly what to do. The smell of laundry soap and the touch of warm fabric ground me back to the present moment. I empty the dishwasher, and each plastic cup gives me purpose: I take comfort in the ease and order of placing each in its appropriate place. *At least this cupboard still makes sense.*

At midday, I bike my dark-haired daughter to preschool. Chloe is a steady sunbeam in the dark storm front of my life, a ball of happiness that can't help but skip when she walks. There's so much light bursting through her tiny being, it simply can't be contained. Her giggles are her natural soundtrack and a wide smile, her easiest accessory. Sparkling blue eyes peer out over the adorable dimple that winks at me from the top of her full, rosy left cheek.

I know I'm failing her. My heaviness is so hard on her sensitive heart. As we drive to everyday errands, I swear she can feel the grief rise in me like a tidal wave, often for no apparent reason at all. As tears prick my eyes, her tiny voice will chime from her car seat behind me. "Don't cry, Mom… Please, Mom, don't cry! Don't cry!" She doesn't even have to see my face. She is soft and warm and so empathic, a happy little sponge who can't bear the frequency of my crushing sadness. I try to blink away tears and swallow the sob in my throat, but I can't make it go away, and she hates it.

So, I often unload my daughter at preschool with guilty relief, feeling permission to finally fall apart. I've never been more grateful for a preschool teacher: Miss Jenny is competent and kind. When I drop my daughter off with her each afternoon, gratitude overwhelms me. I need Miss Jenny in ways she can't possibly understand. Miss Jenny is helping my Chloe survive, giving her the sunshine and safety I can't, protecting her from my unbounded grief.

I often bike away from the preschool with tears streaming down my face, not even caring that everyone driving down the street can see. The demons in my head circle hard: *Why can't you stop crying? Get it together! He is going to leave you! You are so pathetic! He's trying…he's going to therapy and 12-step and all the things. He isn't on porn, and he's got no contact with the woman. So, what's wrong with you??! What do you want? Why can't you just get over it? Look at you. You are the worst. You are ugly, you are controlling, you are bitchy and fat and pathetic. And that disgusting acne. And no boobs. He is going to leave you. And this time it will be your fault. The kids will want to go with him because you're always crying. Sooner or later, you're going to be all alone. And nobody will be surprised.*

These demon voices fly like bats through my psyche, and I tremble under their cruelty. Sometimes a voice from the past rings in my ear. My dad, my hero. When Nate asked him for my hand in marriage, my dad joked, "Are you sure you want her? She takes herself pretty seriously."

I know he thought he was being funny, but that's what he said, and those words seem like a prophecy now. *My own Dad.* Shame envelopes me, and I choke on a guttural sob and pedal. *Everyone who really knows you decides sooner or later that they can't love you. You're too much. Just deal with it. Suck it up and stop crying. You can't change it. It's just who you are. Get it together. Get it together and be what he wants you to be, or he is going to leave you.*

So much of my daily self-talk is really self-torture. And even more than what happened, my inner voices are my biggest struggle of all.

By afternoon, the household tasks are complete, my toddler is napping, my preschooler is delivered, and I am left to myself for an hour or two. Some days, I sit at the computer and gaze out the window, pouring my current confusion onto hundreds of journal pages. Some days, I sink into my cushy red recliner—the one that's rocked my babies to sleep with me for the past twelve years—and I read 12-step literature and books about trauma and addiction, and I cry and sleep. Sleep has become my voracious appetite, my never-satisfied craving for relief...for just a brief moment of *not feeling*. I have never spent more daylight hours sleeping in my entire life, and yet I always greet my pillow with an almost desperate hunger for escape.

When my toddler wakes from his nap, I collect him, soft and cuddly, and head back to the red recliner. Jayden is a Love Note from God, his disposition naturally content and unassuming. I know he's up when I hear his tiny voice calling from under the basement stairs: "Mo-o-om! I'm awake!" Every time I open the door to his napping cubby, he is sitting in his playpen with a grin on his chubby face, happily waiting for my arrival. There's no climbing out of cribs and breaking down doors like my oldest did. Jayden is pure contentment. Patient. Kind. Gentle. Our cuddles soften my soul. I spend hours simply holding him, stroking his hair, and feeling his breath against my body. His sweet and calming spirit is happy to be held. Without effort, he brings me back to the sanity and refuge of the present moment.

By late afternoon, I am off to teach University fitness classes. I often drive like a half-drugged zombie with tears streaming down my face. My face has learned to somehow recover quickly from red splotches and puffiness, and I wear waterproof mascara. When I arrive, I sit in the car, feeling the firmness of the steering wheel in my hands as a means to collect myself. I am unsure of whether I can make it through two hours on stage, leading students through fast-paced cardio with a cheery voice and a smile. Each day, before I leave my car, I pray, *God, please give me the strength to do this today. Please, just give my students what they need through me. I don't know if I can do it, God, but I know You can.*

This God of mine hears me. He shows up for me every single day as I teach through the worst of my trauma. Each time He does, it's a miracle I cannot deny. He gives me the energy to stomp and move and dance, even to smile and encourage. And He not only gives me the energy, but He transforms my work into a vehicle of my healing. Each stomp and swoop becomes an expression of my grief, my powerlessness, my pleading, and my rage. Emotions I don't even consciously know I am carrying bubble up and out of me as I move on the stage. I organically start to use my breath to express and release the tightness in my chest and the dread in my stomach. My teaching becomes a dance of sweet release, and often I am brushing tears away and letting my hair fall in my face to disguise my unfiltered emotion in front of my students.

Brick by brick, one class at a time, this period builds an internal fortress of trust in a God capable of showing up in such primal and practical ways. It's really quite miraculous to know down to your bones how powerless and limited you are and then watch yourself do something you have no capacity for. Experiencing this grace daily—it changes me, humbled and awestruck at how unfailingly my utter dependence is answered by a Power greater than myself.

By the time I walk to my car after class, I am in a different state of consciousness. I feel calm. I feel the ground underneath me. I am here. I can go home and greet my kids with a genuine smile on my face. I can show interest in their day and prepare a meal and help them do homework. After my workout, life doesn't feel quite so tragic. While I don't have a name for this magical shift, I am aware that peeling myself off the couch and getting myself to class is a prime stabilizing force in my life.

I'm also shaken with the potent awareness that people around me are suffering. At the grocery store, behind my neighbors' front doors, in my classes—everywhere I go, there might be people just like me who are barely surviving, who are drowning in darkness. Now that I know the depth of this pain, I am completely overwhelmed at the thought of it, and I cannot let them do it alone. *God… Please let them feel Love through me. Please let Your Love move through me somehow and help them know that they are not alone.*

Perhaps I feel this urgency because I feel so acutely alone myself, and most particularly at the place I've always felt the most belonging: at church. When we moved to a new home just three months before Rock Bottom, we also moved into a new ward with new people. Nobody knew the bright and shiny me that had secured her place as responsible, faithful, friendly, and service-oriented: clearly a "good member of the church."

So, when a service activity is planned on a Saturday morning for the Women's Relief Society in our new ward, I'm determined to participate. I will myself to pull it together and make it a good day. I am one of the first to arrive at the gym, where round tables are set up with sewing machines and scissors, and I survey the near-empty room with anxious bubbles in my stomach. *Maybe I should go back to my car and wait until others come.* But I quickly pluck myself up: *Just choose a spot, Becky. Just sit yourself down and start cutting fabric. People will trickle in and join you. It will all be okay.*

And people do, in chatty groups of twos and threes. I watch them enter the door through my peripheral vision. Each group walks through the door and surveys the room before choosing a table amidst laughs and sighs, lightly dropping their bags and picking up projects. There is much waving to others and running over for quick hugs as the room fills with a cheerful buzz. As each group enters, I feel their gaze circle the room, and I feel myself like the clumsy child on the playground field: *Please—pick me! Please don't let me be the last one picked.*

But nobody does. The room is nearly full now, and still I sit, all alone at my round table with my eyes down and my hands now shaking as I force myself to keep cutting fabric. If I was a normal person, I would just get up and move to another table, put a big smile on my face, and introduce myself. But I am not a normal person anymore. I am a psycho. And this is more than I can muster. My body is stiff and hot, tightness creeps up the back of my neck, and my throat clamps down desperately to avoid the sobs that want to erupt from my deepest belly. *Oh no, this was a mistake. I should not have come here. I should not have come here; I'm going to lose it. And everyone is going to see.*

I can feel the tailspin coming as I try with all my might to brace against it. But the voices in my head keep getting louder, and I am nose-diving into a full-blown trauma response that I can't pull out of. I can't breathe, my chest so tight it might explode. I escape to the freedom of the hallway and lock myself in the single-stall bathroom. I let the sob burst and call Nate to come pick me up. I lay my head back against the bathroom wall and try to get my chest to release its grip, try to release the air from my lungs so that the pressure inside my head will soften. I shouldn't have come here. This was a mistake.

I don't belong. I don't belong. I don't belong. I am Hester Prynne, wearing a Scarlet Letter. *But how do they know? How do all these women already know?*

63

They've barely met me, and they already know I'm an outsider. They already know I don't fit here; I'm not like them. They already know I don't belong. And I have no one to blame but us. We chose this through our sinful choices. It's my own fault. I deserve this.

What used to be the most stabilizing force in my life now feels like a painful reminder of all that I've lost, of the inherent unworthiness I'm trying to somehow fix or understand, and the shame of having a terrible secret to hide. These deep feelings of shame and hiding are new sensations for me, and the coping strategy that emerges becomes another surprise.

It's sex.

My traumatized hunger for sleep may only be matched by the same urge for sex. This primal sex drive catches me off guard. It makes no sense in my logical mind. After all, I pretty much hate my husband. And myself. And I definitely hate sex. Sex is what got us into this mess in the first place. Whose idea was that, anyway? *Worst. Idea. Ever.*

I spend most of my days avoiding or ignoring my husband. He works in his home office, and I stay as far away from him as possible. My heart wall is as thick as the walls between us. But at night, after my workout-stability-glow fades and the kids are in bed, Nate and I usually end up in the bedroom, trying to work things out. Some nights, our talks are calm and even hopeful. We each share what we are learning in therapy and the Twelve Steps.

But so often there is new information to make sense of or old questions to answer, and I unravel. Sometimes I am raging chaos, other times I am excruciating despair and self-hatred. My husband is either bracing himself against my blows, emotional or otherwise, or trying to comfort the vast ocean of emotional pain that sucks me under.

Either way, this nightly dance inevitably turns into a mad sexual wrestle. I have never felt more erotic heat, more tangible longing, more desperate need. It's like sex is the only tool I have to dim the unbearable neon flashing light of fear and abandonment that pulsates inside of me. There is so much I cannot control; so much sharpness in the abandonment; so much darkness in the unknown; so much loathing for myself. The sex numbs it all. The sex quiets the screaming voice in my head that says, *"He is gone! He left you! You are alone! And you deserve to be!"*

The sex is desperate, clinging, grasping, reckless, and lusty. It's different than any sex I've known before. It's a medication. An escape. An illusion of safety. And for now, I'll take it. I'll take this illusion over my reality. Today, sex is getting me through. It's keeping my head above water. And if there's sex today, it feels a little more likely that he will still be here when I wake up tomorrow.

So, it's funny the shock I feel when I recognize the familiar sensations of early pregnancy: three months after Rock Bottom, two weeks after we sold all our baby furniture and clothing in a garage sale, and seven weeks after my husband's vasectomy.

There's no way...it couldn't be. There's only been one time we didn't use protection, and I was on my period...

Crazy and impulsive, the week before his vasectomy, a mid-afternoon tryst where I felt he'd pressured the unprotected encounter. Afterwards, I half-jokingly told him, "If we get pregnant, I'm going to be so mad at you. I'm so sick of you and your stupid penis ruining my life." At the time, we laughed in each other's arms at the ridiculousness of those words and the ridiculousness of our crazy situation.

But when I feel the familiar tenderness in my breasts, I cannot imagine adding to the chaos of this situation—bringing a child into the mess we've created. After all, I am still unsure about staying in this marriage, very aware of my possible need to establish financial freedom. I'm doing the math. My youngest is two. In three years, he will be in school, and I could more easily pursue a career, a way to support myself if this thing—*us*—doesn't work. We're three months from Rock Bottom, and I can't deny the persistent urge to establish a backup plan.

But a part of me already knows. I've had four babies, so I recognize the signs in my body. I talk to Nate, call my sister, and buy a pregnancy test. I wait until morning to get the most reliable reading, and when the white stick shows positive, I sit on the toilet feeling numb. I don't know what to do, so I call my sister.

"I'm fucking pregnant," I say.

"That's wonderful!" she says.

We laugh. I cry a little. I don't know what to feel. I hang up the phone and plod, dreamlike, to Nate's office door window. He gazes up from his computer, and we lock eyes. I nod my head, half-heartedly raising the plastic stick in the air, like a white flag of surrender.

Nate's face lights up. He leaps from his desk, throws open the office door, and sweeps me into his arms, nuzzling soft kisses into my neck as I melt into his strong embrace. "It's wonderful, Beck. It's wonderful news and I'm so happy." His whispers soften my swirling resistance.

Part of me feels stuck. *It's this man and his selfish, horrible, destructive, thoughtless sex drive! He doesn't have to worry about how this will affect his life! He doesn't have to think about how this affects his freedom! Maybe he did this on purpose to trap me! Now I am years further from a place in my life where I have the freedom to make it on my own without him.*

But despite my internal ranting, I can't deny the part of me that has always wanted this baby. Part of me knows I bought five matching frames when I planned the kids' school picture wall in our new home. Part of me knows that every miraculous soul that's come to our family is my life's greatest joy and purpose.

For a moment, I flash back to fear and the drawn-out cycles Nate and I created together, concluding that my pregnancies trigger his addiction. *Isn't that why we got the vasectomy in the first place? Am I walking right into another round of hell?!*

But a larger part of me is starting to understand that I am one hundred percent not in control. Seven weeks after Nate's vasectomy, I am eight weeks pregnant. *Of course I am.*

I take a deep, shaky breath. *Okay, God…thank you for this baby…but what the hell are you doing?!*

DRIVING HOME
BECKY MOLLER, MARCH 2014

It is late.
Later than I thought I'd be.
My stomach starts to tighten.
I pick up my phone.
I press his name, catch my breath to hear his voice.
I will know if everything is okay.

No answer.
I set my phone down. Surely, he is not in bed.
I pick my phone up. I press his name.
My chest tightens as I wait for each unending ring.

No answer.
I set my phone down. What is he doing?
What if he got mad and left?
I am late.
Later than I thought I'd be.
What is he doing? Why won't he pick up?

I pick up my phone. I press his name.
I wait. No answer. My throat clenches.
Is he on the other line?
With *her*?

I turn the corner.
I see our house. Is the office light on?
Is that the glow of the computer screen?
What is he doing in there?
Is he making the mistake that will end things forever?
Because I am late?

Will I feel like this every time
It is late?
Later than I thought I'd be
For the rest of my life?

CHAPTER EIGHT

WORKING WITH
BETRAYAL TRAUMA

Like most people experiencing pain, almost from the second my life fell apart, I was anxious to get on with it and be okay again. I longed for a return to my former "bright and shiny" self. But Pandora's box was splayed open, and I could no longer hide from the myriad things in my life that didn't add up. Like it or not, there simply was no going back. I was in new territory.

Initially, my husband and I turned exclusively to our church for help. This was where we had always turned for answers. The church generously helped us pay for church-sanctioned talk therapy, but after several months, we felt like we were talking in circles and going nowhere. We diligently attended church-sponsored 12-step support groups, but over time felt stuck there, too. Nobody seemed to actually be getting better.

I diligently read scriptures. I prayed more fervently than ever before...and I'd always been fervent! I filled out workbooks and completed assignments and wrote hundreds of journal pages. I followed all the rules and advice offered by my accepted authorities. But I wasn't better. I was barely treading water, just keeping my head above triggers enough to survive day to day. I began to believe that this was the best I could expect from now on. I would never be happy again.

This was my test from God, and I was failing it.

At the time, this was the only way I knew how to frame my situation. It never even occurred to me that I hadn't been given the right tools. Eventually, my former college roommate (who happens to be a therapist) handed me my first power drill: the name for the unwelcome ocean I was drowning in. Betrayal Trauma is a condition supported by a growing body of research showing that spouses of people with secretive sexual behaviors often experience PTSD symptoms in the aftermath of disclosures. This was a revelation.

Could it be that my experience was something more than my own failure? Could it be that there were legitimate reasons I was acting completely nuts?

Betrayal Trauma. The label itself offered immediate empowerment.

I dig deep into books like *The Body Keeps the Score* and *Your Sexually Addicted Spouse* and learn that I am not alone in my violent internal struggle. I learn that my brain is wired to keep me alive, first and foremost. When threatened, the limbic system takes over, and the rational mind goes offline. This setup ensures survival when the lion attacks in the jungle: We don't have time to think about it—we just instinctively run. Trauma kicks us into the same limbic mode: freeze, fight, flight. We aren't thinking—our body just reacts.

My crazy reactions don't mean I am defective or dramatic. They mean I am human. I'm not choosing my reactions. I'm being hijacked by my limbic system. My body is not betraying me. It thinks it's protecting me.

Just having the word "trauma" meant the difference between saying *"I am crazy"* and *"This feels crazy."* For me, this distinction was everything.

Betrayed partners certainly aren't the only ones who've been wrongly cast as crazy. It wasn't so long ago that irrational behavior in post-war veterans was also misunderstood. Vietnam-era physicians named "shell shock" as an actual mental disorder in the 1970s. The DSM-III deemed PTSD an official diagnosis in 1980. Now, PTSD is household terminology and there are ample resources and funding for veterans who struggle.

It makes sense that a war veteran would experience panic if a sound, situation, smell, or sense of claustrophobia mirrors a traumatic wartime incident. Their body responds to the trigger as if the life-threatening incident were occurring in the present. This reaction is an evolutionary embodied response: the brain stores the sensory data of the experience and hard-wires itself to protect them from similar threats. And what's more, it turns out that everybody's brain works this way.[1]

Today, this essential understanding continues to influence the cutting edge of psychology and neuroscience. Science is discovering more and more about the connection between mind and body (something the yogis have understood for centuries, by the way). The implications are almost universal: Big or small, we all experience embodied reactions that are attached to memories or subconscious beliefs. To me, these responses shouldn't be categorized exclusively as a "clinical" thing; they should also be compassionately held as a supremely human thing.

The more I learn about Betrayal Trauma, the more relief I feel. Finally, what's been happening inside me makes total logical sense. Having the language of trauma is the first step toward regaining my sanity. Now, I at least have a name for it.

This isn't me. This is my trauma.

This mantra becomes a crucial first line of defense: my protection from the daily tailspin. Until now, my swinging emotions have felt shameful: I know I appear melodramatic and pathetic. Well-meaning loved ones and authority figures keep advising me to "get over it" with obvious frustration at my struggle to do so. After all, my husband ended the extramarital relationship—what more do I want? I can't give them an answer.

But my self-compassion grows as I realize that trauma is far from a refusal to "get over it." Trauma is physiological: affecting my brain and body in powerful and predictable ways, every minute of every day. Trauma doesn't play games; it wreaks internal havoc, and it doesn't "get over it" on any timetable other than its own. And because trauma arises naturally from our deepest subconscious, it carries a deep, embodied wisdom with a highly attuned bullshit radar. When honored and understood properly, I believe trauma can become a valuable part of our wise inner compass.

Having the awareness to name trauma helps me start to claim this compass for myself: My body knew, even if my logical mind and the people around me didn't, that nothing had changed. I could feel it inside me, like

---

1 Van der Kolk, B. (2014). *The Body Keeps the Score: Brain, Mind and Body in the Healing of Trauma*. Penguin Books, p. 45.

screaming bells and whistles catching my attention in no uncertain terms. Nothing had been healed. Not really. Everything in our relationship and our minds and hearts that had gotten us into this mess was still there. Even if I couldn't explain it to anybody else, something in me knew: I wasn't yet safe.

This was a lonely knowing: One that I didn't even know how to hear. One I was too afraid to defend. So instead of listening to it, I mostly just wished for someone to step in and rescue me, to tell me what to do. But there was no one else who could do that for me—though church leaders, parents, podcasts, and friends offered well-meaning advice with the best of intentions. I was going to have to step into my big girl shoes and learn to hear and trust my own inner voice. No one else could tell me my next right step.

Trusting my inner voice was no easy task, and particularly difficult because I had been loudly validated in so many ways by doing the opposite. Conforming to family, cultural, educational, and religious ideals is exactly what had given me any power I'd secured thus far in my life.

Be the responsible big sister! Lose twenty pounds, lose your period, and people like you better! Jump through the right hoops and you get the A and the lead in the high school musical! Over-perform and validate your authority figures and you receive the church title! Get on board. Play the game. Follow the rules and just see how far they promote you!

But I'm not interested in their promotions anymore. I'm not interested anymore in winning anybody's game. I am done with the bullshit. I just want to somehow reclaim my Self.

In my trauma, this appears to be an impossible task. My loudest inner voices scream self-loathing taunts and fearful threats. If I give them an inch, they take a mile. With so much insanity in there, why would I ever want to trust myself?

This isn't me. This is my trauma.

The more I make this separation, the more I realize there isn't just one voice in there. There are many. And underneath them all, a Stillness that feels like something bigger than any voice: it feels like God right there inside me. The sense of it is fleeting but the juxtaposition is drastic. The chaos is uncovering something I've been previously unaware of: the difference between my True Self and all the voices in my head.

This isn't me. This is my trauma.

I start to recognize the chaos as it's happening and ground myself before the demons sweep me away. I learn to slow things down to one breath at a time, one moment at a time. I find that this simple pause is the key to my freedom: I must pause long enough to realize that the crazy thoughts running through my brain aren't *me*. I'm learning to become an observer, making space to get curious about what I'm feeling and why. The simple mantra, over and over, helps me:

This isn't me. This is my trauma.

The mantra grounds me in the moment. It also helps me to find some self-compassion in the aftermath of embarrassing emotional outbursts. And I have plenty of opportunities to practice with my husband working in his home office all day. With the constant buzz in my wiring, my triggers often unleash the entire contents of the trauma folder instantaneously. What might seem to my husband like a small lapse in judgment hits me with all the weight of his years of betrayals combined. We struggle to communicate.

"I simply forgot to call!" he insists.

"This isn't about this one phone call. This is about all the times you didn't call and all the things you were doing instead of calling for the past ten years of our life together!" my trauma screams.

It's impossible to reconcile what an appropriate reaction should look like under the weight of so much emotional baggage. My body is constantly waving flags and blowing whistles to protect itself: "DANGER! DANGER! DANGER!"

From the inside, this creates internal havoc in all directions, from sleep disturbance to crushing anxiety and depression to gastrointestinal problems to spinal misalignment. From the outside, it looks like deranged, irrational behavior—at least, I'm pretty sure it does. When I look back at who I was in these months, I see the very worst version of myself. She'd been backed against a wall and was flailing desperately to survive.

There are few things easier to do than to pass off a traumatized woman as a crazy bitch.

EMPATHY
BECKY MOLLER, OCTOBER 2014

I never knew someone could feel this much pain,
Could feel this much pain and still live.
I never knew that there were places so dark,
Relief wasn't out there to give.

I never imagined a knife cut so sharp
It would pierce me right down to my soul,
It never occurred to me someone could hurt me
And leave me a wide, gaping hole.

I remember just yesterday, or so it seems,
How invincible life's path appeared,
Just follow these rules and nothing can hurt you.
Be righteous, you've nothing to fear.

But now I lie broken and bruised on the ground,
With righteousness still in my hand.
My dreams have been shattered, my strength has been sapped,
And there's no sure foundation to stand.

Because love him or leave him, my choice is the same,
It's a path that is littered with pain.
My righteousness profits me nothing right now,
All my "doing" seems now done in vain.

So life settles into a cadence again,
And the pain settles deep in my heart,
More aware of the faces of others I see,
Who may carry a burden that's hard.

I just didn't realize people felt this much pain,
They could feel this much pain and still be.
I see the world different, forever I will,
Empathy's the gift life's given me.

CHAPTER NINE

RELIGIOUS TRAUMA

Most Sundays, our family arrives twenty minutes late to church these days. We sit in the back rows of the chapel, where I keep several children between myself and Nate so I can focus on the speaker and try to cultivate some inner peace.

Often by the end of the meeting, my face is strewn with tears. There's a particular sting to the triggers I feel in the former safe haven of the chapel, a certain weight to my circumstances held against the dreams and expectations of my religious upbringing. There's an inaudible loneliness in looking around at happy families in church pews and facing that I never actually had what I thought I did. There is a deafening sense of failure and confusion as I listen to rhetoric that once made perfect sense but now only further exposes all the ways it didn't add up in reality.

Sunday used to be my favorite day of the week. I had always loved my church life and felt beloved by my church family. But all of the identity and social status I had accumulated through years of church service and titles were irrelevant in my new neighborhood and life situation, and this shift felt disorienting. Interestingly, I often caught myself mentioning my previous leadership positions in conversation with my new neighbors. A part of me needed them to know. I needed them to see: *Hey… I'm special. I may not look it now, but I used to be capable and important. Bright and shiny.*

I don't look special anymore. I'm not on the front lines or behind the microphone delivering insights that validate and uphold the cultural script. So many comments that never even fazed me before now seem to loudly confirm my new status of un-belonging. The promises of honored covenants and eternal families that used to bring comfort now feel like a slap in the face, a constant reminder of my personal failure.

I gave my everything. I put all my eggs in the basket. And yet, here I am, a pitiful mound of broken promises. We are outside the narrative, and it's obvious in almost every word that floats over the pulpit. Sundays have become a weekly shame bath as much as a plea to regain the clarity I used to find here. I must somehow make it all make sense again.

But as I sit in meetings week after week and hear people testify of the safety of the gospel, I feel both bewildered and betrayed. *What about me? I did everything I was asked to do. Why didn't your guarantee work for me?*

The dissonance churns in my stomach as I swing between wanting desperately to somehow fit back into the box and feeling defiantly double-crossed that I no longer can.

This particular Sunday is already such a painful affair as we make our way from the main worship service to the Sunday School class that follows. Nate and I settle into our seats and my insides are scrambling to get away from him. He tries to sit next to me like everything is okay, like we are just like everybody else, normal people who keep their promises and honor their marriage vows. I am sitting on a padded chair next to him and my whole body sends me alarm signals to get away. It's all I can do to keep it together and not have a complete breakdown in the crowded classroom.

And then the teacher begins, asking us to open our scriptures to the Old Testament. The teacher begins breaking down the story of David and Bathsheba: a well-known biblical account of lust and adultery, deceit and cover-up. My mind swirls and my heart is pounding. Each time a hand is raised for comments I feel more infuriated and humiliated, more exposed and angry.

Who do these people think they are? Who are they to be analyzing why David did what he did? Why don't we even mention Uriah, Bathsheba's husband, and how he must have felt about the whole thing? Who are we to be sitting here scrutinizing these people and their thought processes and choices?

How did David's wives feel about what happened? And what the hell—he already had six wives when he slept with Bathsheba?! And he is supposed to be a prophet of God? A holy man? What the hell, God?! Is this your plan?! Is this what women are to you?! Just toys?! Just property?! Just conquests to be consumed?!

And now I am hyperventilating and the tears are streaming and I am pinching my arm with my nails to the point of bleeding like I often do in times like this. I'm intuitively trying to bring myself back down, to somehow distract myself from the emotional hell that's swallowing me up in this very public place, and I am losing the battle.

My husband squirms in his seat and tries to put his arm around me to calm me, and my whole body tightens and hisses. "Don't touch me!" I whisper-hiss.

I am a coiled snake, and I will strike. All the bells are going off, and my rational brain is no longer driving. "I hate you. This is you. This is *your* story!"

Sometimes, I just can't stop myself. The fear and pain come spewing out of me like an erupting volcano, and I say terrible things. It's like watching myself from the outside, while the rational me sits there shaking my head and saying, *You are being totally irrational. Stop talking. Take a deep breath. That was mean. You don't mean what you're saying. Calm down.* But I just can't.

Sometimes, I just want him to feel, just for two minutes, the pain I feel from what he has done.

My husband gets out of his chair and leaves the room. A neighbor sits a few seats away, and she is witnessing my distress with compassionate, concerned eyes. She slides over to the now-empty chair. "Let's go outside and ditch this, hey?"

Her voice is a kind whisper, and I am suddenly a little child who is lost and afraid. I look up at her and nod my head, and she gently guides me out the door of the church, a soft hand on my elbow.

We end up sitting outside on the ground, knock-kneed in our Sunday dresses with our backs against the cold brick of the church building. Tears run from my eyes, and my face feels tight and itchy from the drying salt. This is a common sensation these days.

She offers small comforts, tokens of empathy. Mostly, she just sits with me and helps me to feel like this is normal. Like it's okay that I just had a mental breakdown in Sunday School. Her calming presence creates the space for my rational self to go back online.

I start to talk, no gruesome details, but enough of the story comes spilling out that she can pretty much piece together the gist of my situation. This openness is new to my situation. It feels scary.

I haven't talked to anyone in my real life about what is happening. I've told my parents and my sisters who live states and oceans away. I meet with a therapist. I attend the church's 12-step group. But in my day-to-day existence, I am utterly alone, trying to hold it together and maintain some sense of normalcy for my children in our new neighborhood. I've become a secret-keeper, another new and unwelcome role. But my neighbor feels safe, and it feels so good to be real with somebody.

She eventually ushers me to my car and encourages me to get some rest. I settle myself in the warmth of my minivan with the sunlight pouring through the windows and take some deep breaths. I've got to be normal by the time the kids get out of church.

Suddenly, my phone buzzes, and it is our bishop, the head of our ward, asking me to come to his office: Nate has been in to see him. I don't know what to make of this, and my heart starts pounding. *What the hell? Did Nate go tattle to the Bishop? You've got to be kidding me.*

I respond that I will come, and I take another deep breath. Maybe he is just checking on me to make sure that I'm okay. I've met with him twice before.

He was the first person I officially reached out to the day after Rock Bottom. He had dropped whatever he needed to in his personal life to show up at the church building and meet with me for an hour on a Monday afternoon. He was kind and offered supportive condolences. He shared his great love for his own wife, and tears filled his eyes at the thought of having to tell her what Nate had to tell me. He acknowledged the courage that had taken, and I appreciated the perspective and was grateful for his time.

Then, shortly after, Nate and I met with him together. He had assured us that he believed we could work it out; that after meeting with both of us, he could see that we loved each other and wanted things to work. He encouraged us to go on walks together and talk more. He helped pay for our therapy appointments for a while as we settled into our new mortgage. This was a much-appreciated safety net.

But I'm also aware that this bishop doesn't really know me at all. I had spent hours in planning meetings and teaching capacities with my previous bishop in my previous congregation. He knew my heart; he saw how committed I was to the church and how much I gave to the people I served. The only thing this bishop knows is that my husband cheated on me. So, as I make my way toward his office, I feel tenuous at best.

I knock on the door, and he opens it. My husband is sitting in a chair, hands folded in his lap, shoulders hunched forward, gaze down, like a wronged puppy-dog. Just at the sight of him sitting like that in this office makes my blood pressure spike and my guard go up.

The Bishop nods at Nate, and Nate meekly leaves the room. I watch him exit with skeptical eyes and sit slowly in a seat as the Bishop gently shuts the door and sits behind his desk. *What is going on here?*

"Well, your husband tells me that there's been a bit of a problem in Sunday School today."

I nod, slowly.

"It sounds like you attacked him. It sounds like you went right after him. It sounds like you were judging him, like he is David or something. Your husband is not David, Sister Moller. Your husband did not go down to Bathsheba."

His voice is very strong, very firm. He is looking right at me with the authority of a man who believes he has authority. He is almost pounding his fist on the pulpit.

I am suddenly a fourth-grade little girl who has been called out by the teacher for speaking out of turn. Tears spring back to my eyes, and I fumble for words.

"I'm sorry. I just feel so confused. I don't know what happened to me. I just feel so confused."

"Of course, you feel confused! I hear you've been speaking to all sorts of people about this. Don't you remember I told you expressly not to talk to anyone about this when we first met? Don't you remember that I counseled you to keep this between you and your husband? And now I hear that your mother knows. And you're going to therapy as well. So, talking to a therapist every week. And I hear you go to 12-step groups as well. So, you're talking to all sorts of people about this, Sister Moller. Of course, you're confused! Now, I distinctly remember I told you to keep this to yourself."

He goes on and on, and as he talks, I find myself beginning to float away from the fourth-grader inside of me. I feel a familiar detachment, the same drifting feeling I had all those years ago when Jared sat me down for a similar talk: *You're not perfect. So I don't want you.*

This...is bullshit. I realize. *All the words that are coming out of his mouth are bullshit. I know more about how to handle this situation than he does.*

This feels like a revelation to me: a never-before-considered possibility. That this man, this institution, this authority figure could be wrong, could even be questioned. That my job could be anything other than to show up and get in line and exceed the expectation that is put upon me. The possibility that I could say no. That I could have and hear my own voice. This is something utterly new.

And suddenly, I am not the fumbling fourth-grader; I am a grown woman. I hear his voice going on and on with conviction and clarity, and I hear it like I am underwater. His words are fuzzy, but his energy is clear and passionate. And I know that he is speaking from his best understanding. That he honestly believes his words are true and helpful.

But he doesn't understand. And his words are not true or helpful. At least, not for me, not in this moment. And every cell in my body knows it.

And this knowing, this calm, embodied knowing fills me up: this little woman in this little chair in this big office at this hardwood desk of "God-given" authority. And suddenly, I am big enough to open my mouth—I may have even cut him off.

"With all due respect, Bishop, I know that what you're saying isn't right."

"Excuse me?"

"I don't mean to be disrespectful. But I know that what you're saying isn't right. I can't worry about my husband's reputation right now. He's made his own bed, and he can lie in it. I'm struggling with thoughts of harming myself most days. I can hardly eat, and I don't sleep more than a couple of hours most nights. Right now, Bishop, I've got to do what I need to do to be okay. For me. And I need those support pieces you're talking about. I need to have people I can talk to. I need help finding my way through this. I can't do it by myself. And what you're saying, it's just wrong. I'm sorry."

My bishop doesn't know what to do with me. He fumbles through a few more remarks of his own, and I thank him for his time and walk out the door, calm and grounded.

WHO ARE YOUR DAUGHTERS TO YOU?
BECKY MOLLER, SEPTEMBER 2014

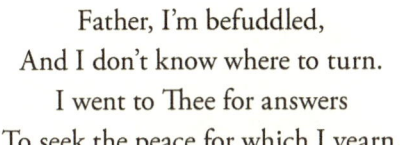

Father, I'm befuddled,
And I don't know where to turn.
I went to Thee for answers
To seek the peace for which I yearn.

I went unto the temple
Feeling sure I'd find them there,
But what I found just left me
Feeling burdened with despair.

For you created Adam,
And then you gave him Eve, a gift,
For companionship and helpmeet,
To support and to uplift.

"It's not good for man to be alone,"
You said to him, not her.
You made him Lord of all the Earth,
Of fish and fowl and fur.

You sent your servants to him,
"To the man Adam" is how you sent,
They conversed and counseled with him,
Eve was sidekick, silent, spent.

She never speaks again after she's
Made her covenant,
To follow after husband,
She just follows where he went.

It doesn't seem right, Father,
How you never speak to Eve.
Was the plan designed for Adam?
Were we an afterthought? I grieve…

How do you see your daughters, Lord,
Were we created for
An embellishment for husbands,
I always thought that I was more…

I've felt you speak right to me
And use me as a tool in hand,
Am I sinful in my wish to be
More than a tool for a man?

Why did you put this appetite
In them and then adorn
Your daughters with these bodies
That they lust after in porn?

Why did you make us faithful
And command us to unite,
When you knew their carnal nature
Would be an everlasting fight?

Why program us to nurture
And then program them to roam,
For when they give into their nature,
It destroys a happy home.

Why are we just an object
In your plan, for men and Thee?
Am I just another dominion?
"Lord over all," including me?

So, Lord, I'm starving for your answers
And I'm slaking from the thirst,
Of the living water promised,
Because I can't believe the worst.

I can't believe my role here
Is to fill a husband's need,
Be defined by any person,
I think you have a plan for *me*.

I think I'm as important as
The man created prior,
I think you speak right to me,
Not through men, am I a liar?

I want to be content, accepting
All your plan entails.
And, Father, I pray your answer
Will not cause my faith to fail.

CHAPTER TEN

Boundaries

W hen I walked out the door of the Bishop's office, I felt an initial euphoria. Like I had just stood up and done something heroic for myself that I had never done before, but it wasn't long before I talked myself back into my cage. It wasn't long before I let all the voices in my head seep through my deeper wisdom and taint my clarity. It wasn't long before I trusted my bishop's authority more than I trusted my own gut.

That very night, I package it all properly in my journal. Back to resolves. Back to vows.

Three main insights I learned today from my counsel with the Bishop:

- *I cannot keep going back to the affair. I can't keep dwelling on it. Nate and I shouldn't discuss it anymore, I shouldn't ask questions about it. Nate has been as honest and complete in his confession as he can possibly be to both me and the Bishop, and nothing else good can come of discussing it further. Now it is time to put it behind us. Now it is time to move forward. As the Bishop said, if I cannot put it away, it will destroy our marriage. I am choosing to forgive.*

- *The Bishop feels strongly that I cannot detach from Nate during my process of recovery. He wants us to do as much together as we possibly can. The Bishop said if I don't rebuild with Nate as I rebuild myself, he doesn't think our marriage will be able to work. I don't know what I think. I just know that I keep swinging back and forth, from fear to faith, to faith to fear, to feeling safe to feeling so triggered. I know that I feel like my best hope is in following the advice of those who have been where I am, and in trying to decipher what the Lord is telling me. It is still so hard for me to trust these feelings. When things are good with Nate, it feels so good to feel so close to him. I don't know if that is spiritually good, or if it is good because it feels good to feel loved by him again. I am so confused.*

- *Today, I have been blessed with feelings of gratitude that things didn't go further with Nate's affair. I have fought against those feelings because where he did go was still so unbelievably painful to me, and I didn't feel like he should get credit for manipulating the situation to go as far as he could possibly go without actually going there. But the Bishop is right. Nate did not go down to Bathsheba's quarters, though he was sorely tempted. And he is still in good standing with the church. So, I am blessed.*

I keep trying to convince myself that if I just arm-wrestle my emotions down and get in line, everything will be okay. Deep down, I've accepted the belief that a good woman is forgiving, patient, long-suffering, and above all—*nice*. But my body is not cooperating with this logic. Four months from Rock Bottom and I still find myself awake at 4 a.m. Something inside me knows that *nice* isn't safety here. *Nice* isn't Goodness.

Again and again, the same basic abandonment story plays out in my dreams. Sometimes the story is lusty and crude, sometimes old boyfriends show up, sometimes I am back at the moment of decision on our wedding day. You'd think my subconscious would expect it by now, but my heart still races when the nightmares come. My mind won't stop replaying all the moments that somehow got me here. It keeps envisioning how it's all going to end. One way or another, I will catch him at it again. Humiliation. Heartbreak. Rage. Loneliness.

Tonight's episode sneaks up on me: in my dream, I see Nate across a crowded hall. I make my way towards him, my little one in my arms, my older ones yanking and pulling at me. They want to go here and there, they want an ice cream cone, they need to go to the bathroom, they want to go home. But I see him from across the foyer and long to reach him. I need him.

When suddenly I realize…he is talking to *her*, so intimate, heads close together. They look into each other's eyes and laugh softly. I see her slide her hand down his arm, an easy and familiar gesture. Their fingers lock, and he glances over his shoulder to check if anyone has noticed. They glide through the crowd towards the door at the other end of the hall.

He is leaving me. He is choosing her. He is choosing her right in front of my face.

I watch them walk off hand in hand. I am still holding my youngest in my arms, my older ones still giggling and laughing, pulling at my arm, teasing, whining. But I am staring, fixated at the disappearing forms in front of me.

How will I ever move from this place? My feet are rooted to the floor, my heart and stomach crashing, free-falling out from under me. My child slips from my grasp. Everything is sliding out from under me and still, I stand frozen in shock, in helpless fear. I am floating in space as I somehow turn myself around and shepherd little heads towards the door.

But tonight, in my dream, a new sensation arises. Instead of staying stuck in the familiar sinkhole, I feel something new deep in my gut: a resolute understanding that I must pull it together. My little ones need me, and I must be their solid ground. Somehow, I must figure out how to keep breathing—for them. Tonight, somehow, I stay grounded: a piece of me vitally awake and aware, even amidst the nightmare.

And now my actual breath catches in my throat, and I snap back to the darkness of my bedroom. My husband is breathing easily beside me. I sit straight up in bed, and the vision in my mind is fresh and real enough that my heart pounds through my ears. I quietly pull back the covers and swing my feet to the floor.

The gut-level strength is still there, still with me. For a moment, I am not crumbling. I am facing it. I sit, hands on heart, and name the unbearable terror of having no control over what happens next. "This is hard," I whisper.

These relentless nightmare visions are like an invisible prison cell nobody else sees. I am so tired of feeling alone in a dangerous and upside-down world, always waiting for the next shoe to drop. I feel a building, churning, bubbling anger in my gut, creeping up through my chest and clutching at my neck and shoulders. A red-hot, valid anger. A vehicle for change.

No more. No more waiting.

I make my way in the darkness to our small office. I take a deep breath and open my laptop. *What do I do with this powerlessness? With this rage?*

I pray to God. "God, show me what I need in order to feel safe. Help me know what I need so I can sleep through the night." I open up *What Can I Do About Me?*, a book written by Rhyll Croshaw, a betrayed partner, that I've devoured over the past weeks. Most of all, it has given me someone to follow who has lived through a similar experience and found a path to healing. Her counsel is so different than my bishop's.

"You need boundaries," she says. "Boundaries aren't about control, they're about upholding your integrity. They're about establishing safety. *What boundaries do you need to feel safe?*"

"Boundaries need to be 'If, then...' statements," she says. "They are intended to guide your *own* behavior, not his. If *this* happens, then I must do *that*. Clear boundaries help you in moments of trigger and chaos, because you've got an action plan. You've got a response."

"You must include God in your boundaries," she says. "God will help you know what you need to find safety. Boundaries are the most loving thing you can do."

So, here I sit, at four in the morning, laptop open, prayer in heart. *What do I need to feel safe?*

I begin to type, fingers flying on keys, and with each sentence, I gut-check myself: *Does this feel right? Is this coming from a place of fear and control? Or a place of integrity? God, how does this feel to You?*

Protective Boundaries:

The behaviors I list here feel unsafe due to the trauma I experience when they happen. If these behaviors continue, I know they will further damage my trust in you (Nate) as a person and in our relationship. They will also decrease the likelihood that our marriage will be able to move forward. I recognize that I cannot control your behavior or guarantee your honesty, but I can ask for what I need. And I will take action and use my voice when I feel that things are off. Ultimately, we both have to trust each other to show up fully committed if we want to make this work, and over time, I trust this commitment will become evident. I'm taking things one day at a time.

If Nate feels triggered by lust or has a slip with pornography, I need him to tell me about it within the day. If he fails to disclose the trigger or slip, **then** he will need to stay in the guest room for a night.

If Nate crosses one of his personal boundaries, I need him to tell me about it and discuss what happened within the day. If he fails to share with me within the day, **then** he will need to stay in the guest room for a night.

If Nate is exhibiting addictive behaviors such as excessive anger, irritability, blame, stonewalling, defensiveness, selfishness, detachment, etc., **then** I will detach from the situation and write a letter explaining what I'm seeing and why it triggers fear for me. I will give Nate the letter, and we can discuss it at an appropriate time. **If** the discussion goes well, **then** we will both come to a place of greater trust and understanding. **If** the discussion does not go well, **then** we will both need some space to reflect. We will sleep in separate rooms until we can resolve the feelings and behaviors.

If Nate habitually acts out with pornography or habitually exhibits addictive behaviors that create a toxic atmosphere in our home, **then** we will separate.

If Nate has an extramarital affair of any kind, on any level, **then** we will begin moving towards divorce.

The inherent consequence of any of these actions is further damage to the trust I feel in him and in our relationship. These actions will further prolong the healing of our relationship and decrease the likelihood of our marriage being able to move forward.

Positive boundaries:

These are things that Nate can do to help increase feelings of safety and security in our home and relationship. When these things happen, I can feel that I am more able to trust him as a person and have hope in our relationship:

If Nate shows commitment to his own personal recovery by proactively attending 12-step meetings, personally working the program with a sponsor, initiating a couple of check-ins, showing a personal commitment to his own healing, and meeting long-term with a professional counselor, **then** it will help me believe that his heart is in recovery and he is not just going through the motions.

If Nate continues to be patient with me and my recovery, to take accountability for the pain and fear he has brought into my life, and to show remorse for the way he has hurt me, **then** it will help me to believe that he could truly love me.

If Nate shows consistency in being patient and loving towards our children (particularly our oldest son), **then** it will help me believe that his recovery efforts are creating a change of heart.

If Nate can establish a new way of thinking where his sexual needs are not the predominant force in his life and the predominant demand and problem in our relationship, **then** it will help me to trust that he is healing and that we can build a healthy relationship that I can trust.

If Nate can fulfill his role as husband and father with a sense of gratitude and honor rather than feelings of resentment or self-pity, **then** I will feel more trust that he is a safe person for our family.

I finish typing. I press print. As early morning light starts to filter through my office window, I notice that I can feel the chair underneath me. I can feel my feet on the floor. I have a list. It's not perfect. It's not certified or validated by any authority other than my own gut, but it's currently my truth. Even before I hand it to my husband, I know it is the safety my body needs right now. It doesn't matter what anybody else thinks.

Even as I grasp at Rhyll Croshaw's guidance and paste together basic boundaries from the blueprint of her book, I am baby-stepping my way towards my *own* power. I am learning to trust my gut. This is *my* life. I get to decide what I can and cannot live with. I get to decide what I value and where my limits are.

When Nate pads his way into his office an hour or so before the kids will be up, his face is wary. If I am already up, if I am in here typing, he knows it's been one of those nights. I hand him the paper with a sense of steady calm—without anger or threat, guilt or fear. So different from the passionate threats I sometimes make in our late-night sparring matches.

There is no passion or proving here. Only a grounded knowing: *This is where I stand. These are my lines in the sand. And I'm sharing them with you because I love you. Because I want this to work. Because I'm all in, and in order to be all in, this is what I need you to know.*

In the hazy stillness of this early morning, we can both feel that I have the strength to follow through on every word I have written. I can do it because I feel God with me in it. No matter what happens next, I know He has my back. He can and will provide a way. In writing my boundaries, I have just taken one huge step away from fear. One huge step away from desperate reactivity. I have put my trust in God and in myself.

I watch Nate read over the paper, and then he meets my eyes, steady and clear. "Thank you for taking the time to put this together, Beck. I'm going to put this up where I can read it every day."

As we move forward, this simple piece of paper, these boundaries, become the foundation of our healing relationship. They become the cheat sheet to Nate's attempts to show love at a time when his spoken "I love you's" add insult to injury. They become the trampoline that bounces me back to sanity when small shifts in his attitude could send me into a tailspin. They become the magic pills that allow me to sleep through the night once again. They become the floor underneath me and the framework for our recovering marriage.

I am instantly less afraid. There is suddenly a safety net to catch my heart, my stomach, my spine, when it all feels like it is falling out from under me. I don't need to waste hours on "what-ifs" anymore. I have a ground. I have my integrity. I have a voice. I have boundaries.

SHACKLES

BECKY MOLLER, AUGUST 2014

"The greatest lie ever told about love is that it sets you free."
—Zadie Smith

The shackles that bind me are heavy,
My shackles I carry with fear.
They weigh me down, hold my soul captive,
They fill my eyes always with tears.

The shackles keep me from forgetting,
From letting it go, pushing through.
The shackles I wear keep me suffering,
My chains are my deep love for you.

It's not that I cannot forgive you,
It's not that your side I can't see,
It's that I still see all that's in you,
All the good that endeared you to me.

It's that I still need your sweet friendship,
That I crave all your innocent heart,
That I feel so connected to your soul,
And the pain of it tears me apart.

If I just could shake off these shackles,
And feel my soul scream, "I don't care!"
My burden feels like it'd be lightened,
And the weight of it floats in thin air.

It's not that I want to feel anger,
But the relief it can bring seems not bad,
When I labor in grief from these shackles,
Because loving you makes me so sad.

I still see you the way that I fell for,
Your innocence, humbleness, smile.
You still are unceasingly hopeful,
Still, in most ways, like a child.

But I just don't know how to get past this,
For the love that I feel makes me cry,
I chose you and you up and left me,
And now I'm just left to ask why.

I beg from my Father deliverance,
To give me a place I can rest.
I am drowning in deep pools of sorrow,
I have tried, but I'm failing this test.

The shackles I fear bring me terror,
You've power I cannot ignore.
I can't live with the uncertain future,
Will you love me or leave me once more?

Dear Father, help me find the grounding,
To find peace in this miserable place.
Can I find peace and still wear these shackles?
Please help me learn how through Thy grace.

CHAPTER ELEVEN

BIG-T, LITTLE-T

Typically, people associate trauma with life-threatening events: war, terrorist attacks, car wrecks, death, rape, natural disasters, violence. Such defining moments organize our lives into two parts: before and after. I call these large events Big-T Traumas. My husband's disclosure, although not physically life-threatening, was emotionally life-threatening. At least it was to me, a Mormon woman who'd been taught that my role as a wife and mother was my most important existential purpose. Overnight, *before* and *after* came to define my newly narrow world. When Big-T Trauma hits, life will never again be the same.

But trauma comes in different shapes and sizes. Big-T Traumas are obvious, but little-t traumas are also impactful and potentially life-altering. They're just sneakier about it. Little-t traumas are what I call the "normal" life experiences that lead us to internalize false beliefs about ourselves or draw incorrect conclusions about the nature of the world or our value in it. These are the small moments when we feel abandoned, cry into a pillow, and get up never to put our heart out there in the same way again: the oft-forgotten potholes that make us believe, one bump at a time, that there is something inherently unacceptable about who we are.

Until I experienced a major life-changing event, I never gave myself permission to be bothered by such potholes. But over the course of healing my Big-T Trauma, I learned just how significantly my little-t traumas had impacted the way I function. In fact, when I dug deep enough, each discernible thread leading to my painful Big-T Trauma eventually traced back to little-t traumas that had been internalized in my childhood without my conscious awareness. *(Remember that Trauma Egg?)* For most of us, these little-t traumas go undetected, slip in quietly through the back door, or get shoved under the bed for weeks, years, or lifetimes.

Before Big-T Trauma hit, I didn't have the tools or reasons to name the subtle dissonance that drove my striving; so, like most of us, I brushed aside nagging feelings of unworthiness. Instead of facing and naming these feelings with awareness and curiosity, I moved through life turning up the treadmill, working even harder to exceed everyone's expectations. This is where safety seemed to be secured, however temporarily.

I compulsively compared myself to others to know my place: Was I better than? Or worse than? I didn't know how to be one in a family, simply a member of the human race. As the 12-steppers insinuate, I was always scrambling for the top of the heap or else I was hiding underneath it. And like most of us, I felt that this way of being was completely normal.

But Big-T Trauma gave me permission to unplug from the rat race and challenge what I was willing to accept as "normal." And I *did* begin to challenge—even as I wrestled to rein myself in through pretty-packaged journal entries and resolutions. I couldn't unsee the holes in the logic I had so easily accepted in the past. All of my life, I had felt secure in the validation I got by staying safely in someone else's lines. I began to see how heartlessly my whole identity was rooted in functioning at top-level to meet an ideal. New and troubling thoughts began to swirl through me:

Whose ideal am I meeting?

Who decides what normal is?

Am I really the sovereign of my own life?

Or am I so busy trying to please I don't even stop to think about where I am going, or who decided on the destination?

I had spent my life meeting other people's expectations and couldn't deny the fact that it had landed me here. Maybe obedience wasn't safety after all.

Big-T Trauma blew the whistle on the incessant forward motion. Although the world kept turning, everything inside me stopped. This created the pause I needed to ask the questions that would transform my life. But in the fast-paced, outwardly validated environment that we all live in, even Big-T Traumas are often trampled over without ever getting the healing attention they really require. Society tells us: "Suck it up." "Get over it." "It's not that deep." We often think that by burying our pain, by denying or minimizing our struggles, by acting like we don't care, we are strong. We move on. We leave the past behind.

But that's not how trauma works. Pain that is not transformed eventually gets transmitted to others. As Eckhart Tolle wrote in *The Power of Now*: "Every addiction arises from an unconscious refusal to face and move through your own pain."[2] The coping strategies we unconsciously use to numb our discomfort often end up traumatizing the people we love the most. And we are helpless to change the cycle and blind to our part in it until we're aware enough to recognize our own traumas and do the work to heal them.

The fact is, there is no agency without awareness. And when we are reacting to life in an unconscious state, whether from addiction, trauma, or just plain humanity, we are blind. This is why the process of healing is so crucial—a beautiful restoration not to be missed, even when it seems easier to skip over pain or stuff it down. Without the healing, our blinders grow darker and wider, accumulating emotional baggage that blocks us from our true nature and purpose.

And that's why no one else can do the healing work for us. The peace that we long for is not separate from us. It is hidden underneath the walls we have painstakingly built within our own selves. Unresolved trauma becomes a part of the very cells of our body, an invisible filter on the lenses through which we experience life. Without healing, we become unconsciously driven by fear. Everything we see, hear, and experience is colored by beliefs we aren't even aware of. These beliefs grow unseen over weeks, years, and lifetimes into vast forests of dysfunctional behavior and self-defeating coping strategies, anxiety, and depression.

And relational trauma creates a particularly potent type of blindness, a thunderous culmination of Big-T and little-t trauma combined. Big-T disclosures tend to drop after years of little-t manipulations and gaslighting have slowly eaten away a partner's self-worth, let alone their ability to see straight or trust themselves. So, when Nate came forward with the admission of his

---

2 Tolle, E. (2018). *The Power of Now: A Guide to Spiritual Enlightenment.* Hachette Australia. Pages 152–153.

affair, it was only natural that I would feel responsible. His actions were not only heartbreaking to wrap my mind around, they were the fruition of all my greatest existential fears.

I am unlovable.

His Sunday night Big-T disclosure was the consummation of my entire life's little-t traumas combined. Trauma took this Mother Lode and feasted on it. At the time, it seemed I had no other choice than to succumb to the voice in my head.

I am unlovable. I am not enough. I am a failure.

These were *my* beliefs; how *I* interpreted and internalized what had happened, and I actually invested great amounts of time and energy building them out and deepening their roots in my mental landscape. My chosen identity became an outgrowth of my own faulty conclusions:

I am unlovable. I am not enough. I am a failure. Nothing can ever change that.

I repeated these words over and over until they were wedged deep into my soul. I crumbled and collapsed under their weight. I willfully constructed a cage that was paradoxically intended to keep me safe by keeping me in excruciating pain. And I couldn't remove the blinders. For a long time, I couldn't see it any other way.

But I did have a choice. And over time, I began to realize it. The unlikely gift of being stuck in such a suffocating worldview was that it made me aware I *had* a worldview. We all do. This was an awakening in and of itself. And every choice I made was on some level an attempt to either run away from or confirm the core beliefs I carried about myself. When we're unconscious, we all do this. Trauma just made it more obvious for me. My trauma made my core beliefs conscious.

It wasn't what happened that had me in prison. It was what I *believed* about what happened, and what it meant about *me*. My misery was actually very self-centered. I was terrified of my little storied self, my ego. And in my trauma, it had all the power.

Over time, I gained the grounding skills to name and separate from my egoic thoughts and stories. I learned how to ground into a deeper Self—a Self that existed beyond story or circumstance or form. I began to find the *Deep I* that lives within me. This Deep I was there when I got very quiet, mentally.

I was finding it through my fitness classes, when I was in my body, in the present moment. It felt like space and freedom. It felt like me—the *real* me. These brief moments of mindfulness were the beginning of my liberation.

To find them, I first had to recognize the fear-driven and self-loathing narratives that played in my head. Next, I had to own these narratives as my own stories, not as immutable Truth. And then, I had to accept that only *I* had the power to free myself from them. This took weeks, months, and years of mindfulness practice, coming back daily, even moment by moment, to breath, to center, to stillness, to a Deep I, to a Higher Power. This practice still forms the foundation of the way I try to move through the world.

Before trauma, I was doing what everybody seemed to be doing: trying to master "normal." Trauma snapped me out of the trance. It was an invitation to begin doing things the way that I, uniquely, was designed to do them. Trauma actually brought me back to my Self. Betrayal didn't shatter my perfect life and perfect self; it arrived right on time to highlight what was already out of balance in my life and self. Trauma came in to course-correct my soul, to redirect me onto the path for which God truly created me.

My pain came as an unexpected glacier to carve out a spectacular, breathtaking terrain from within. It opened my eyes to the fact that all I was ever looking for was already right here...and it couldn't be taken from me. Not by my husband. Not by my life situation. Not even by my own despair. When I began to find the wholeness underneath the rubble, I began to know my true home.

DOOR COUNTY WOOD

BECKY MOLLER, JULY 2017

I am a Door County wood,
A patchwork quilt of darkness and light
Filtered through to the forest floor.

The dead and rotting things
That once meant tragedy and loss
Dissolving with time and stillness
Into a creeping, verdant bed of growing greens.

A soft pillow for my troubled head,
Bringing me back from my too-busy mind,
Whispering, "Be Still" with every perfect
Breath that hangs in the dewy air.
Whether this day dawns
With darkness or light,
I will rest in the knowing.

That all pain dissolves in time
Into the perfect pillow
For an open, trusting heart
And, behind whatever clouds come,
Shining through the canopy of this mortal existence,
The sunshine is constant,
Just waiting to peek through.

CHAPTER TWELVE

WHERE DO WE GO FROM HERE?

E very summer since we got married, we take our annual family trip to Wisconsin, the safest of all my heart's places. This will be our first trip back since the Trauma, and this alone feels daunting. But even worse, we are also scheduled to spend a week in Nauvoo, Illinois, where Nate's parents are serving an 18-month Mormon mission in the reconstructed temple.

This temple also happens to be where Nate and I were married twelve years ago and where, a year ago on a similar trip, Nate and I knelt across a sacred altar in remembrance of our wedding vows. And now I know that this all was happening right smack dab in the middle of his affair.

As the trip approaches, I vividly relive the previous year: arriving at his parents' missionary apartment at one in the morning after an eighteen-hour drive. Always generous and eager to show care, they had couches and air mattresses waiting for our arrival. Six cramped passengers piled out of our minivan, exhausted and relieved to finally stretch our legs and breathe in the damp, firefly-dotted midwestern night air.

We all wasted no time in crawling under covers, and I was half-asleep before my head even hit the pillow. But Nate kept rubbing himself against me. Soon, he was hissing in my ear because I'd resisted his sexual advances. Our four little ones were mere feet away from us. This type of dynamic was so status quo at the time that it hadn't even fazed me. Now, with the context of his online relationship, the memory infuriates me.

I distinctly remember how Nate was in a particularly sour mood all week, sniping at the kids and me at every opportunity. I remember feeling so frustrated, trying to manage his outbursts along with our four young, squabbling kids. My blood boils.

But even more painfully, I remember how sacred and special I held the whole visit. How I made sure in advance to carve out an entire day to return to the very altar where we were married twelve years earlier. I can still feel our fingers interlaced as we walked, sweaty hand in hand through the sultry air till we reached the solemn doors of the Nauvoo Temple. They stood to me as a solid reminder of our vows to be faithful to God and each other for time and all eternity. At the time, I felt genuinely happy. I felt like everything was good—at least reasonably so. I really did feel close to Nate.

How was I so stupid? A scratched record, I keep reliving every detail of the week against the backdrop of his affair, tasting and twirling each memory. Obsessively. Feverishly. I keep looking for a hint, a sign, a reason. *How did I not know that even as we were driving the day before, he was thinking about her? Texting? Sexting? How did he hide it? How could he look into his parents' eyes? How did I not know, as we sat in the temple, that it was all a big lie? How could I be so stupid?*

The closer the trip looms, the worse I feel. One day, I sit in a parked car talking with a friend before our weekly 12-step meeting. I am going on and on about the trip, about Nauvoo, about my fear of seeing Nate's parents again, when she gently interrupts me—the only way for her to get a word in edgewise tonight.

"Why don't you just stay in Wisconsin?" she suggests.

"Stay in Wisconsin? You mean, not go to Nauvoo? Well... I mean... I don't think Nate would like that. And, I mean—what would Nate's parents say?" I stammer in confusion. *What does she mean by 'not go'? Doesn't she realize everyone expects me to go? This is a family vacation. I'm the Mom. How could I possibly not go?*

"Well, it just seems to me that you don't have to go to Nauvoo. It makes sense that you wouldn't want to. So, don't go. You have that choice."

I sit in shocked silence. In all my weeks of worrying and fretting, of reliving the past and predicting the future and hating my husband and then myself for all of it, the possibility of not going has not even occurred to me.

"Hmmmm..." I say, slowly nodding my head. "I'll have to think about that."

And I do. All through my support meeting, I think about not going. But it feels like letting everybody down. Embarrassing Nate's parents in front of their friends. Disappointing or even scarring to my kids.

No. *No.* Not going would be selfish. Unimaginable. Unreliable. I would never do something like that.

I go back home, and over the next few days, I think more about not going. And the more space I give the notion, the more it feels like blessed relief, like a two-ton weight lifted off my chest. It feels radical—to not take responsibility for everybody else's feelings and okay-ness. Rebellious—to put down my self-sacrificing role. Beautifully irresponsible—to not be guided by others' expectations. It feels like letting the balls drop and allowing myself to just be a person who simply can't do this. Or maybe, a person who just doesn't want to.

In all honesty, asking what I want feels like such a strange question! *What is expected of me? What does everybody need from me?* These are the questions I know how to answer. But what do *I want*? This seems almost impossible to compute. *Is it okay to want? Is it safe to?*

I close my eyes and imagine the possibility of staying in Wisconsin and sending my family to Nauvoo without me. Of sleeping in the room I grew up in. Of waking up in the morning with nobody to take care of except myself. Of winding my way through my old forest haunts and watching the sun set over familiar dairy farms. Of going on walks and pushing strollers with my sisters. Of going to lunches with my mom. Of breathing and reading and writing and crying and praying, all in a space where nobody expects anything from me.

And the cells of my body tell me. *Yes! We want this!* And my heart feels like it is cracking open as it tells me. *Yes! It feels like I can breathe here!*

I let myself marinate in this cellular wanting right up until just a few days before we leave, when I approach Nate gently but firmly.

"Nate... So, I've been thinking about this a lot...and I think I need to stay in Wisconsin this summer with my family. I'm not going to go to Nauvoo with you. I want you to take the kids. Your parents are so excited to see them. But I can't go there, Nate. I just can't. It's too painful. It's too hard. And it feels really good to me to give myself permission to just stay home."

Nate is shocked, perplexed, fearful. This is wholly unexpected. Unprecedented. And once the words are out of my mouth, I find even more clarity and courage.

"And, Nate, I think it would be really good for me to stay in Wisconsin for most of the summer. I think that space will be good for me. For both of us. I think we need it."

"What does that mean…for us? I mean…what am I supposed to tell my parents? What are they supposed to tell their friends?" His face goes white with protests and pleadings.

"I don't really care what they tell people, Nate. And I guess you'll have to decide how you want to explain it. It's not my job to manage that for either one of you."

There's a calm grounding in me that feels far more solid than the desperate threats and outbursts I've previously gotten lost in. This is my next right step, and the cells of my body know it. It's an energy that can't be argued with.

Within a few days, he reluctantly concedes. "I get it. You need to do what's best for you. I'll figure it out with my folks. It's not your problem." I reach out and squeeze his hand in gratitude, even as I look him straight in the eyes, without apology. *Damn straight.*

He pauses, then takes my face in his hands and pulls me in, tenderly, nose to nose, eye to eye. "Beck, I need to say something to you… The fact that you feel unsafe going to Nauvoo is evidence that you've been hurt by my behavior in the past…"

Tears spring to my eyes. He's rehearsing a script he's learned from Rhyll Croshaw's book, *What Can I Do About Me.* I recognize it immediately. Even though the words are rote, they pierce me straight to my heart. I close my eyes to hide from both his gaze and the pain that's now rippling up from my belly into my throat and face. He kisses me softly on the nose.

"Look at me, Beck, please…" he whispers. I reluctantly open my eyes to meet his steady stare and my tears spill over. "No wife should ever have to go through what I've put you through, and I'm so, so sorry. I want you to know that I'm fully committed to recovery. I'm doing the work, and I'll keep doing it as long as it takes. I'm so sorry, Beck. Truly. Whatever you need, I'm here."

His eyes are shining as he wraps my shaking body into his arms and lets my sobs collapse into his chest.

* * *

Once we arrive in Wisconsin, I find that even my safe place at the lake feels marred by the ugly scars of Nate's betrayals. So many of our memories now seem soiled and unreal, all our traditions littered with triggers. The safety and respect I feel with my parents and siblings only make my own life situation harder to bear. This feels particularly true in regards to the men: my dad, brothers, and brothers-in-law. In my heart, I know they would never have done this to their wives. Never in a million years. But then, none of them is married to *me*. My shame is overwhelming, and the secret-keeping feels unbearable.

All day long, I just want to get away from Nate, but he follows me around like a lost puppy, uneasy in the loud chaos of my large family. One night, he tells me that a conversation he had with my dad here a year ago was what made him decide to end the relationship. They were out on the lake, just talking, when something clicked and he realized how much he was putting at risk. He ended it with the woman shortly after we got back from this Wisconsin trip. My stomach twists in fresh disbelief that this is who he was a year ago, in these very walls. At this very lake. With all the people who've wrapped their arms around him and loved him like their own.

That night, I end up kneeing him in the nuts in crazy rage. Another night, I sob uncontrollably, and he makes love to me to put me to sleep. On our family's treasured adult date night, I cross my arms and slide as far from him as possible. I can't even look at him as I compare his lack of devotion to the happy marriages around us. All week, I quiver on the edge of violent reactivity, feeling trapped and suffocated. I'm sure he feels alone and abandoned. It's an excruciating week for both of us.

When Nate leaves for Nauvoo at the end of the week, we are at a point of desperation, of pain too great to manage. As hard as it is to see our minivan pull away from my parents' driveway with my husband and kids in it, the larger part of me is utterly relieved. I settle into my old bedroom at my parents' home and am just myself for the first time in twelve years.

For a week, I sleep as long as I like and move through my days without an agenda. Within a day or two, I find that I remember this girl, and I like her depth and independence. I practice asking what I want, asking what I need. I'm gently remembering how to organize my life around my own inner compass rather than Nate's or my kids' expectations and desires. It's like stumbling to speak an old, distant language. There's more freedom in each breath. I'm remembering what it is to be me.

A week later, my kids return, and Nate leaves for the airport. I am glad to see him go.

The coming weeks are pivotal: a separation, a self-defining. Nate and I don't even talk on the phone. Instead, we send occasional emails that express our hearts: what we're learning, what we feel, what we want—for ourselves and our relationship. But mostly, we are alone: unhinging ourselves from the ping-pong werewolf patterns of insanity that have carried us through this trauma so far. Instead of desperately grasping at or pushing away from Nate to escape my fear, I am learning to sink into myself and face it. I am learning to root into God.

Most days I lace up my shoes before my kids are awake. I head down the hill into thick Wisconsin air and listen to the trees whisper. I walk and run down the same highway I walked and ran down fifteen years ago. The same highway where I learned to hate myself, to pound myself into submission: the desperate drive to achieve, to perfect, to perform. *You are fat, you are ugly, you are fat, you are ugly.* A mantra that effectively shaved off so much of my tummy and my soul but won me the validation I was looking for at the time. That was supposed to be safety.

But it wasn't. And now, this same road beats that illusion right out of me. This morning ritual on this life highway carries me so gently, teaches me how to willingly surrender. This road is just here, a steady constant, bridging me from who I was to who I am becoming.

Fifteen years ago, I thought I was mastering the road. I thought I was mastering myself. I was eighteen and claiming scholarships, titles, smaller pant sizes, and admiration from boys. I was leaving my homeland behind with an arrogance that imagined I had already conquered this simple midwestern life and was on my way to far bigger and better places.

Today, I am stunned by the world and its cruelty. Today, I am utterly defeated and empty. Today, I plead with this road to still have me, if it will. This road, this space, this pure and heavy Wisconsin air. This family, this sure foundation, the manicures and outings and lunches. It all gives me space to heal. It gives me courage to want. Those years ago, I thought I wanted to be bright and shiny. *What do I really want?*

As I breathe in this clear country air day after day, I realize: I want the simple goodness I feel here. All of the real and honest beauty I took for granted before. All the quirks I used to criticize. *I want what's real.* Bumps and all.

Just give me a life that's good, God. Not perfect, not righteous. Not bright and shiny. Just good. It's so much harder than I thought, and I don't know how to get there. But You do. Please, show me.

This simple surrender slowly settles my racing breath. It loosens my grip on the need to hide or push away from what's happening. It clears space for God to do something; it opens me to His possibilities.

But as this newfound willingness starts to sink into my soul, a clock hovers over my head: Nate will return in a few short weeks. I feel the weight of the timeline as much as I relish the freedom of it.

Will I have things figured out by then? Will I be ready to go back?

It's not the separation that scares me. It's the reunion. There's something so fragile here, so sacred in the space we're creating: I in me, Nate in himself. Will we be able to do all we need to do in this time apart? When we come back together, it's got to be different. Will it be?

Before I know it, summer is over. Our separation has ended. What does life look like from here?

THIS ROAD

BECKY MOLLER, JULY 2014

Sun low in the early morning sky,
Each day, this road has greeted me.
No questions asked.
No matter the state of my battered heart,
This road takes me as I am.
Some days, anger churns in each pounding stride,
Other days grief overtakes each faltering footstep,
Gasping for air, chest heaving, heart pounding, body shaking.

Whatever my beleaguered spirit cries out,
This road reminds through soft breezes blowing bulrushes,
Wild geese gathering by still water,
Sparrow spurting to bright blue skies,
That there is peace.
There is love.
Steady through the uncertainty of the future,
All this is here to comfort my troubled soul,
And wrap me in God's glorious creation.
No matter how darkly fear threatens my dreams,
There is always this road, steady and strong,
Ready to take my pounding punishment,
Willing to wait for my bubbling brain to calm its
Train of worries.
Until it tires and simply sees
All that is right in front of me.
This Road.
His Love.
He takes me as I am

And shows me He is there.

PART TWO

Through
The Muck

CHAPTER THIRTEEN

A RECOVERY COMMUNITY

U ntil glaciers retreat, the depth of the resultant damage is largely hidden. A frozen glacier appears on the surface as a smooth, floating field of ice. But its heavy weight, up to millions of tons, has been grinding down the earth below, resulting in a mix of gravel, rocks, sand, and mud called *till*. As the melt begins and the till is dumped and deposited, the former landscape is randomly reshaped at Mother Nature's will.

Glaciers will leave behind anything they pick up along the way, and sometimes this includes huge rocks, termed glacial erratics or erratic boulders. Until the ice freeze has melted, you never know how far a major boulder may have been moved—even hundreds of miles. If you've ever seen a massive boulder seemingly dropped from the sky with no geologic context, you are likely looking at a glacial erratic.[3]

Whether you like it or not, suddenly something large, immovable, and unexpected has been dropped into your formerly familiar and orderly horizon. Until the glacier retreats, until the moment of crisis has passed, you might not realize how drastically the underlying landscape has been rearranged. There's no way around it: making your way through the muck is going to be messy.

When my family and I finally pull into our driveway after the long trek west across I-80, it feels like pulling up to piles of till freshly unmasked from the receding crisis. Something inside me senses that despite our summer

---

3   https://www.nps.gov/articles/erratics.htm;
    https://www.nps.gov/articles/glacialtillandglacialflour.htm

respite, we've got layers of excavation ahead of us. In truth, it will take years to unearth them all.

Less than a week earlier, Nate flew back to us in Wisconsin. My parents kept the kids, and Nate and I spent two days wandering The Dells and boulders of Devil's Lake, trying to create a new topography between us. My baby bump is now showing, and it makes our reunion all the sweeter. Our trajectory is hopeful, but when we load up the kids and I hug my parents good-bye, my courage fails me. After the refuge of parents and siblings and daily outings with Grandma, it feels like a monumental task to return to my strained reality far across the country.

When I first see our home under the heavy summer moonlight after being so long away, the stonework on its front face seems to glare at me with ominous tones, the dark soffits sharp and threatening. I feel like I'm being returned to prison.

Oh God, I don't want to go back in there. This sentiment is truly a prayer. I shield my kids from my bloodshot, teary eyes with sunglasses and prod them to help unpack our luggage and gear. As soon as I walk through our garage entryway, I immediately feel a sense of revulsion. *The smell.* We've only lived in this home for eight months, and I can still smell the previous owners and their untrained cats when I open the door—especially in this summer heat. It seems too much trouble to try to scour out their scents and stains, to update the ugly dark brown paint on the walls and heavy iron light fixtures. After all, we don't know if we're even going to be married a year from now.

For a moment, I let my mind wallow again in the darkness: *This doesn't feel like our house. This shouldn't be my life. I hate that this is my life.*

But as the days continue, it's a little easier to release the old resistance. I settle in and try to recapture the freedom I felt in my Wisconsin summer. There are plenty of positives to focus on if I let myself: The kids are starting another school year, Nate is doing well in his career and staying sober from his self-defined "weapons of war" (pornography, masturbation, and browsing social media), and I've got another semester at the universities to prepare for. Not to mention the baby!

Days turn into weeks and months, and we find a steadier rhythm, less of a crisis energy about us. Trauma outbursts are less frequent. It's beginning to feel like a New Normal. As the weather grows cooler, I find myself planting tulips, which I see as a significant act of faith. I'm daring to believe we might still be here to watch them bloom next year. We even schedule a painter to update the dark brown trim inside the house.

Each day is another faltering step forward and back—usually both directions at different moments on the same day. But now we have a scaffolding holding us up. Our pillars are the weekly and daily support systems we've established: 12-step meetings and therapy appointments offer safe spaces to ease the tension and breathe. We've also found personal practices that help ground us when our bottom falls out. Between mothering and teaching fitness, I spend hours journaling, sleeping, reading, walking, thinking. Nate has created his own routines: daily check-ins, reading, writing, reaching out when he feels triggered. He is learning how to better care for himself and recognize his triggers. An acronym he's learned in recovery is HALT (Hungry Angry Lonely Tired), and he often takes breaks in the middle of the day to go outside and pull weeds or find other healthy ways to shift his energy. It feels good to have a toolkit.

We seem to be mostly out of the danger zone. Nate appears to be safely sober, and I am no longer clawing my way through the days the way I used to. But I still feel like I'm treading water with my head barely above the surface. Yes, I'm surviving, but I'm going nowhere. I doubtfully wonder: *Will I ever feel happy again?*

With the fresh hope of our recent reunification, Nate and I feel cautiously ready to attend a Recovery Conference in Salt Lake City. I'm most interested to hear Rhyll Croshaw, a scheduled speaker and the author of *What Can I Do About Me*, the book that helped me formulate my initial boundaries.

Attending the event is a game-changer. We see acquaintances there, and it's the first time people we know have seen us in this addiction recovery space. Instead of feeling ashamed, we embrace each other with relieved fondness. It all feels hopeful and alive, and there are so many resources there I've never even heard about, including a 12-step program founded by Rhyll and her husband Steven. I take home the information and plan to attend, reassured by the fact that they are members of my religion. I don't want to get lost. I don't want to be led astray.

The women's meeting is only twenty minutes from my home, straight towards the mountains. Next Thursday, I pull into a gravel parking area littered with minivans and hedged by horse pastures, and cautiously enter a beautiful lodge, dimly lit. I immediately hear the same friendly buzz I felt at the Conference. I make my way through a spacious living area, past a huge oak table with sturdy, luxurious chairs, and toward a seated circle of fifteen unfamiliar faces. I find a chair on the outskirts and hope that no one notices me.

Although I know Rhyll is a member of my religion, this program is not church-sanctioned, and that makes me nervous. It already feels strange to be in a beautiful home with high ceilings and mammoth couches instead of a utilitarian church classroom. It feels even stranger to observe these normal-looking women greet each other with hugs, laughing and chatting with familiar, affectionate ease. These are not the silent strangers with forlorn faces I've been sitting with at my 12-step groups this past year. I'm perplexed. At first, the levity feels disconcerting: *Don't they know why we're here? What could possibly be funny?!*

As the meeting starts and I survey the circle more carefully, I realize with dismay that I recognize a few people from my own church congregation. But when I make eye contact, they look straight back at me with a nod, a smile, even a wink. They don't seem a bit surprised to see me, and this fact and their lack of shame unsettles me. I'm trying to wrap my mind around the rules. *Well, I suppose if they're not worried about seeing me here, I shouldn't worry about seeing them here?*

The meeting follows a script that sounds strangely ritualistic, and I struggle to keep an open mind. It all makes me nervous. I am afraid of being deceived, afraid of failing the test. I am afraid of looking anywhere but toward the church, afraid of doing this wrong. I am afraid to lose anything more. I am afraid that I will never get better or feel joy again. I am afraid that despite his strong start, Nate will never stay sober, and that somehow this community, like the last one, will only reinforce the fear that nobody ever does. I am afraid that people like us don't ever really get better.

As people introduce themselves by first name, the openness in the circle touches me, and I feel the sudden urge to be known. I am so tired of carrying this shame, of feeling like an imposter in my skin. When the group moderator welcomes me as a newcomer and invites me to tell a little bit about myself, I find myself asking permission to share my story, something I've never done before.

Before I know it, the highlights of the past year are tumbling out of my mouth while customary tears roll down my cheeks. But as my story unfolds, I feel a strange disquiet. Details that would have shocked my past group dissolve into the collective presence of the circle. The faces around me are kind but unresponsive. They are neither appalled by my husband's exploits nor impressed by my tearful professions of enduring faith. I can sense it. Eventually, my words trail off, and I sit in the deafening quiet. *That felt weird.* The group facilitator kindly nods and thanks me for sharing, then moves on with the agenda. I sit silent as we study from S-Anon 12-Step literature, and I marinate in a fresh vulnerability hangover.

I am baffled. There's something altogether odd about this place: something different, an energy I've never before experienced. I'd grown familiar with hopelessness and stoic suffering. I'd leave my past group each week with both the quiet pride and humiliation of being the unequivocally wronged party. I'd grown professional at professing the wish to endure my trial more faithfully. I'd grown empty from endless stories of partners relapsing repeatedly in seemingly endless cycles. In each meeting, there was a holy martyrdom in the air.

But here, people don't talk like that. And I don't feel judgment or pity or fear or comparison or self-righteousness or anything else recognizable to my current map of what recovery is supposed to look like. In fact, as I sit back and really listen, I feel the strangest sense that this is not about my story at all. Embarrassment creeps into my face. *Why did I go on and on like that?*

My share sticks out like a sore thumb. People here aren't making pretty speeches. Many don't even talk about betrayal or relationships at all. Instead, they are blatantly honest about their *own* journeys: What are they learning? How are they coping? What do they need to be accountable about? Some are unapologetically pissed. Some are openly sad. It's more honest and raw than anything I've yet been a part of. There's a quiet confidence, an almost tangible serenity that hovers like a light above the circle and fills the room with power and peace. Soon, my curiosity overshadows my self-consciousness. *What do these women have? What do they know that I don't know, to speak so differently than I do?*

And what's more, people are getting better. There's more sobriety in offending partners and less victim mentality in betrayed ones. Up until now, Nate's year of sobriety was the anomaly, giving him an almost celebrity-like status amidst our former 12-step circle. This created a weird sense of pride accompanied by a deep fear that inevitably, relapse was coming for us. Nobody seemed to actually get better and stay better. But as I talk to people after the group, I learn there are many people here whose partners have years of sobriety. Even a decade. I didn't even know that was possible. It occurs to me that, thus far, the Twelve Steps has been a place to share the suffering. I didn't know there was a path that led to real recovery.

When I receive parting smiles and hands on the shoulder that encourage me to come back, they don't have to sell me. I am already sold. Although I have my qualms about the potential danger of a non-church-sanctioned resource, I *am* certain of one thing: They have something that I don't have. There's something here that I need, that *we* need. I'm not sure what it is, but my soul is thirsty for it. I am hooked.

When I get home, I tell my husband that this will be my new recovery group. We're both a little nervous about the church issue, but I really believe the proof is in the pudding. There is sobriety here, and that fact is undeniable. So, I make a commitment to guard my testimony of the church. To be a good example to the group, to help them understand who God really is. After attending my first meeting, that's my one sticking point: I'm not sure that they quite understand Him. (*What a joke!*)

My unconscious arrogance becomes the crowning irony of all the miraculous healing that eventually unfolds. Week after week, I show up and am schooled by these experience-made experts. Month after month, my self-righteous superiority is ground down to a stupefied humility, an uncovering of my own brokenness: the holes in my belief systems and perceptions, in the way I hold myself, the world, and yes, even and especially, God. But there is progress in the pain, and with each new touchpoint of self-awareness, I feel myself loosening the knot I've been tied up in since that notorious Sunday night.

My teachers in the Group are women who've been working recovery for years, even a decade. *Why do they keep coming?* I can tell it has less to do with their husband's sobriety dates and more to do with the inner freedom they find in this circle. From their easy shares and insightful discussions of each step, I learn new vocabulary and build a powerful roadmap forward.

I am introduced to the practice of surrender: the counterintuitive power of letting go. I recite the Serenity Prayer a dozen times a day and apply its wisdom to navigate moments both small and big. I learn more about boundaries and I witness people using them each week to find greater safety, less reactive codependency, and deeper personal integrity in everyday life. I get a better sense of how to flex and bend with boundaries, how to watch them to see if they serve, and not make them black and white and rigid. I hear about qualified therapy and full disclosure and come to recognize the many rocks Nate and I have left unturned on our current recovery path. I learn names and numbers of the most qualified therapists in the field, and Nate and I get our name on a year-long waiting list for the apparent best-of-the-best.

I learn there is a difference between sobriety and recovery, between white-knuckling and healing. I learn more about addict behaviors and cycles and why Nate's moods and actions trigger me so badly, even when he's not acting out. I learn that Nate is very often at my center, and I am taught how to recognize the chaotic thought patterns and behaviors in myself that can tune me into this fact. I learn that I can put God at my center instead, and I begin to experience the peace that results when I do.

I learn more about sponsorship: a mentorship-of-sorts with someone who is further down the recovery path. I hear about people reaching out and using their sponsors to get through their very weakest moments. It's hard to imagine myself calling somebody in the middle of a trauma spin-out, but week after week, I hear people share that they've done just that, and how it helped them find their center again.

Holly is a staple at my weekly meeting: blond, beautiful, uncommonly wise, and larger than life. From the first time I walked into the lodge, the light seemed to radiate around her. Each week, I found myself wishing and willing her to speak throughout the meeting. Every word she said was so profound, like nourishing food to my starving soul, filled with wisdom, love, insight, humor, accountability, and compassion. I'd never met anyone who resonated more with me, so eventually I ask Holly to be my sponsor, and she kindly agrees.

For the first time since Rock Bottom, I feel hopeful and empowered, like I'm finally getting all my recovery ducks in a row. One week after the meeting, I somehow mention something about Nate's year-plus of sobriety—even without a sponsor—to the group leader.

"Well, that's great, but if he doesn't have a sponsor, he's not in recovery," she says, simple as that.

When I return home, I mention her comment to Nate, who is initially offended. But as he sees and feels my progress, he decides to try their men's groups. Suddenly, there are people with much more experience he can learn from. He gets a sponsor, and things get even more on track between us. Week after week, we both witness people getting better. We use "I" statements rather than "you"-stories. We find ourselves speaking the same language more than ever. Suddenly, we are swimming in liberating and unapologetic honesty rather than hiding and shame.

Before long, Nate is as engaged in this new community as I am. His weekly meeting is a top priority on his calendar, and he starts meeting his 12-step friends for lunches, bike rides, and golf outings. He's often on the phone with his sponsor, and soon he becomes a sponsor himself. He loves sharing his experience and helping other people find sobriety. He's never been more connected, and happiness and self-confidence begin to grow from his insides, out.

The additional support network for both of us gives our healing relationship much-needed breathing space. When we're in a bad way, we can ask one another if we've talked to our sponsors. Getting feedback from a sponsor before we come together on tough issues creates an emotional filter: a new space of humility in our perspective. By reaching out, we become more autonomous and accountable for the energy we bring to our interactions with each other. The cylinders start firing; in moments, it seems as though we actually know where we're going.

Over the next few years, this community becomes the framework for our healing. We learn from others' experiences, we soak in their energy, and we learn a different way of being almost through osmosis. As we make healthy choices, we are validated and supported. As we share struggles, we are validated and supported. Even when we fall flat on our faces, we are validated and supported, without being given any excuses for our behavior. This community embodies the reality of unconditional love, and it's a collective energy that's like a magnet, drawing us away from old paradigms towards new, healthier mindsets. It gives Nate and me a soft landing for both the hills and valleys along the rocky road of rebuilding our life, our marriage, and our individual sense of self.

I am learning what it means to be a fellow among fellows: a revolutionary sideways orientation that's a radical shift from my previous climb-the-ladder, follow-or-become-the-authority-figure approach to life. Here, in the mess, we are all just human beings, figuring things out together, one day at a time. Our brokenness only connects us all the more. Over time, it helps shift me from a broken self-concept to an empowered one, showing me that I *do* have something valuable to offer—not in spite of my ugly path, but even *because* of it. The sting of my wounds softens each time something I share in the Group helps another person to feel heard and seen.

I am no longer an island. Everywhere I turn, a new Divine messenger has been sent to guide my path. No matter how tipsy and unsteady I feel on the unstable ground, there's a whole army of true spiritual friends to prop me up. I cannot fall; I am supported. This community shows me, one step at a time, how to walk through hell without turning to ash.

BEAUTY FOR ASHES

BECKY MOLLER, JANUARY 2015

My heart, it feels to sing today, and sing forevermore.
For what was broken, buried, gone, begins to be restored.

You face the ugly in us all and hold us in our grief,
You take our pain, remorse, and sin and offer your relief.

All you've asked is willing hearts, to change and understand,
To say, "Please teach me, Lord, for surely, I am just a man."

Your plan of mercy in my life is beautiful to see,
For in the beauty of your plan, you've rescued him and me.

You let us choose and make mistakes, you're there to catch our fall,
And then you take our broken souls and mend them, heart and all.

And miracle of miracles, and what still leaves me floored,
Is how we walk through fire and emerge with so much more.

The wisdom, understanding, humility, and softened hearts,
We never could have known without the dark and lonely parts.

You give a fresh today, you are a God of second chances,
You give us more than we deserve, it's beauty for our ashes.

CHAPTER FOURTEEN

My Body, My Friend

Before I know it, it's January and I'm at the hospital getting hooked up to tubes, my contractions intense and close together. There is a sinking fear deep underneath the familiar hum of the labor and delivery orchestra. This may be baby #5, but it's my first baby since Rock Bottom, less than a year since my life fell apart.

How has life changed shape so drastically in such a short span of time?

My soul has whiplash and my body is on high-alert. But I find comfort in this safe and familiar room. All my babies have come to me at this small, intimate hospital, under the watch of experienced doctors and nurses so capable it's been easy to relax under their care. And yet, I've spent so much of the past year kicking and screaming that I can't deny the addictive anxiety bleeding into this moment. My fear demons are vigilant: *What is God going to take from me now? Am I going to die in childbirth? Will I lose my baby?*

I'm also guiltily aware of all the trauma in my body. *How many stress hormones has he absorbed? Will something be wrong with him? Will it be my fault? Will he come out twisted?* My guard is up, and I am tensing for another hit, another pang, another loss. There is too much at stake, and I feel like a sitting duck waiting for the worst.

But labor progresses uneventfully, similar to my other deliveries. I am a'slow and a'steady, and my blood pressure drops predictably. I drift off to sleep after the epidural. The doctor comes in to chat football with my husband in the midnight hours as I doze in and out. Before I know it, it's time to push. This will be my last baby, my last time to perform this miracle and meet the little soul who's been swimming inside of me, carrying all my pain and grief with me over the past nine months.

What will I say? *I am sorry. I am sorry. I am so so sorry.*

It always seems to be four in the morning when babies decide to be born, and that is the hour when Tyson bursts into my life. He is born with a healthy set of lungs, ten fingers and toes, a perfect round head with wisps of dark hair, and the same Moller face I have seen presented to me four times before. When I see him, tiny hands grasping empty air, hungry rooting mouth, warm body ready to nuzzle into me with complete trust, different tears spring to my eyes, and my tragic apologies evaporate into the air, irrelevant. My heart bursts as gratitude overflows and begins to trickle down my cheeks.

So, you are the one who needed to come. You are the one I needed, after all my efforts to keep myself from the risk of being hurt again. Thank you. Thank you for being willing to come into this mess. Thank you for carrying this pain with me. I love you, I love you, I love you.

I breathe in his sweet fragrance and wonder what he knows about me, about himself, about life, about God. His giant eyes are shut newborn tight. He is perfect.

I look at my husband and see that gratitude is streaming down his face, too. He squeezes my hand, and the meaning between us is as deep and true as the ocean itself. *We don't deserve this.* After all we have been through and all we have done, we are blown away by the goodness of God. We sit, hands clasped tight, in a perfect moment where time stands still. We have never felt so undeservedly blessed. We have never experienced such tangible grace. This perfect little miracle in my arms is a living, breathing manifestation of second chances and new beginnings, of innocence and trust. No matter what happens tomorrow, we will always have this moment.

* * *

It's the middle of the night, and the baby is crying. By the time it registers that I need to actually swing my feet to the floor to get to him, my husband is already walking towards me, holding our little bundle of hungry lungs. I grin in spite of my exhaustion. I adore this tiny creature, but I'm grateful that Nate was the one to heave himself out of bed to fetch him tonight.

I reach for Tyson with both arms, and as I feel his small weight rest into my outstretched fingertips, a sharp and shooting pain ripples through my spine from the back of my left ear all the way down my back. I collapse into the pillow as my little one latches on, and we drift back to oblivion, nestled together.

But when I open my eyes the next morning, I cannot move. Even the slightest tinge sends a searing pain down the left side of my body. I feel paralyzed, and it terrifies me. *What is wrong with me?* My voice quivers, "Nate? I can't move…"

I have never been to a chiropractor, and I rarely visit the doctor. Most of the time, I don't even have ibuprofen in my house. Something in me just likes to give my body time and space to figure itself out. Even through the crazy trauma pendulums between depression and rage, I had no desire for medication. In my view, my body was clearly trying to tell me something—and I didn't see how numbing its signals would solve the problem.

Instead, my group exercise classes became my happy pill; a coping strategy that lifted my mood and stabilized my spinning mind. The only time I could remember canceling class was the day after Nate's *Sunday Night Disclosure.* Other than that dismal day, I was onstage jumping, kicking, and punching my way through trauma and pregnancy, all the way up to my due date.

So, it's significant when I wake up frozen in pain and line up substitutes for an unprecedented week. Later that day, Nate holds my arm as I shuffle into the chiropractor's office. When the chiropractor orders an X-ray, it startles me to see the very crooked line of my cervical spine in black and white. *How did this happen?* I've never had neck or back problems before. *I am so fit, so active, so healthy—I teach Pilates, for crying out loud! How can I suddenly be so out of alignment?*

My chiropractor starts referencing possible reasons for the problem. Eventually, he asks if I've recently experienced a trauma. Maybe he's referring to a car accident or injury, but I am caught off guard by his word choice.

Of course, I think. *Of course. How could I be so full of stress hormones for so many months and not expect my body to be affected? What do I think happens to the toxic levels of cortisol and adrenaline I keep dumping into my system? Of course, my body is locking up! Every cell in my body is kicking and screaming in one massive temper tantrum.*

The doctor continues, explaining how emotions can be thought of as energies stored in our bodies. When they get stuck, they can create imbalances and blockages, even a heart wall. As I hear his words, I feel sure of the emotional connection to my locked physical condition. I commit to regular chiropractic visits for the next few months and know this is not a healing for my cervical spine alone. The crucial questions that must accompany this process of alignment go way beyond my vertebrae and into my soul: *What do I still need to let go of?*

* * *

In my senior year of high school, my body became my shield against the world. I lost twenty pounds in two months, and suddenly the world saw me as adorable instead of intense and overbearing. I was less intimidating and apparently more worthy of love when I took up less space. People were more interested in what I had to say when I was more interesting to look at. From then on, my body became the blanket I desperately grasped at to secure love and acceptance in an adult world. In my mind, nobody could criticize me when I was too thin to get a period.

Betrayal Trauma complicated this already-exposed thorn in my side. My husband's sexual behaviors poked at the most vulnerable parts of my body: both outwardly (*I'm not pretty enough*) and inwardly (*I'm not sexual enough*). My physiological trauma reactions made my body feel like the enemy. More than ever before, I was split inside: at war with myself.

Enter yoga: an embodied practice I was a stranger to, despite my nearly 15 years in the fitness industry. I had always been too focused on the efficiency of my precious workout time: I had fifty minutes away from the kids, and I needed to get the most calorie-burn bang for my buck. But my sponsor Holly taught a regular yoga class at the public library, and the promise of learning more from her was enough to motivate me. So, as baby Tyson grows older, I carefully carve out space to attend weekly. I have no idea how deeply this simple ritual will change my life.

Yoga quickly becomes the safe and sacred container to recraft this broken relationship with my body, and Holly becomes my spiritual gangsta guide to do so. From day one, when I settle my mat on the nubby carpets of the library common room and take in the faces of the measurable crowd, I recognize that I am in new territory. Under Holly's nurturing guidance, I learn that true yoga is more about spiritual transformation than acrobatics. Her classes are simple and straight-forward, sprinkled with new questions to consider: What does it feel like to be in my body without some intended outcome? Without pushing my body and ignoring its voice? What does it feel like to move into different postures and positions without framing these by their function: *this is a leg toner, this one is for upper body strength, etc.?* What does it feel like to just *move?* To just *be?*

Holly frames each practice with a sacred and self-reflective intention, inviting me to honor my body as my teacher and most loyal friend.

"Your body," she says, "is very literally the container of your soul. It has miraculously stored every thought, emotion, experience, and belief you have put into it from the moment you were born, and it holds each one for you with fierce loyalty. The very cells of your body are hard-wired for self-protection and will go to almost any length to safeguard the values, purpose, and sense of identity you have entrusted to its care. This includes depleting itself to the point of chronic illness or injury. Therefore, it is up to you, your own Higher Self, to give your body permission to release the thoughts, beliefs, and memories that do not serve it. It is up to you to give your body conscious permission to let go."

So, each week, with Holly's gentle guidance, I learn to breathe into the places in my body that want to tighten and clench and gently invite them to relax. I learn to feel my mat underneath my feet, deepen my breath, and check in with my body: *What are you trying to tell me today? What needs my attention? I love you. I'm listening.* As my body starts to let go, my Spirit is finally able to do the same.

When there is discomfort, pain, or even just a sense of unrest, I watch, feel, and witness. My body points me to the underlying need asking to be met. As I learn to respond mindfully, I am able to actually attend to my needs rather than drown out the complaining. A headache is often best answered by a drink of water or a nap. Tightness in my shoulders might point to emotional burdens that need to be set down, heard, or supported. A locked neck often points to trauma reactions that need to be acknowledged, held, and surrendered. When I listen to my body, I am brought more quickly into the

127

cognitive awareness of what is going on with me. My body always knows before my brain does.

Yoga means unity: at-one-ment. I start to realize that since high school, my fear has been tearing my body and soul apart, making us enemies. But over time, yoga reunites us. Even amidst emotional turbulence, I find that I have the capacity to be with the pain. If I can stay conscious enough in my body to relax and allow the emotion, I can watch the sensation rise and fall like a wave on the ocean. I can find the part of me that is big enough to hold it.

Thoughts come, and physical sensations follow. *I feel the fear as tightness in my chest. It's so tight right now, like I can't even breathe. It feels sharp and tight, and bright, bright white.*

But if I stay with the sensation and let the thought pass, my experience changes.

As I stay here and breathe, I can feel it changing. Each exhale seems to soften its hold on me. Here it goes now. Hmmm. My hand is on my heart. It feels warm. The color is softening; it's more gold now than that bright white light. It feels more open. I can breathe better.

I am shocked at my capacity to be with hard things, amazed to witness how quickly the pain moves through if I stop thinking about it and just watch it pass. Moving into my body moves me out of my mind, where most of the trouble seems to start. I can sense the wisdom there, and instead of looking to books and bishops, I start looking inward for my answers.

A few months into my yoga practice, I pop a rib out of place, creating spasms that literally take my breath away. I schedule an emergency session with my massage therapist, and she talks to me about how rib issues can point to feeling caged in or trying to control things. Immediately, I recognize the ways my chronic perfectionism has snuck into my mindset again, the strain of trying to make my life fit in perfect, tidy boxes. I'm doing it in my relationship with Nate. I'm doing it with my work. Before I could see it in myself, my ribs had called my attention in no uncertain terms. Yoga is teaching me a new way to be in my body: with kindness, curiosity, alert attention, and deep respect.

Towards the close of each weekly yoga class, Holly guides us into Supta Baddha Konasana or Reclined Butterfly posture, an intense hip opener. Week after week, I try to settle in, the soles of my feet kissing each other, my knees splayed open to the side, my back reclined, and my arms wrapped elbow to elbow above my head.

But each week as I lie back and try to breathe, my body and spirit tense into violent revolt. Lying in this posture, I feel more than unprotected. I feel like a sitting duck. This posture embodies all the eggs that have shattered in my life's basket. My heart rate quickens, my breath goes shallow, and tears begin to leak from my eyes. Dark narratives start to swirl: *How dare you, God? I'm not safe with You... I'm not safe with anyone. I don't want this life!*

My unshielded body reveals the parts of my soul that still feel betrayed by God, unsafe with life, and this is crucial information for what still needs healing. My mind likes to believe the story that "I'm fine now and it's over," but my body knows better. As I listen to my body, I learn so much I didn't realize about myself, and I can heal what's broken on a deeper level.

In yoga, it's easy to see my progress or regression, because it's all there, stored in my body as plain as day. Each time I practice, the same postures feel different, and they manifest the internal energy of clinging or surrender that either causes my body to tighten or relax.

One day, as I settle into Supta Baddha Konasana, I find that I am able to grasp my wrists overhead, press the soles of my feet together, and allow my knees to gently fall open without a fight. For the first time, I lie still here, completely exposed and utterly surrendered. I breathe deeply for a solid moment before I map the significance of the feat. *Oh my gosh, I'm doing it!* I ask my brain to draw a map to this peaceful place so I can find it again, and my mind takes note: *Today, I am not afraid. Today, I am willing to surrender. Today, I am ready to trust. Today, I relax into His care. So, this is what this feels like.*

Over the coming weeks, this position becomes my craving each time I practice. Supta Baddha Konasana becomes a gentle and trustworthy barometer of my healing.

Another day, Holly guides us into a sitting butterfly position: "Take a moment to deepen your breath and see if you can use that breath to soften and deepen the pose." My legs butterfly up and down, further opening my hips. My gaze falls naturally to my feet. They are short and stubby, and I've laughingly called them my "hobbit" feet for years. I've always hated them, hiding them when possible. But today my gaze takes them in as though I've never seen them before. I notice their short, round shape, and register in my chest how this familiar critique mirrors a much deeper internal fear: I am too short and round myself... *You are fat, you are fat, and nobody will ever love you.*

Hearing that old voice in my head triggers sadness and regret, and my mind-body-spirit is making connections, showing me something I've never truly understood before. I am seeing how my own ego-fear has hurt them, has done violence against *me.* How I've tried to fit even my feet into a box to meet my desperate need for acceptance and validation. How I've been afraid that they aren't right, that people won't like them. Afraid they will give me away and everyone will know, no matter how skinny I get, that really I am just short and stubby and irrelevant underneath.

Before I know it, there are tears dropping onto these short, round little feet. My throat chokes with palpable remorse at the harshness I've hurled at them all these years. *I am sorry. I am so sorry I have been so unkind to you. I am so sorry I have hated and used you. I am so sorry that I have never truly seen you and all that you've done for me.*

With breath and acceptance, the sadness moves through, and slowly, I fill to the brim with a different emotion: overwhelming gratitude. Each curve of every toe-knuckle, the swirls of skin on each toe-print, each miraculous detail appears magnificent, like newly discovered appendages I've never taken time to notice. My entire being bursts with praise and thanksgiving: *I love my 'hobbit' feet. These are the feet that God has given me. These are the feet that have brought me to where I am today. Thank you for carrying this burden with me, feet. For carrying me through my trauma. Thank you for all you have done for me. I love you.*

Later that night, I walk through the hall with a basket full of laundry and my eyes rest on the family picture taken right in the midst of Nate's online affair. I pause and breathe, and let myself take it in for the first time in over a year. And I notice it's a little easier to see this image from the painful past. There's a little more capacity to feel the sting and freely let it go.

If I can accept and love my "hobbit" feet, maybe I can also love the other less-than-ideal parts of my life, including my journey with my husband. Maybe I am growing closer to this AA promise: "We will not regret the past nor wish to shut the door on it."

Yoga

Becky Moller, November 2016

Every longing is a
longing for
You.

Every wanting
is a wanting
Your way.

Every ache is the aching that comes
from being far from
all that You are.

CHAPTER FIFTEEN

SURRENDER

I'm driving in my car, baby Tyson asleep in his car seat after dropping kids at after-school activities, when I realize that my hands are squeezing my steering wheel so hard that my knuckles have gone white. My chest and shoulders are tight, and I can't turn my head because the left side of my neck is locked up, again. The latest row of back-and-forth arguments between Nate and I are looping in my mind. No matter how many days of sobriety he piles up, I still find myself mired in the frustration of feeling unheard, unsafe, overlooked, and powerless.

I can't believe that he can't understand how he's still twisting things and gaslighting. I hate that he is so numb, so unfeeling. I hate the unfairness of feeling so much when he's the one who caused all this pain, and he is so cheerfully oblivious. I will never open myself up to him again. Never, never, never. I feel hard and closed, my heart locked in iron-clad chains, keeping me safe and protected.

But I am not safe. I am miserable. I tell myself that I will be free of him, but it's my own obsession that has me in chains. I can't not care that he doesn't care. I can't not see that he doesn't see. I cannot free myself from the suffocating pain that still sometimes feels like it will never heal.

As I drive, the most oft-repeated word from my 12-step group surfaces in my brain: *surrender.* "God grant me the serenity to accept the things I cannot change…" *Is there anything I am more powerless to than this pain and obsession?* But acceptance seems impossible. My whole being tenses up at the thought of it.

If he can't see me, if he can't feel what I feel, then I can't be with him. That's just all there is to it. But even as I think these justified thoughts, I sense their instability. This does not feel like Truth. *This does not feel like Truth.*

I take a deep breath and decide to surrender. I pull my car over and pull out my phone. I scroll through my contacts to find Holly's name. Even though I love and trust her and I've called to surrender dozens of times, my heart is still beating fast. Every time I do this, I feel like I'm about to stand naked in front of a crowd. *What am I going to say?* Before I can second-guess myself further, I push Holly's name. The phone rings and I pray she doesn't answer.

But she does, on the second ring. "Hi, Holly. It's Becky. From Group. I mean, 12-Step. I am so sorry to bother you. Is this a bad time?" I stutter clumsily.

"Not at all. What's up?" she asks kindly. There's no getting out of it now. I start to talk, words spill out and I am not even sure where the narrative is going. I am all over the place. She lets me talk through my feelings until I finally run out of words to say.

"Is that all?" she asks without a hint of irony. "I think so," I say.

"Let's take a breath together," she says. I slowly inhale and feel a calming energy start to swirl inside me. On the exhale, I can feel my feet again. I can sense where I am sitting. I am no longer lost in the labyrinth of my mind. We breathe again, together. I am slowing down, growing clear.

"What do you need to surrender?" she asks. "What are you afraid of?"

I am not certain, but the question itself invites me to step even further out of reactivity. My curiosity calms me, and I begin to observe my emotions and thoughts at arm's length. "I need to let go of needing my husband to see me. I am afraid that I don't matter. That he will never see me. It feels like I'll never be seen. And that scares me, and it makes me so sad." Tears fill my eyes.

"Who is at your center?" she asks.

"Nate is," I answer with clarity. "I need to surrender Nate and put God at my center. I know God sees me. I can let that be enough. I can let that be enough today." I feel different now. I am in a different place, a steadier state of mind. Suddenly, what seemed so insurmountable has become less significant.

"Thank you," I say. I hang up the phone. I sit for a moment and soak in serenity like the sun through the car windows. Even with tears on my cheeks, there is a freedom in my heart that wasn't there before.

Now, what else am I supposed to do when I surrender? Ah, yes, I am supposed to pray.

God, I surrender. I surrender my need to be seen. I surrender my need to be validated and right. I surrender my need to be a victim and the cheap satisfaction it brings me. I let go of Nate as my center. I know he can't fill me. I know that no matter how sorry he is or how much he hurts, it will never heal this huge hole inside of me. I ask You to fill me instead, God. Help me to know that You see me. Help me know that I matter to You. Help me know that You are feeling this with me. Let that be enough.

As I speak the words, my heart begins to overflow with warmth; a warm-honey love expanding through my chest and spreading throughout my entire body. I feel Him with me, so strongly it is as real as if I could reach out and touch His face.

"I see you," He says to my heart. "Not a single tear will go unnoticed. Not a single tear will go to waste."

Tears roll down my cheeks as I sit in my car in this strip mall parking lot in between errands. *This is enough. This is…everything.* For this moment, I am free. Nothing outside of me has changed, but in this moment, my entire Universe has shifted. This is Grace. This is freedom. *This* is surrender.

And when my Tyson wakes in the back seat, I am there. Present enough to playfully reach out and squeeze his toes, cooing loving words to welcome him back from his nap with a clear mind and an open heart. And that's what it's all about.

Thousands of moments like this one teach me: The healing I seek is not a destination I can measure by checking boxes or counting journal pages at the end of the day. It's not about global issues or even about whether Nate and I end up together or apart. Healing is about this magic that is happening inside of me; the magic that nobody else can even see. It's a daily practice of progress, not perfection—and progress is not a linear slant. It's a slowly ascending Ferris wheel, and every small ascension relentlessly requires my full attention to the present moment. All I can do to prepare is…to *be. Right here. Right now.*

With the bells and whistles of physiological trauma still making their share of noise, the tool of surrender teaches me Presence: to bring all my awareness into what is happening inside me, right here and now, and then ask: *What do I need to let go of?*

I See You!

Becky Moller, October 2017

I see You
In every fallen leaf
Drifting softly through the chill,
Telling me to not be afraid
To lose the parts of me
I relied on to feel safe
And important.

Your bare branches
So willing to lose all their breathtaking beauty
And stand in their nakedness
For all the world to judge and scorn,
To dismiss and overlook,
Without the verdant garb of sunnier days.

My prayer is for my heart
To dissolve and soften in Your hands,
And become so willing
To sacrifice all that which the world may applaud,
To stand bare, vulnerable, unprotected,

Trusting,
To learn and grow and sleep
As long as the frigid season lasts.
For it knows,
That this is the price
One pays for
Spring.

What would it be like
If every gentle breeze
Dropped another piece of ego from my soul?
Oh, brown, ruddy branches,
Do you ever sigh and wish for your
Leafy greens once more?
Or are you so much more
Enlightened
Than I?

CHAPTER SIXTEEN
A CENTERED PRESENCE

Slowly, my definition of success is changing. Instead of asking, "What did I get done today?" I'm asking, "How connected did I feel to my true Self today? Can I feel my Higher Power with me—right now?"

I'm learning to observe myself without judgment, but with kind curiosity. Whatever thought or feeling is happening inside me is okay. It belongs. I meet each observation with a conscious, softening breath and this simple mantra: "Hmmm, that's interesting."

My chest is tight? *Hmmm, that's interesting.* My feet feel heavy? *Hmmm, that's interesting.* Just the awareness softens what's happening and brings me back to my Self. I start to realize that noticing is everything. If I'm not aware enough to notice the tightness in my chest, I *become* tight—mentally, emotionally, physically. If I'm not connected enough to feel the heaviness in my step, I *become the heaviness*, lost for hours or even days. One moment at a time, the *awareness* of what's happening in my being alerts me to the recovery tools I need to come back to my Self.

Presence has become the anchor to my inner freedom, and it's a word I initially learn from Eckhart Tolle, the spiritual teacher who offers me a whole new vocabulary. I first discover his spiritual talks on YouTube and immediately recognize that his teachings precisely describe the mystical unwinding that's been happening inside of me. When I read his book *The Power of Now*, his teachings shine so much light on all that I've experienced: The clarity that comes and goes between moments of grounded presence and trauma tailspin.

The never-ending voice in my head. The suffering. As I devour his book, my understanding and my freedom deepens and expands.

Practicing presence brings new mental discipline. Eventually, I am able to choose what my attention focuses on rather than getting hijacked by every song on the radio or intrusive memory. The safest harbor for my weary mind is the present moment, and my body is my consistent anchor to get there. In moments of distress, I learn to drop the story and drop into my body. As I deepen my breath and hold my attention to the felt-sense of my physical experience, I eventually find my center.

Where do I feel this in my body?
What is the quality of the sensation?
Does it have a color? A texture? A temperature?
Can I be with it?

The peace and calm of presence stand in stark contrast to the chaos of my mind, which often spins into what might happen in a month, if I'll still be married in a year, how I'll pay my bills, or how long before my husband relapses again and with whom. As this difference becomes more and more clear, I realize that part of healing means stopping the compulsive mental noise and starting to live one moment at a time.

Do I feel serenity right now, in this very moment? This question becomes my number one priority. Serenity is still a new word for me, a 12-step word, and it encapsulates the deep feelings of peace and equanimity that I find through the 12-step pathway of recovery.

We recite the full Serenity Prayer each week at Group, and its words paint a new vision of success: *Acceptance, Courage, Wisdom, One Day at a Time, Accepting Hardship, Trusting, Reasonably Happy.* These words work like a drug to settle my being, calm my fearful heart, and encourage me to lower my self-protecting gloves. As I feel this ethereal effect week after week at Group, I begin to get greedy. I don't want to wait a week to feel this way. I want to be able to find this peace for myself, any time I want to. All day, every day. Finding serenity becomes like air to me. It becomes life.

So, one day at a time, I learn to focus on just this moment, and I find peace even amidst the great uncertainty. I begin to recognize the routine daily activities that are landmines for my emotional breakdowns and realize I have the ability to break the mental patterns underlying them. It's about taking ownership of where I place my attention. Can I fold clothes without letting my mind wander to my husband's illicit exploits from the past? Can I go to church and look for treasures instead of incongruencies? Can I go to a soccer game and not predict what the other soccer moms would think if they knew who we really were? These questions become key to my ability to function. I've been trapped in a mental prison, and only I have the key to the cell. The patterns are there. It's up to me to investigate.

What am I feeling RIGHT NOW? Again and again, this question refocuses my attention. Getting curious about my emotions helps me separate my Self from them. I begin to clearly see: these feelings aren't who I am. *I am the awareness* that feels them. With practice, I get a clear felt-sense of the difference between the spaciousness of my true Self and the tightness of all the false identities I've been living through.

Slowly, presence moves me from chaos to consciousness. I feel things differently; life appears richer and more alive. I feel a connection to the entire Universe, from the ant crawling across my floor to each leaf quivering from my backyard trees. It is all unfolding, awakening, just like me, and every bit of it is so sacred, so beautiful. I fear suffering and discomfort less. Even my ugly and searing pain is becoming a vehicle for beauty.

I begin to teach my fitness classes differently. As I walk down a hall full of university students, I can feel their true presence. I begin to study people's faces and notice what's there. *Who are you in there? What are your hopes, your dreams, your worries, your fears? What burdens are you carrying? Do you really know that you're right here, existing?* Instead of letting the clock and calorie-burn govern my teaching, I let my heart lead. I spend more time talking to my students. I try to feel their energy and give them what they need, rather than lock in a planned agenda. I choreograph breath and movement to release emotion and build energy, and craft in plenty of time to replenish and restore. Even if it's just for forty-five minutes, I want to offer one place in their life where they can be wide awake, experiencing the present moment fully. I want my class to be a refuge.

I begin to parent differently. I hold my babes in my arms and just hold them. I notice how their soft hair feels against my cheek, how their warm bodies rise and fall against me in rhythm with their breath. I am entranced by their laughter and get lost in their shining eyes. I learn what it means to truly delight in each one of them.

I notice sunsets and go for more walks. I gaze up into the sky more often and for longer periods of time. Inspired by Holly's example, I begin to look for secret love notes from my Higher Power in the clouds, the birds, the breeze. I can suddenly see Him everywhere, and I start to whisper, "I see You" every time I do. The truth is, He was always there…but I wasn't looking. I wasn't on His frequency; I was always looking to the next achievement or event rather than looking inward and upward, here and now, with nothing to prove and everything to learn.

I find myself *responding* to people and situations rather than *reacting* from my emotional state. My life begins to shift from an endless striving to get somewhere, to an endless practice of coming back to the Now, where a Higher Power and purpose are already here, right at the center of me.

But I didn't figure all this out on my own. *What is at my center?* It is a key question we ask in 12-step meetings and one I work with often when I reach out to Holly. It's become a powerful mindfulness tool to help me recognize my mental state. When I'm centered, my mind is clear, my body relaxed, my heart feels open. Serenity is the true north on my inner compass.

Conversely, when my mind is chaotic and spinning, my body is tight or reactive, and my heart feels closed, these are the signals that I've lost my center. As the wisdom of AA suggests, I learn that whenever I'm dysregulated, for any reason, there is something off with *me*.[4] There is reason to investigate, and an opportunity to take ownership of the way I'm relating to my circumstance. No matter the apparent cause, my own disturbance is a sure sign that:

1. I'm trying to regulate myself with something that cannot satisfy…or

2. I'm trying to control something that I cannot control (which is anything other than me).

In either case, I'm grasping for fulfillment and safety where it can't be found; I'm grasping at illusion. The Mindful of Center Models below are tools I've developed for the mindfulness courses I teach. I use these models to track what's happening internally in moments of struggle, and they can

---

4 *The Big Book of AA*, Acceptance, p. 417; and *12 Steps &12 Traditions*, Step Ten, p. 90.

help bring clarity to where I'm stuck. They can help me realize when I've lost my center and remind me how to find it again.

WHAT IS AT MY CENTER?

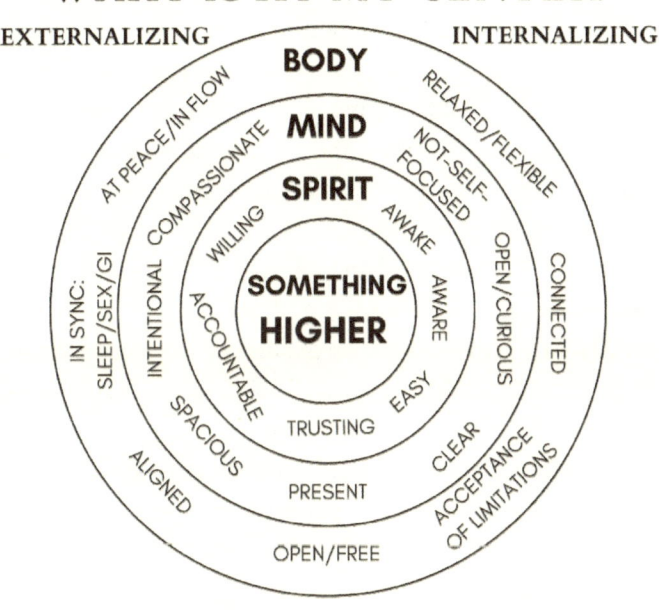

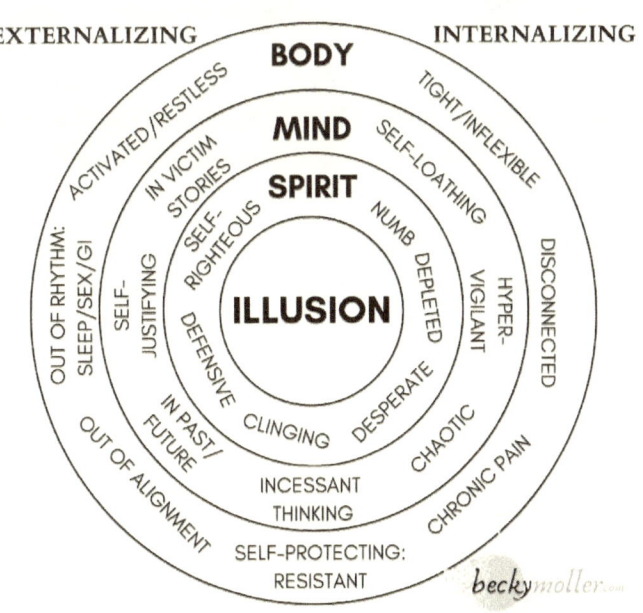

These Mindful of Center Models are a visual expression of a very Eastern notion. The core concept in Buddhist and yogic philosophy is that all conditioned existence is marked by Dukkha, or suffering, and that this suffering is caused by attachment; by grasping at or clinging to illusion.

The circle on top is a circle of alignment, peace, and right action, highlighting the fruits that naturally unfold when we're centered on the Real: that One Divine Intelligence that flows through all things as our innermost essence. The markers listed in body, mind, and spirit help us recognize when we're in this centered state. They also remind us how to find that center: calming the mind, breathing deep to release bodily tension, bringing acceptance and curiosity to what we can't control and offering a willing heart to whatever it is we are experiencing.

The circle on the bottom is a circle of Dukkha, highlighting the suffering we experience in mind, body, and spirit when we center ourselves on Illusion. What is Illusion? Anything that's not real; that's temporary, fleeting, corruptible, self-serving. This might be our own ego desires. Or it might be that we center ourselves around another person. Either way, we create our own suffering when we become attached to that which cannot last and cannot satisfy, when we cling to illusion.

What might "finding your center" look like in everyday life?

Running late is a common occurrence for me, and it's been a great place to practice. When I started, I would often find myself rushing to my minivan, slamming the door, feeling my heart pound in my chest, trailing too close to the car in front of me, cursing whoever had kept me from leaving on time, and obsessively glancing down at the clock as though my glare would somehow slow the minutes and make me less tardy.

I started to catch myself and name what was happening: *I feel off. I'm dysregulated.*

What is at my center?

When I would pause to feel into my heart-space, I found it was often centered on the opinions of the people at the other end of my drive. I didn't want to disappoint or inconvenience anyone—this was the top, most present layer of the feeling. But over time, I could sense the trace of my dad's voice from my childhood, chiding my mom that she had "no concept of time." *Hmmm, that's interesting.* I would take a deep exhale and recognize this deeper layer of conditioning: a shame, a belief, or a shadow that I'd clearly internalized in my childhood. With another deep breath, I would consciously release these thoughts and fears and relax my grip on the steering wheel.

"I'm late," I might say to myself in the quiet of my car. "I accept that I'm late. I can allow the fact that I'm late. It's pointless to fight against it because it already is. I surrender to people's opinions of me. I surrender my shame. Being late doesn't make me a bad person." I would focus on my breath through the remainder of the drive, and by the time I arrived, I would usually be able to engage fully and without excuses—late, but present, unguarded, and available for whatever the situation called for.

This is one example of what it looks like for me to *surrender:* to let go of my resistance and take ownership of my center. It also shows how the practice of surrender can help us become more deeply aware of the unconscious beliefs that are creating our everyday feelings of shame and give us a tangible tool to release these beliefs if we so choose.

Other times, surrender has looked like navigating the challenge of co-parenting teenagers with Nate. There have been times I would wake in the morning and register tightness in my chest and shoulders, dreading the impending drama of skipped classes, explosive outbursts, and unpredictable crises.

I'm aware of the fear I'm already feeling about what might happen today.

It meant noticing the narratives that crept up in the face of such chaos: inner voices calling me a failure, that my teenager's struggles were my fault or Nate's—stories that led to feelings of despair and depression. *I'm aware of the stories I'm telling myself.*

What is at my center?

When I've investigated my heart, I've found the compulsive need to control what I cannot: my child's choices, attitude, happiness. My husband's reactions to my child. Other people's perceptions of me.

I've also found things I *can* change: My own definitions of what a good mother is or isn't.

What is at my center? My child. My husband. My own role identity as wife and mother. Illusions of safety. Illusions of identity.

What happens if I let go and put Something Higher at my center? I breathe space into the tight places in my body, and release control, placing my child, my husband, and myself in the care of a Higher Power with limitless capacity to meet each one of us in all our messiness. I take all the energy of trying to control others and channel it into aligning my own heart with what is and trusting God.

What is my next right step? What is mine to own?

I ask God to show me how to offer love, presence, and space to the moment, exactly as it is. I focus on my own reactivity and the energy I contribute to each convoluted interaction with my teenager or husband. As I do, I can feel the tightness in my chest relax and release. I keep my attention on the sensation of my heart-space and away from my mind-stories.

Through finding my center, my breath, body, and a willing heart become my greatest tools in the very moments of conflict, anxiety, depression, anger, or panic. I've learned that I'd best take ownership of my life by taking full ownership of my center. Through simple actions and words, I can choose to trust in Something Higher. I can refocus my attention from the pandemonium to the Source of peace.

This embodied practice is so simple, it is tempting to overlook or dismiss it, just like the bronze snake that Moses mounted to a pole in biblical days. "Look and live," he was told, when his people were perishing left and right from deadly snake bites. "Simply look, and you will live."

One moment at a time, over and over again, my healing happens exactly like that.

One moment at a time, I surrender. I look and I live.

THE SERENITY PRAYER
—REINHOLD NIEBUHR (1926)
(Reprinted with permission)

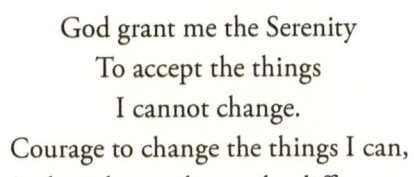

God grant me the Serenity
To accept the things
I cannot change.
Courage to change the things I can,
And wisdom to know the difference.

Living one day at a time,
Enjoying one moment at a time.
Accepting hardship as the pathway to peace.

Taking this sinful world as it is,
Not as I would have it.
Trusting that He will make
All things right,
If I surrender to His will.

That I may be reasonably happy
In this life,
And supremely happy
With Him forever in the next.
Thy will,
Not mine,
Be done.

CHAPTER SEVENTEEN

JUMPING ALL IN

One hot summer evening, our full family of seven is out walking, making our way along the paved river trail that winds behind our house and up into the canyon. The kids are laughing and chasing, bickering in their easy and familiar way. They ride scooters to keep up as Nate and I walk briskly along, pushing the baby in a stroller. The earthy scent of cow manure floats through the heavy breeze, and the steady sound of gently pressing water creates a backdrop as we make our way through the green canopy of trees.

Today is a good day. I feel the sun on my skin and the ground underneath my feet. I feel the breath move through my lungs and into my body.

Here I am. I'm right here. There is a gorgeous freedom in this simple awareness. I feel the earth support me with each footstep, and it is enough to hold me up. *I am not alone, I am supported. And I am right here.*

All the recovery work I've been doing has helped me find this steadiness in myself. From time to time, when it feels right, I reach out and interlace my fingers with Nate's, even just for a moment. Sometimes, it feels good to reach out to him. Sometimes, it feels safer to hold my distance. I'm growing more in tune with these signals, trying to honor them as they come. He has been kind and steady. He is putting in the work. This helps.

We may not yet be out of the storm, but there is a ground underneath us now that increases our capacity to be with the mess; to make our way and feel glimmers of hope shining through, especially on days like this when the sun is beaming and the river is running cool and clear.

"What I love most about rivers is, you can't step in the same river twice…the water's always changing, always flowing…" These words from Disney's *Pocahontas* bubble up into my mind and heart. *I'm just like this river,*[5] I think. From one day to the next, I am being rearranged, and despite the discomfort, there is a strange exhilaration to it. I'm learning to stop fighting the current. I'm learning to surrender to the bumpy ride. Little by little, I can feel the sun peeking through and as strange as it seems, I am experiencing something utterly new and unfamiliar. I've been offered a new pair of glasses and am seeing the whole world with fresh eyes.

"Mom! Mom! Mom! It's the rope swing! Can we do the rope swing, Mom?" My oldest son bounds down the trail to announce his triumphant discovery. Sure enough, as we catch up to the spot where he and his younger sisters have now stashed their scooters, there it is: a rope swing dangling from sturdy branches across the way. The river seems to pause and pool here, and before I can say a word, my little ones are crashing down the brush-filled banks to cross over.

My oldest is up to his knees, halfway across before the bottom gives out, and his white, bony shoulders are swallowed up in the river's depth. He gives a shout as the cold water prickles his skin, but it's a shriek of delight and a siren call to his younger siblings. Soon, three little heads are paddling their way through the deep pool to get to the rope swing—each one desperately calling back, "Mom! Watch me! Did you see that, Mom? Watch—*WATCH*!"

And now they scramble up muddy banks, and Nate is pulling out his phone and promising to film the footage. For all his excitement, my oldest son is unsure, and his younger sister eventually pushes him out of the way to be the first to take a running leap, find the edge of the arc, and sail herself gracefully down into the cold pool of water beneath her. Once she has safely emerged, the others are quicker to try.

The air is filled with giggles and shrieks, the light is the golden wash of almost sunset, and suddenly, I feel the urge to be in there with them. It's so unlike me to willingly step into discomfort. I am the Mom who sits in the hot tub or waves to her splashing kids from the pool's edge. I am too fettered with responsibility and burdened by messes to make any myself. No, I prefer

---

5 Goldberg, E., & Gabriel, M. (1995). *Pocahontas*. Buena Vista Pictures.

to keep things efficient and tidy. To hold the towels and keys and remember where we parked. To gather the dirty clothes and shoes before anyone steps on the clean carpet.

But as I sit here on this perfect day and bask in the blessed peals of laughter ringing through the air, I feel a release. A deep desire to let go. *To live.* I *want* to feel the icy cold water wake up my senses. I *want* to know what it is like to fly through the air. To *play* with my kids. *To be in this* with them. To *experience life.*

I gently secure the stroller into Nate's empty hands, and his eyes drink me in with a surprised twinkle. "Are you for real?" I return his gaze and playfully raise my eyebrows, then twirl around and make my way carefully down the riverbank, weeds and branches scratching my legs. When I step into the water, everyone is thoroughly astonished: "Moooomm!?! What are you doing?!"

"Hey—I can do this, too!" I say, enjoying their shock and surprise. The rocky river bottom feels sharp to the soles of my tender feet, but the current is soft and gentle. The water is cold enough to send a shiver up my spine and numbness down my legs. I draw a sharp breath in and keep walking, my mind distracted by securing my safe passage across. When the bottom disappears from view, I know I'm fully committed. I take a big gulp of air as my foot lands on nothing and the cold river welcomes my gasping body, bobbing now up to my shoulders.

My kids and Nate laugh at my stunned face as I paddle across as fast as I can to the other side. My kids are waiting for me with open arms, anxious to yank me out and drag me up the riverbank. As they pull me toward the rope swing, they are all talking over each other, squabbling over who gets to show me the right way to do this and whose technique is best.

I take it all in as I stand here and shiver, the fading sun too cool to offset the frigid shock to my liking. I listen to their advice and instruction as best I can, nod my head, and say, "Let's count to three."

"1-2-333333333!!!" I grab hold of that rope and swing my body up onto it, squeezing my legs tightly and finding the seat under my rump. I swing back and forth a few times to get a feel for the arc, sensing my unease with the empty space as the bank drops out from under me. My kids are laughing and teasing and complaining, "You've got to let go, Mom! When you're at the top, you've got to let go!"

On my next swing back to the bank, my kids catch me and help me reset. I find my feet underneath me again, take a big breath, and make promises. I'm going to let go. I'm going to do it. I promise. I'm not cold anymore. I'm not worried about the shivering or the disappearing sun. *I'm right here. And I'm living, damn it.* I lean my weight back, take two running steps forward, and launch myself into the air.

"Now, Mom! Now!! Let go noooowwww!!" They are jumping and clapping and shrieking, and I somehow find the courage.

I let go. I am flying through the air with nothing to hold me. I am trusting their voices and the feel of the arc and the cool running water below me. I am trusting this life to catch me. I am embracing the mess. I am learning to let go. And I've never felt so damn alive.

* * *

There's a funny story about mindfulness I love to share with new students: A well-renowned therapist sends their new patient to a week-long mindfulness retreat. When the patient returns, he reports on the grief, stress, repressed anger, and fear that came up during all the silence and contemplation. Eventually, he says, "I don't think it worked. I thought I was supposed to feel better!" And the therapist says, "Oh no, it worked great. Don't you see? You *are* feeling better! You're *feeling* your grief better, your stress better, your anger and your fear better. It did just what I wanted it to do."

It's undeniable that becoming more mindful results in *feeling* better, and despite the inherent discomfort, there's also an enthralling energy of awakening in every aspect of my life. Suddenly, I am reaping the rewards of the depth of pain I've opened myself to, because on the other end is an intensity of joy I've never experienced before. I'm coming to realize that the highs and the lows are interconnected: one can't exist without the other. To me, this intensity feels like truly living for the first time.

But living with this kind of passion is a two-sided coin: its cost is the willingness to keep digging up the stuff most people ignore, a process Nate and I are about to accelerate with our new specialized sexual addiction therapist. After waiting a year on his waitlist, we are far past the crisis and well-established in our recovery routines and support network. *Why even go here at all?* we sometimes wonder. But I'm all in, and I know there's more in me to uncover. I can feel it.

At our first meeting, we explain, "Nate is doing really well… He's been sober for two years, so that's amazing. At this point, we're really just here to try to help Becky."

Our therapist devises a treatment plan. Nate and I will rotate weekly for individual sessions: I will work on my trauma; Nate will work on his Full Disclosure—a term we've heard from 12-step friends as an imperative of long-term recovery.

"Full Disclosure," our therapist explains, "is recommended protocol in the aftermath of betrayal, and I require it for all my patients. I'll work with Nate for as long as needed to create a document that recounts his full sexual history—from his earliest memories. And then, when he's ready, he'll share it with you, Becky, here in my office. My job is to prepare Nate to give a Full Disclosure in a healthy way, and to prepare you to receive it in a healthy way. How does that sound?"

Nate and I meet eyes and nod. I feel naïvely confident that I know all I need to know about his online affair and pornography use. I figure Full Disclosure will just be a formality for us.

"Yeah, Nate's already told me everything, and he's been sober for over two years, so, you know, I think that will be fine…"

So, for months, my sessions focus on Trauma Egg and EMDR while Nate works on his Full Disclosure. And every so often, a big enough conflict arises that we end up in session together. After many sessions, I walk out with a hangover that lasts for days. Our therapist's specialized expertise makes all the difference, and I leave each time with a deeper understanding of the faulty ways I've constructed my worldview. Every appointment feels painfully productive, an intentional low that I trust will eventually engender our highest highs.

I am up. I am down. I am all over the place; most days, a violent mismatch. With the deeper awareness I'm gaining from therapy, I sit on a precipice between two landscapes: empowerment and freedom on one side, temper tantrum on the other. There's a part of me that sees the possibility of soaring open-hearted toward a whole new way of being in the world, and another that clings to the notion of going back to my old comfort zone in both mindset and life situation.

Humiliation is a visceral presence in my life. It's become my constant companion as my eyes open to the holes in my logic, the coping woven into my perceived strengths, the unreliable crutch of the identities I've built for myself. At every appointment, it becomes clearer that everything I thought I knew, I don't. All the ways I thought I was being good are often the very things that have caused the most harm. Everything I was sure about, I'm not anymore.

This humiliation is perhaps hardest to swallow when we meet for a couple's session. I feel a slight nausea every time Nate and I settle in on separate couches in our therapist's office, because our body language manifests so clearly the turbulent gulf that still often separates us. The measured space we leave between our bodies provides a detailed compass to how the previous week went, as do the ways our arms are folded and the angle at which we cross or uncross our legs.

Sometimes, the distance feels impossible to traverse. We've made so much progress and done so much work, but there's still so much under the surface that I don't have a handle on—in my *own* self, let alone *us*. I feel like a geologist in the Grand Canyon: fascinated but completely overwhelmed, a tiny ant facing insurmountable granite walls.

One day, as we make our way to the car after a particularly tough session together, my body trembles. A cloudy sky casts a gray and hopeless light over the valley, and the dark mountain peaks appear sharp and dull. I silently step into the car and slide myself all the way over to the door, as far as I can possibly get from my husband. I have been holding a "No-touch, No-words-of-affirmation" boundary for the past weeks, as his behaviors and attitudes have felt painfully mismatched with his intimate advances. In fact, every time he utters a pleading and expectant "I love you," it fills me with rage. Those words are a slap in the face when they're so dissonant with his attitudes toward me or the kids. I simply cannot stand it.

So, I've armored myself in a castle of resolve, and I'm terrified of making the wrong move. On one hand, I'm afraid that if I don't hold the right boundaries, he will return to his addiction. On the other hand, I'm scared that if I'm too punishing, he will return to his addiction. I see the faces of our five children in my mind. I can't let them down.

It's up to me. I've got to do it right. I'm the responsible one. I've got to hold it together. Everyone is counting on me, and I cannot disappoint. Everything depends on it.

Even without realizing it, I am still trying desperately to control the outcome, still trying desperately to do things perfectly, so I won't be abandoned. So that I will be worthy of love. The work I've done in therapy is helping me see this narrative in every facet of my life. The perfectionistic pressure hurts so badly, and I feel so damn broken and fragile. And as I breathe and let myself feel the pain and observe the narratives in my head, it occurs to me…maybe the pain I'm feeling isn't all Nate's fault. Maybe this is a pain that's always been with me.

Somehow, as we silently make our way towards home on the twenty-minute car ride, Nate's hand slides over to the empty seat where my legs would be if I weren't huddled fiercely against the door. And I can feel that he is trying to reach me. And suddenly, my pain melts into the deepest longing to let him hold me. I feel every inch of his pinky finger as it crosses into my space like an anxious teenager on a first date. But then I'm no anxious teenager; I am a woman. And I feel the palpable heat of desperate desire deep in my body like a grown woman—more of a woman than I've been in a long time. Maybe more so than I've *ever* been.

What is this pulsating heat?

Suddenly, it's all I can do not to jump out of my skin and lay my body on his, begging him to love me, to want me, to need me. I have never felt the depth of this throbbing thunder inside me before, never felt my sexuality like this ravenous, wanting beast. It's been a role, a responsibility, a way to manage moods and chaos, fueled by the desire to please. In trauma, it's been a numbing compulsion, an anguished, frenzied escape. But this—this fire is wild and pressing. It wants… It wants so much it is all-consuming. It cannot be overridden by logic, or even by fear.

We ride in the car and the seconds pass like hours as I feel the heat of his hand and the heat of my body and I wrestle inside of myself with the rigid religious girl who is so afraid of doing the wrong thing, who is so frozen by believing she can guarantee an outcome by doing everything right. Until eventually, I cave, just a little, and give in to the animal-like drive to feel his skin against mine.

I allow myself the tiny indulgence of touching his hand with caution, but the warmth of his skin only pulls me in harder and soon my hand is pressing into his with feverish passion. My body is trembling with yearning as I hold my gaze out the window and my hand makes love to my husband's. I feel the texture of each hair on each knuckle, the comfort of his familiar fingertips, and I am lost in a crazy whirlwind of wanting that sends my heart pounding out of my chest.

We pull into the garage and the car comes to a halt, the weight of uncertainty heavy in the air as we sit with hands clasped together for the first time in weeks. He stares ahead at the blank wall in front of him, and I finally allow my gaze to turn in his direction. There he sits, this man who is fighting so hard for this marriage, for us. Who keeps diving deep, willing to dig down to the molten core, willing to try, willing to talk, willing to work on his own recovery, willing to face his mistakes, willing to hear my pain. As I take in the sight of his face, tentative and exposed, I don't see him as the asshole who hurt me. I see the tender boy giving his all to fix this. I see the man who is showing up and owning his mistakes. What is left of my restraint unravels and I throw myself over the center console and onto his waiting body.

Our mouths are wet and sloppy, and we are swept away in a wild and reckless holy communion. Somehow, we stumble and shove our way to the door of our house and make our way down the hallway to our bedroom, driven by madness and heat and the deepest, most primal instinct to connect and own and desire that I have ever felt. And as we make love, it is the sacred expression of the deepest longings of my human heart. I'm following an impulse that was always too vulnerable, too selfish, too messy, and unmanageable in my previous life. With mind, body, spirit, I express my whole Self's yearning for Nate, for Love, for God, for Home. Of all the wanting, of all the millions of shiny trinkets in this world, this union is the reclamation of what I want most, and the surrender of any thing or thought that gets in the way.

I want You. I want You. I want You.

When the madness has climaxed and we lie spent amidst blankets and pillows, our limbs and longings intertwined, we rest in the softest, most tender landing. Without words, we lie eye to eye, breath breathing breath, and he traces each tear that escapes my eyelids to run down my cheek. I don't care if I did the wrong thing. I don't care if I should have held my boundary or made him meet some measure. This feels so good, so deep, so connected, so real. This was right. And I let my heart lead the way. I feel so brave.

This may be the first time I have ever truly listened to my own longing. I let myself want, and I trusted my desire. And at least for right now, it feels so good: a high of such intensity I know we could never have found it without our lows. This is what it is to be *me*, alive and wanting. Another new awakening to add to my map of the person I want to keep choosing to be. Another new practice…another new freedom…another spectacular gift of jumping all in.

HEALTHY SEXUALITY
BECKY MOLLER, FEBRUARY 2017

I want to please my parents.
Make the right choices.
What school
What major
What boy
Will everyone clap for?

I want him to like me.
I want them all to like me.
I want everyone to like him.
I want him to want me.

I want to please him.
Be a good wife.
Keep him happy.
A good wife always says yes.
Never says no.

I want to feel free of this pressure
To not always be in charge.
I just want to be left alone.
Give me a day
Just one day to breathe
And not be punished for it.

What's wrong?
So much anger,
So far away,
Sleeping miles apart
Under an ocean of covers.
What is wrong?
I want to know the truth.

No, I don't want to know the truth.
I want to escape.
I want to stop feeling.
I never want to see him again.
I hate him.
I want him.

I hate him so much I want him to die.
I want him so much I think I might die.

I want to be wanted.
I want to be like those other women.
Women he wants.
Women who want.
What would that be like?
I want to know.

I want to be able to say, "I want."
I want peace.
I want You.
I want nothing else.
Just You.

I choose You.

And then,
I choose him again.
Choosing him is choosing You.
At least for today.

Now this messy, painful, beautiful, relentless sex
Becomes more than wanting.
Becomes choosing.
Becomes giving.

Choosing You.
Choosing him.
Giving my Self.
Not because I have to
To be good.
Because I want to.

I want to share myself with someone.
I want to open myself to him.
To You.
Fearless.
Raw, naked, vulnerable.
No more masking.
No more obligation.
Choosing.
Trusting.
Flaws and all.

This union has become holy.

CHAPTER EIGHTEEN
REARRANGING

With every heart-guided experience, I'm like a toddler learning to walk a new way in the world, and each messy step seems to expand my capacity to love. Sometimes, it seems I can physically feel my mind click into the present moment or sense my heart growing bigger in my chest. And these qualitative sensations of clarity and expansion start to formulate my new definition of spirituality. The more I experience their magic, the more I recognize the many traditions speaking to the same power. Born-again Christians call it grace and surrender. Daoists refer to it as simply "the way." Yogis call it the third eye. Eckhart Tolle calls it Presence.

Whatever you call it, one surrendered moment at a time, it becomes my new way of life.

I discover teachers from all different times and traditions who speak this same language: Buddhist monk and peace activist Thich Nhat Hanh, Catholic priest Richard Rohr, meditation teacher Sarah Blondin, yogi Michael Singer, the ancient Tao Te Ching, and the sublime poetry of the Persian Sufi poets, Hafiz and Rumi. Each perspective brings its own terminology and emphasis, but the core message of these teachers is the same: they describe the same Divine Love, deep knowing, and messy path through unconscious conditioning, uncertainty, and fear, toward inner freedom. It's the gritty reality I'm coming to know in my own bones, and this enthralls me. This awakening feels so universal, so deeply human. We are all so much the same.

And to me, it all lines up seamlessly with the words and life of Jesus Christ, my own spiritual home. I read the New Testament with new eyes and am convinced Jesus is also a yogi! His life, a living archetype of freedom through suffering. His cross, a symbol of the vertical dimension of presence cutting through the horizontal dimension of time. His invitation, to look inward and upward: "For behold, the Kingdom of God is within you" (Luke 17:21, KJV).

Oh my gosh—I know exactly what he's talking about! It's so mind-blowing, I want to shout it from the rooftops: *The window to the Divine is right here, in our very own souls, and nobody can keep it from you!*

Suddenly, it seems all Truth-tellers throughout time have been pointing to this same, un-brandable presence…and it's everywhere—in scripture, in literature, in the seasons, the night sky, the changing trees, my kitten's eyes, my children's smiles…in my own being. My worldview is exploding, and I'm shocked at how much Truth is out there that I was never even slightly aware of, regularly humiliated to realize my profound limitations. I never had reason to look because I believed I already had it all. This fundamental reframe is both empowering and unsettling, and I start to separate the notions of spirituality and religion as two completely separate things, a mind-blowing revelation to me.

For over a year, my 12-step sanctuary has become my most holy house of worship, where my insides come out and I learn to praise the alchemy of pain. Today, I look out of rain-spattered windows and see the wind howling through mountains that stretch wide outside the lodge's safe and sturdy walls. Everything outside is changing. Trees are turning colors. Leaves are falling, leaving branches bare and dead-like. Everything inside of me is changing, too. Becoming bare and dead-like. Everything I thought I knew, I don't. As I sit in my healing cathedral week after week, this much has become clear: I. Don't. Know. Anything.

Week after week, I've come to sit on overstuffed couches, swallowed up in deep pillows and the even deeper wisdom of this honest, open-hearted circle. When I sit back, my short legs leave my feet floating far from the ground, like a little girl sitting in a big grown-up chair. And that's how I feel most of the time. Like a very little girl, sitting in a very big, grown-up chair. I've never felt so small.

What I do here excavates my soul, a spiritual grapple so different than the pious and buttoned-up "plan of happiness" I thought I'd mastered in my previous life. This spirituality feels like mud-wrestling God, kicking and screaming, as life tries to rip all my false security, prideful identities, and illusory attachments from my grip. The same sweeping passion I feel now for Nate I feel also in a sacred way: this gut-level need for God; this kind of desperate longing. And what's more is that in all my religiosity, I realize I have never known Him like this. Not in this raw, real, embodied way. I'm not sure what to make of this.

All I know is that week after week, I sit with women navigating betrayal, addiction, even illegal activity at times: situations I never predicted myself facing or relating to. No, I saw myself as far above this kind of thing, these kinds of people. But now I am privileged to witness each one of us feeling our way with surrender and trust to our next right step. More than anywhere else I've ever been, I've witnessed God's hand here in this circle. And every single path looks different.

My mind is blown with this clear realization: *I don't know what's right for anybody else. What looks wrong to my notions of goodness might be the exact experience someone else needs to wake up. Might be the right action that only they will know, from their own deepest truth. Shocking.*

I'm growing more aware of how deeply my own judgment has limited me: my ability to see clearly, my capacity to love. My own self-righteous notions have so often been the block that has severed my heart, cutting me off from the Divine Love that I now crave. I'm realizing it's a full-time job just to stay tuned in to my own Source. Keeping my mind present, my heart open, moment to moment, is a completely new level of spiritual accountability.

And it has nothing to do with religion. "Salvation" is not about submitting to someone's authority or being saved from everlasting damnation—it's about being saved from the misery I've been creating in *this* moment. It's about seeing how much joy I can create here and now, about cultivating wonder at the Divine mystery we're all engaged in.

How fully can I surrender myself to Life, exactly as it unfolds? How deeply can I open my heart to each moment? How much of the unreal am I willing to let go of to open myself more completely to the Real?

These questions come intuitively from within as my work of self-observation in therapy, 12-step, yoga, and my own personal study create a clear picture of what inside me leads to freedom, and what keeps me stuck. And what does the main culprit seem to be? My own ego, which I learn to recognize through the teachings of Eckhart Tolle, my most impactful spiritual teacher.

Ego, Tolle teaches in *The Power of Now*, is an inherent part of the human psyche: the mind-made sense of self. Ego is attachment to identity—of any kind. It clings, grasps, and looks for security where it cannot be found—in the world of form. Ego finds safety in being special: its sense of separateness is what allows it to survive, and it's always fighting for survival by building its case. The ego has to be right because being right is what makes it special or above. So admitting a mistake or considering another perspective would be like annihilation itself. Ego keeps us blind, guarded, striving, self-absorbed, and most of all…*afraid.*

The more I learn about the ego, the more blatantly I see it in myself. My need to be extraordinary. My urge to defend when someone disagrees with or misunderstands me. My tendency to compare and compete. My clinging to status—be it tied to my weight, my church title, my neighborhood, my marriage, or my children. My grasping at perceived safety. The absolute terror that's consumed me as my identity—as wife, mother, good person, good woman, good Mormon woman—has been threatened. Even relationally: I've had to be the bigger person, the one who's willing to step back and self-sacrifice, able to manage others from a standpoint of subtle superiority—so subtle, I couldn't even see it in myself. In fact, I thought I was being Christlike.

I have a sinking feeling that my entire world is built on ego.

And Step 4 in my 12-step work, a "searching and fearless moral inventory" of my entire life, gives me the perfect opportunity to investigate. The Step 4 milestone has loomed like an impending thundercloud as I've shown up each week to my overstuffed couches and cathedral ceilings, but there's no getting out of it. Even so, it takes me over a year to build enough trust with my Higher Power and enough compassion for myself to wholeheartedly attempt it.

What am I afraid of?

I'm afraid that facing my inevitable shortcomings will somehow justify my husband's betrayals: that if I lay it all out, I'll have to face the fact that I *am* unlovable and unworthy, and I don't know if I can take it. The imperative thing is to remember: the ego isn't me; it's just the small, fearful *part* of me—the *false, unconscious* me. If I can find the courage to see it, it can help me claim the True Self that's waiting underneath.

So, with trust in my True Self, I bravely zoom out my lens and start to observe the ways my ego is showing up in real time: how I often mention my previous church position as a Young Women's President in conversation with my new neighbors—*What am I doing?* Trying to secure my status and assert my worth. Self-protection. Perceived safety. Ego.

I notice how, when things get really tense and tight in arguments with Nate, it's easy to pull out his biggest mistakes. My ace in the hole—*What am I doing?* Trying to secure my superior position. *You can't challenge me. I'm better than you. And don't you forget it.* Self-protection. Perceived safety. Ego.

I notice how when I take my kids to the waterpark, I am side-glancing at all the other moms in bathing suits—*How do I measure up?* The fear and insecurity, the urge to cover up the softness of my belly... The perceived safety of comparison and perfection. Ego.

I notice how when I talk to people, I often classify them in my mind as either members of my church or non-members of my church. How I tend to interact with people outside my faith as though I'm putting on a performance, like my job is to be an example to them, to recruit them, to convince them of something. How I approach them from the fundamental position that in some way, I know better than they do. The perceived safety of belonging and superiority. Ego.

I notice how, on many Sundays before church, we holler and yell impatiently at our kids so we can get there on time, and then once we're seated, we smile and nod at the other families with our arms around our children's shoulders like we're some kind of Brady Bunch. Ego. Ego-o-o.

Suddenly, I can't unsee how my entire sense of self is built upon titles, appearance, and a constant drive to somehow make my life truly meaningful. I have gone from grasping at 4.0s to grasping at numbers on a scale to grasping at the right kind of guy to marry to grasping at church titles to grasping at my husband. And now I can see it all as the incessant fear so dramatically unmasked in betrayal, yet an ever-present current surging through my life all along: my ego desperately grasping for survival.

Without these constructs, these achievements, this sense of being in control, this striving to be a "good person," who am I? I don't even know. I don't even know what it looks like to relate to life any other way. Without this drive, this incessant push for more, without the approval and validation, it feels like I might evaporate into thin air.

But instead of evaporating, I just get quiet. *What do I know?* Nothing.

My main objective: free myself of this incessant ego grip. I start paying close attention to my notions of certainty, my black-and-white thinking, or as we say at Twelve Steps, my attitude of "I know best." When I feel my ego insecurity kick up with a need to defend, complain, criticize, or prove, I try to just *be still* and let the urge pass. I may not know what to do next, but I don't want to do what I've always done...and this creates a holy pause. My closest relationships don't know what to make of me. I am a puzzle piece changing shape, and it disrupts the system, unraveling old patterns.

This empty space of stillness is where God rewrites me, where old neural pathways are diminished. It's the power of *not* knowing, and God is in the void. I start to feel in my day-to-day interactions the wisdom of the Zen empty cup. When I let go of my notions of certainty, I'm making room for God to pour the tea. I'm making room for possibilities and insights beyond my own. *Be still* and *know* that *I Am* God. It feels like I'm starting to understand what this scripture means.

But as I witness these good fruits in my relationships and mindsets, I can't ignore how obviously the same concept relates to my religiosity. Something suddenly feels so unsettling about the oft-repeated declaration I've made hundreds if not thousands of times in front of an audience: "I know my church is true." Even as a tiny little girl who could barely reach the pulpit in tights and on tiptoes, "I know my church is true" has been the standard statement of belonging, met with nods of approval from not only parents but an entire congregation.

There's always been something so secure in having this faith community where I've known exactly what to say. And up until rock bottom, it all seemed to work. Up until now, absolute certainty here has been a given. But after tasting the expansive fruits of stepping back from my other opinionated stances, a sliver of curiosity wiggles in. *Why would it be any different here?*

I can objectively see the ways my religious conviction has served me—keeping me safely *out* of potentially harmful behaviors and *in* the mindset of serving God and others positively. For heaven's sake, I was one of the few designated drivers at my high school, and I know my firm moral compass was a rock to many of my friends—and myself, too. I have no regrets for the clean life I've lived and the many mistakes I didn't even consider making. Yes, growing up in the church was a gift for me in so many ways.

But I can also see the shadow of my certainty: how it created an invisible veil between myself and honest self-reflection—not to mention, anyone outside of the group. With newfound awareness, I can see the unconscious traces: anyone outside my religious box was always a potentially dangerous or inferior "other." I was superior and separate. I was right and they were wrong. My mind and heart were closed to any perspective at odds with my already-secured convictions: my cup was full.

And now I can see that this is the same ego, the same fundamental separation, the same soul-split. And because I know its rotten fruit in my own soul, I can't unsee the way this egoic mindset has helped to land me where I am. It's a realization that deeply disturbs me.

What did I know—really? In tights and on tiptoes? And why was I so encouraged to claim certainty rather than explore, experience, discover, and question?

And so, I sit, unraveled, not knowing anything but the visceral awakening I feel inside myself.

Why was I so stupid? Why did I just get on board and trust that the system would keep me safe? Why didn't I look more deeply at the things that weren't adding up?

But until rock bottom, I couldn't see any of that. I didn't know how to look inward and get curious about my own experience. I'd learned to compartmentalize and push aside what didn't fit my model. I'd overlooked, justified, and ignored, telling myself we had a "normal marriage," and I needed to be a "good wife." I never even thought of challenging my perceptions or the role I'd been told to play. Such critical thinking would be considered "dangerous" or unfaithful.

But my definition of faith is changing. Because faith to me now isn't about never questioning. It's not about turning a blind eye to what doesn't add up: just like there would be nothing enlightened about pretending I was unaware of Nate's betrayals. Faith is about being boldly unafraid to *ask* every question, to *investigate* every dissonance, and to *trust* that there's Something out there that's big enough to hold it all up. That's holding *me* up. That there's Something out there, *and in here*, that *is* Real and in perfect alignment; and it's indestructible. This Something is not a theory. It's what I've started to feel within me and what I'm coming to trust in completely. It's a deep knowing. A peace. A trust.

"Nothing real can ever be threatened," my heart echoes this line from *A Course in Miracles*, and there is nobody and nothing that can convince me otherwise. Seeing what doesn't add up in my life hasn't destroyed my *faith*; it's destroyed my *delusions,* delusions I *had* to see to operate in a deeper, more honest, and free way. With that kind of faith behind me, I can look life square in the face and surrender to it, and so can you. My *faith* has never been stronger.

The more clearly I see the harmful impact of my egoic mindsets, the more frustrated I feel with the ineptitude and inconsistencies of my supposed spiritual path. It seems to me that seeing more clearly is only dangerous to people whose power depends on controlling the narrative. In terms of faith, there should never be anything you're not allowed to look at. You should never be told to stop asking.

And the more progress we make through our new recovery path, the more obvious it is that our religion had so little to offer both Nate and me in our darkest hour. I feel shocked and betrayed that so much of our trusted system was devoid of any real spiritual tools: the tools we've had to stumble upon through other sources. Tools to recognize why and how we've been coping and what we've been running away from. All that religiosity, all those years, without ever getting close to knowing our own hearts or mindsets. Or having any awareness around the self-absorbed, fear-driven small self that got us here: our ego.

What kind of spiritual pathway leaves these types of disconnects largely unchallenged?

The kind that is more interested in maintaining the power structure than in providing a pathway toward true freedom. There's a fire in my belly, and I suddenly want nothing to do with the bullshit, in the power structures or in myself.

So, day by day, I stop feeding my ego, and its hold on me softens. I stop trying to fit my expanding awareness into religious rhetoric. I inwardly detach my identity from the church, and a Deeper Self starts to emerge. I begin to feel empowered and clear, to see what I've never seen before. The only thing I trust is what's right here in front of me: the fruits I'm actually experiencing in the here and now. And that's what I wholeheartedly study: not doctrine, not scripture, but my lived reality and the reality I witness unfolding in others.

Am I creating goodness in my mind, heart, and actions right now?

Is my heart open?

What is my body telling me?

What is at my center?

What are the fruits of my behavior? The fruits of my attitude?

The void of my old identities sometimes feels frightening, but there's a freedom on the other side of my painfully shattered self, and I've tasted too much of it to turn away now. Bring on the pain of disillusionment. I want growth. I want freedom. I want God.

And as I strip down in all my brokenness before Him, I discover He wants me, too. Not just the bright and shiny parts, but all of me. I feel it in the very cells of my body. I feel it in the love and acceptance of my sponsor Holly when I eventually share my Step 4 inventory with her. I lose my fear of facing myself and fall in love with the divine deconstruction of self-inventory. There is nothing too shameful or scary to look at. There is nothing that cannot be held in compassion.

Underneath all the clutter, I am finding my own essence: it is deep, Divine, and vast as the widest horizon. It is Love itself.

How could I not be safe? How could this be threatened? This Love is right here within me, and nothing I do or don't do could take it away. It is who I Am.

This is my seed cracking, my worldview disintegrating, the beginning of miraculous and tender green shoots of new life. It's another painful oblivion of the world I have known: a new bottom to my empty cup. All my black-and-white narratives around sin and worthiness begin to lift like a mist on the horizon, like the illusion they've always been. I finally start to accept that my "perfect" life story was always a fantasy, a self-sabotage of True Self. My life was littered with little-t traumas long before I even met my husband. Each faulty belief I internalized along the way fueled my ego identities. Each impacted the way my Big-T Trauma hit me when it swelled into shore.

And because I can see now that it's *mine*, my pain is not something I am powerless over. It's something I can do something about. I can let go of my false selves to make space for my True One. I can take my pain to a Higher Power and allow His empathy to be enough. I can work with Him to correct the faulty beliefs and coping behaviors that make me hurt the way I still do. I can choose the beliefs I want to hold onto by the Truth that resonates in my own soul. I can release the beliefs that don't hold up, whose fruits are full of shadow, hypocrisy, fear, or control.

"By their fruits shall ye know them" (KJV, Matthew 7:16). This verse becomes a foundational comfort: Jesus *wanted* me to hold them up. To learn to discern with my own mind-body-spirit. A radical notion is stirring within me, a strange excitement amidst the fear. This painful, autumn-like, deadening of the surety and self-confident self-righteousness I've built my identity upon: it's the beginning of my glorious undoing; the beginning of months and years of shoveling out all that I think I am, all that I think I should be, all that I think I know, and all the supposed-tos and shoulds. I am shoveling all of it out of my center. I am done playing God. I am learning how to shut up and listen.

I am empowered. I am my own authority. I can forgive myself and others. My breath is deeper than it's ever been, my eyes clearer than they've ever seen. What I know in these moments is not dependent upon a quote from any expert or authority. It has no need to prove anything to anyone. It comes from deep within me. My own Highest Self. My own inner knowing. I see the fruits in my life, my heart, my relationships, and I feel the alignment in the cells of my body, in the shift of my brain waves, in the tangible opening of my heart.

My growing freedom beckons me through the discomfort of my disintegrating security. It feels so good to throw out old labels and burn old boxes that I start using new words. What I was raised to call a Heavenly Father now feels like a sing-at-the-top-of-my-lungs, chain-breaking *FATHER GOD!! Hallelujah!* So, sometimes alone in my car, I raise my hands, throw my head back, and praise.

Feels like Source: an unending well of ability, peace, energy, and Love flowing from my own heart center, through my own breath and body. In yoga, I place my hands on my chest, I bow my head, and I savor the divine current. Namaste.

Feels like the Feminine Divine, a Goddess of softness, nurturance, and strength that sees me with empathy, fierce loyalty, and compassion. I start to place my hands on my soft mama belly with love and gratitude instead of fear or revulsion. *There is room for this, too.*

Feels like the Universe: like everything in nature cohesively working together for my benefit: sending me love-messages through eagles, sunsets, angels, and soft breezes. I pay attention to the animals that cross my path and look up their totem meaning. I hear the leaves rustle on trees and feel the same life force that runs through me. *You are Everywhere.*

Feels like a mysterious and Beloved Higher Power—something beyond my ability to understand that wants to sustain me and propel me towards Goodness. I laugh, I dance, I play, I trust more than ever before, in love with the magical Divinity swimming within me and around me. And strangely, this almost-tangible Divine presence seems to have nothing to do with my worthiness, and everything to do with my hunger for it.

As I let my guard down, I realize it isn't perfection God is looking for after all. He wants me just as I am: raw, real, and desperately wanting Him. Or Her. Or It. There is so much I don't know, and I bask in the wonder of it all. And if this Higher Power, this tangible Love, still wants me in all my messy imperfection, then maybe I can stand to look at myself there, too. Maybe I'm not a disappointment after all. Maybe failure isn't what I thought it was. Maybe success isn't either.

Maybe I'm just a limited human being with strengths and weaknesses, like everybody else. This idea is so foreign, my ego can't even wrap its head around it, so I keep repeating it to myself:

I am a human being with strengths and weaknesses, just like everybody else. A revolutionary mind shift that starts to melt the ego-fear away. I slowly shake the need to justify or compare myself to anyone, quicker to notice my thoughts and feelings without judging them. Instead of being afraid of who I am, I just want to *understand* who I am.

Why do I feel the way I feel? Why do I think the way I think? Why does this hurt so much? Where do I feel it in my body? What do I need right now, if anything?

One moment at a time, I stop listening to my ego and learn to listen to the tender refuge within me. No matter how all-encompassing the tug-of-war, at any time, I have the power to drop the rope. I have the ability to refocus my energy from whatever conflict to my own Divine connection. I am not dependent upon any physical place or outside authority to make direct contact with the Divine.

At my essence, who I am *is* the Divine.

Was I even living before this?

I've been half-asleep, hypnotized by my ambition, my agenda, and my desperate ego striving to get where I thought I was supposed to go. But now, for the first time, it is enough to just be here. For the first time in my life, I feel that I'm already home. And none of it has anything to do with what I can measure or outwardly show. In fact, my life circumstances have never been more of a mess. Astounding.

It is magical. It is more than enough. Deep in my soul, I realize this is all I was ever looking for. All that I have always been.

"For a seed to achieve its greatest expression,
it must come completely undone.
The shell cracks, its insides come out, and everything changes.
To someone who doesn't understand growth, it would look like
complete destruction."

—Cynthia Occelli,
Resurrecting Venus: A Woman's Guide to Love, Work,
Motherhood and Soothing the Sacred Ache

CHAPTER NINETEEN

MEDITATION

My sponsor Holly was such a fascination to me at first. Holly is other-worldly, a spiritual gangsta if ever there was one. I'd always been academic, but even my most analytical self couldn't deny that Holly could often sense my motivations and feelings, whether I wanted her to or not. Her wild, curly blond hair frames a strong face: clear eyes, straight nose, and a smile like the sun breaking over the mountains. She is somehow both fierce and magnificently soft, and every time she opens her mouth, I soak in her words like a starving pilgrim.

Over years of sponsorship, my Holly sees me at my very worst, and yet there is nothing too dark for her to welcome in through the light of aware-ness. In the very moments I'm ugly sobbing, she sits with me on the phone. She breathes with me. She asks me the questions that gently draw me back from blame and point me instead to a Higher Power who can show me, with tenderness and care, the holes in my very own heart. She doesn't shy away from giving straightforward feedback, and this feels like a fully transparent, pay-it-forward kind of love I've never experienced before. She brings my at-tention to the logical fallacies that I was blind to in my ranting and distress. She helps me uncover the beliefs beneath my emotions and welcome my emotions as the guides to the wounds that need to heal.

Holly loves me perfectly and excuses me nothing. When she places her hands on my back in child's pose at yoga, my whole self relaxes, body and soul: her unconditional love is safety. And through sponsorship, yoga, and guided meditation, she opens a world to me I never knew existed, introduced by an oracle of the feminine Divine, my own Holly, strong and untamed. From the moment I stepped into my 12-step circle, she was the yin to my yang.

I never meditated before I met Holly, and she made it easy to start. All I had to do was close my eyes, tune into her voice, and follow her cues. Holly showed me how to truly savor a chocolate almond, mindfully noticing its taste and texture, feeling the coating melt onto my tongue, honoring the hands that plucked cocoa beans to bring it to me.

Holly leads a guided meditation like she's channeling a room, with beautiful flowing narratives that center around light, safe places in nature, and heavenly Beings. She often brings in younger versions of the self, creating deeply personal divine encounters that somehow bring healing in magical ways my logical mind had never before considered. The feeling of Divine Love, like warm sticky honey, naturally oozes from the meditative space within me and becomes second nature.

With time and practice, I realize that I can learn to do what she does for me—all by myself. It's not Holly, but meditation itself that connects me to the intuitive flow that is so abundant in her but also lives within me—and you, too. It taps me into the foreign terrain under my own skin: the body as a landscape of discernment and sensation. As I become more aware of my own energy—in fear, in peace, in happiness, in joy—and where it lives in my body, I am more attuned to the similar energy in other people.

This growing empathic intelligence is extremely helpful. It makes me a better teacher—I know better when my fitness students need to be pushed and when they need a soft place to land. It makes me a better wife—I am more plugged into Nate's embodied signals. I find I can often read him just like Holly can read me—whether he wants me to or not. I am more connected as a mom, a friend, a human, more and more aware of the divine tapestry that connects me to everything—from the birds in the sky to the snails on the trail to the lady in the grocery store. I practice feeling into this connection, acknowledging it every chance I get: *There You are. I see You! You're me! I'm You!*

Meditation also helps me to grow more compassionate and aware of the little girl kicking and screaming inside me in my trauma. I meet her again and again in meditative visions and realize she has been kicking and screaming, in one way or another, my whole life. She is, in one sense, my ego, my inner child: the part of me desperate for love and acceptance. I begin to show up for her, to hold her and love her and let her be heard. And I do this literally—through my own imagination.

I learn to feel where in my body she is hurting: in my chest, the right side of my neck, my upper back. When I locate where I feel the pain of an emotion in my body, I find I can patiently trace back each ache to the memory or belief it is tied to. I learn to use this inner focus and meditative state to allow memories to float up, often pinpointing the exact moment from my past when a faulty belief was internalized. Meditation allows me to actually go back to my little girl self, hold her in her pain, and bring her to a loving Higher Power. This Power can replace lies of unworthiness and fears of abandonment with the Truth of Love. The words my small ego needs to hear are always so much the same:

"I see you, my darling. I see all that you are, and there is room for all of you. You can't be separated from love, my sweetheart…you *are* Love."

Magically, the fear dissipates. Somehow, I am big enough to hold it; God is big enough to hold it and help me feel its weight. Through meditation, I am coming to know my whole soul and find that there is not a single piece of it that cannot be healed through the infinite Love flowing through me.

There is something more delicate and tender inside this messy me than anything I ever experienced in all my rigid perfectionism, a beautiful softness unfolding in mystical ways. The more I allow my pain, the deeper I probe and poke at it, the more freeing the release when I patiently accept and love it. The more I allow that little girl to be heard and held, the more profoundly my Higher Power is able to soothe her heart and fears. The more free the grown-up me becomes.

This simple practice is the medicine, available to me anytime, anywhere. And it's available to you, too: Uncover the pain. Allow it to be just what it is. Bring it to a Higher Power. Engulf it with Love. Meet the need. Watch the suffering magically evaporate. Praise. Praise. Praise. Repeat as needed.

* * *

…Today I am going back in meditation to make amends to my sister. She is my latest discovery in my Step 4 inventory, and I wish so badly that I could have done better for her. My sweet little sister with the big brown eyes and the quick grin. So sensitive and fearful, so soft and gentle, so adored by everyone.

She looks just like my mother, and at six years old, she embraces her role in the family as the cute baby girl. I am the big sister, the responsible one, the smart one. She always wants to play Barbie or dress-up, but these childhood games seem silly to me and I usually roll my eyes and refuse. Even at eight years old, I am sure I have something more productive to do.

But today, through meditation, I want to make things different. Today, I want to make amends for how I pushed her off in the past. Today, I want to be the compassionate big sister that I never was back then. I hold this intention in my heart as I close my eyes, deepen my breath, and make space for whatever vision may come.

After several minutes of breath and grounding, I see myself at my old grade school, sitting at my desk. Suddenly, a small, frightened face appears in the doorway: my baby sister, coming to find me. This is a familiar sight. I feel my chest tighten and my back tense—my natural reaction to feeling my sister's energy clawing at me, seeking me to save her from her substantial kindergarten anxiety. My gut reaction is to turn my back, ignore her, resent her for the weight I feel each time she shows up. My thoughts churn as I feel her presence prickle at the back of my neck. *Why can't she just be normal, like I was? I never went crawling to my big brother when I was in kindergarten. She's such a baby!*

As I watch this scenario unfold, I feel shame at the harshness of my remembered self, but remind myself that today, I get to choose a different response. Today, I get to rewrite the past from a new perspective. So, in my meditation, I choose to get up from my desk and walk gently over to the classroom door.

I squat down and peer up into her frightened face. "What's up, Gin?" I ask in a gentle voice, brushing a hair back from her face, ignoring the whispers and giggles behind me. "Are you having a hard day again?" She nods, her big brown eyes glistening with tears. Her chin starts to tremble. I gather her up in my arms and let her sniffle into my shoulder. "I promise I will save a seat for you on the bus home. Will that be alright?" I whisper into her hair. She nods slowly, face still stuffed into my shirt. "I have an extra fruit snack in my lunch that I saved for you." I lift her chin and stare straight into her eyes, kissing her lightly on the tip of her nose, tender gestures I never had access to before knowing Holly; a feminine softness I've only just discovered inside myself.

Her face steals into a sheepish grin. "Run back to class now, before your teacher notices you're gone." She nods, visibly calmer, and I hold her tight one more second before I watch her scurry down the hall to her classroom. This is the moment I wish I had given her. This is the sister I wish I had been.

But now, my meditation twists in unexpected ways, and suddenly I am me, my thirty-six-year-old self, standing next to my nine-year-old self in the school hallway. I look down at my face, still watching my little sister walk down the hall. My eyes are pools of blue, heavy and intense. I am always trying so hard. I want so badly to be good, to be a good girl. To meet everyone's expectations. To be worthy of love. I squat down, grab onto my young hand, and suddenly understand something I have always overlooked.

"It's hard, isn't it? Being the big sister. Feeling like it's your job to fix everything and knowing you're supposed to fix it. But you don't even know how, do you?" My nine-year-old self looks right through me, like she doesn't even see me, but then slowly sits down and rests her head on my shoulder.

I can feel her. Even so small, such a little thing, she is tired. Tired from the weight of her own expectations. Tired from wanting so badly to make everyone happy. No one will ask her if she is okay today. She's got straight A's, and friendships come and go for her like most third graders. But it isn't always easy. Already she feels the weight of "should" hovering over her shoulder, filling her with fear and resentment, afraid to disappoint, desperate to please.

"I can't fix it for her. It's not fair to ask me to," she says to me. I nod, sincerely surprised to hear these words. They are so true. How I wish I had known this sooner. The harsh judgment I felt for this hard-hearted little me magically evaporates. My heart expands with understanding and compassion: It wasn't fair. It wasn't ever fair to expect her to be the grown-up. No one can be a grown-up all the time. I am shocked by this unexpected revelation: she was hurting, too...

* * *

As I come out of this meditation, tears run from my eyes. My heart wide open, I place my hands with gratitude and reverence onto my chest. *Why is it that every amends always ends up being an amends to myself? And how was I so oblivious that there was so much inside me I needed to heal?*

I didn't realize the truth of the saying, "Hurt people hurt people," until I saw it in my own life. When I first came to 12-step recovery, it seemed odd and unfair that I was being asked to make a "searching and fearless moral inventory" of myself. Wasn't I the victim? But the truth is that the accountability steps were the most transformative part of my healing.

Working the Twelve Steps showed me what I was accountable for—my reactions, my words, my thoughts, my actions, my attitude, my willingness, my resentment, my happiness; and what I wasn't accountable for—my husband's reactions, words, thoughts, actions, attitude, willingness, resentment, and happiness. In the past, I'd had these concepts completely backwards. I was always taking responsibility for the things that weren't mine and often blamed my husband for the things that were.

Taking full ownership of what was mine felt scary at first, but soon became empowering. Seeing where I had done damage showed me the places where pain and fear were still driving my behavior. Hurt people hurt people. I grew less fearful of examining myself, because I realized that I wasn't bad—maybe I was hurting. I didn't need punishment and shame. I needed compassion.

Now, I grow excited when I uncover a belief or relationship nagging at me. I can't wait to take these festering slivers to my Higher Power in meditation and see what magical way He heals the wound. When I go to God with the places I've done harm, He doesn't shame me. He doesn't scold me. He doesn't come down with his sword of justice. Instead, He inevitably shows me where I'm hurting. He says, "Oh, yes. I see. Let me help you understand why you did that. That's where the healing needs to happen."

Once, in all the shame of my crazy trauma outbursts, I fearfully asked God straight-up if I was forgiven. I was in the shower with hot water raining down on me when I felt Him wrap His arms around me with a knowing smile. "Oh, Becky. What a silly question. You were forgiven before you ever even started."

I think we all were.

Relearning God
Becky Moller, October 2016

My God sat at a desk
In a stiff white suit,
It was all business,
Between us:
Contracts and dotted lines,
Signatures and warm handshakes,
Commandments and promises,
"Come see me in your Sunday best."

Neat and tidy. Predictable and secure.
If I kept my end, He would keep His.
Like righteousness was my steering wheel,
And I had the power to drive life where I thought it should take me.

My God was a comfortable King, who followed foreseeable rules,
On a throne looking down, a cosmos away,
Watchfully ticking tally points on a slate gray chart.
An eternity wide as forever between us.

Until my life collapsed and my heart shattered,
And life became too messy for contracts,
Too complicated for fine print.
Spilling out the edges of the neat and tidy boxes,
The contract ripped to pieces that
Would never make sense again.

In my shock and despair,
I found You so different.

Fists pounding in uncontrolled tantrum,
I collapsed to the floor and found Your lap waiting.
Tenderly stroking my hair
No desk between us. No suit to soil.
No measure of worthiness required to bring me near.
Just my desperate want of You.

Come, darling, soak me with your sobs,
Wrinkle and stain my clothes,
I will hold you as long as it takes,
I'll count every tear as it falls.
Not one will go unnoticed.
Not one will go to waste.

You showed me a world so different,
No longer black and white,
But filled with every hue,
Love in a thousand colors,
Deep purples, soft blues, hungry greens,
Shimmering greys.
Playful sunbeams bursting Light,
Obliterating all the neat and tidy boxes,
That were supposed to hold the Truth.

This was a God big enough to hold all my tantrums,
My tears, my rage, and a million mistakes,
This God knew messy and
Enveloped me in His love
Anyway.

And I came to see that discipleship was meant to be
A passionate love affair all along.

I have decided to be done with measured and arduous piety,
And instead run wild through the streets,
Dancing and clanging pots,
To remind myself every day of the
Magic of being
Alive.

O God of my broken soul,
How I hope to be madly in love with You,
For as long as I live.

CHAPTER TWENTY

FALSE INTIMACY

I am sitting in bed next to my husband. We are doing our nightly check-in: AEIOUY.

A—We each reflect on anything we need to be **accountable** for that day. Did I have any triggers or temptations? Did I use recovery tools to respond to those in healthy ways?

E—Did I **exercise**?

I—What did I do for **myself** ("**I**") today? Did I make time and space for self-care?

O—What did I do for **others** today?

U—Are there any **unresolved emotions** I need to express?

Y—What is my **Yay!** for the day? What do I feel grateful for?

This check-in has become the foundation of our growing connection. We both share our vowels each night. We aren't reporting for gold stickers or stars. We are really reporting for ourselves. The ground rules of our ritual help to keep the space safe for both of us: We talk in the "I" and the "me," and keep the focus on our own thoughts, feelings, actions, and reactions. We don't blame, we don't interrupt, and we don't comment on anything the other person says. At the end of the other person's share, we simply say, "Thanks for sharing!"

At least, those are the rules. Some days seem to work better than others. We are trying so hard—both of us, trying to make contact. We keep trying to find a way to feel seen and heard, to have a conversation that doesn't unravel into an argument or meltdown. I am trying to turn towards him when so often the loudest voice inside of me is still screaming, *Run Away!*

Today's check-in is typical. Uneventful. No significant triggers to report. His sobriety is steady by now, almost assumed. I look into his eyes and see the boyful glimmer and the pleading, hopeful light. He wants so badly for all of this to be better. He hates the disconnect, hates the sad cloud that washes over me uninvited, often for no apparent reason at all. So many days I am here, and then I am gone, sucked back under into the vortex of sadness. Demon voices still come flying at me out of nowhere, like cruel waves that crash into me with self-hatred. I am shocked and surprised at their power every time, especially when I feel like I've made so much progress. It's so frustrating to face how far underwater I can still get: it's two steps forward, three steps back.

Nate says he can see it when this happens. How the light in my eyes fades, and my jaw sets like it's bracing. Still, more than two years past the cup-throwing Sunday night that started all of this, there is still a monster inside me that takes over from time to time.

In the soft light of my bedroom lamp, I gaze down at my naked left ring finger. I haven't worn a wedding ring for over a year. It's one way I'm trying to honor my body's signals, and the platinum band started feeling like a chokehold months ago. Years ago, the center diamond fell out, and the cheap imitation cubic zirconia replacement became an all-too-accurate metaphor for our marriage. Seeing the imprint where that ring used to sit evokes a heavy weight deep in my chest, and I start to view the scene with a strange detachment. Soon, it's like I'm floating in a cloud, looking down on us chatting in the softness of our pillows. I see the gleam in his eyes; I know where this is going. I allow myself to be carried into his caresses, and we meet under the sheets in the intimate dance of marriage.

But my mind is still clouded. My heart is imprisoned in hard and heavy walls that I still cannot dismantle. Dark and fiery images from his various disclosures rip through my mind, and I am no longer me. I am no longer in my own bed. I am playing out a fantasy that terrifies and intrigues me at the same time. In my imagination, I am one of the lust objects my husband has so voraciously consumed over the course of his life, a façade that offers momentary escape but always, always leaves me feeling more heavy, more empty, more hopeless, and more full of self-hatred. An unexpressed sob chokes my throat. I am a silent and empty capsule for his pleading efforts to reach me. "I love you," he whispers into my neck as he settles into restful oblivion, draping heavy over my disconnected stomach, limbs, and chest.

I am silent, but my mind whispers, *I don't believe you.* I feel the walls around my heart steepen, straighten, and lock tighter into place. *I don't believe you!* My mind screams in my ears. A single tear stings the corner of my eye and traces a cool line down into my inner ear. I lie underneath him in the secret darkness as I stare unknown at my bedroom ceiling. No matter how much healing work I do, no matter how much sobriety he piles up, I don't know how to change this one insurmountable fact:

I still don't believe you.

DISTANCE
BECKY MOLLER, SEPTEMBER 2014

Sometimes, it's just a symptom of a terrible disease,
It's just something that happened,
Long ago and far away.

It's almost interesting to uncover the nuances,
Of why it happened.
The unmet needs, the justifications,
The holes it was trying to fill.

It's like analyzing a novel,
The hero's descent.
It starts to make sense.

But then you wake from a nightmare,
And remember the nightmare actually happened
And you have to face that it is real.

It's not just a fascinating story.
It doesn't matter if it makes sense.
It doesn't help to understand the psychology behind it.

It just happened.
To me.
And no one can ever make that go away.

CHAPTER TWENTY-ONE

FULL DISCLOSURE

By early September, Nate is ready to present his full disclosure with our therapist's help. With two years of sobriety and our intense involvement in the Twelve Steps, it's easy to think we're out of the woods. But as the day gets closer, I start to feel nervous. I'm not worried about big secrets coming out; I'm quite sure I already know all of them. I'm worried about the trauma. After two and a half years of recovery work, I finally feel removed enough from the crushing tidal waves that the prospect of going back underwater is terrifying. I can't imagine starting over.

Why am I even doing this? I sometimes ask myself. *Because I want Truth. Because I want my life to be real.* And as the day gets closer, this becomes my prayer and purpose: *Let me see the Truth, God. Just help me to see things as they really are.*

On the day of disclosure, I wake to a stomach of butterflies. My older kids are at school, and my youngest is with a babysitter when I arrive at the therapist's office. I've booked a hotel just in case I'm not ready to return home afterward, something my therapist and 12-step groupies have suggested. They are all praying for me today, and that is a comfort.

It's strange to have no idea what to expect or how I will feel two hours from now. I feel naked and raw as I clench the steering wheel on the drive over. I pull into a parking lot overlooking the Mormon temple just a block from my therapist's office to collect myself. The day is gray and overcast, and the temple is perched like a comfort watching over me. I was sitting in that very temple when I felt impressed to ask Nate the question that set this all into motion: "Are you back on porn?" Despite all of the pain, I'm so grateful that I did. That moment of inspiration still feels like an anchor of trust that God has had my back through all of this, and heaven knows, I need that anchor now. I take a deep breath and pick up my phone to call Holly for one last surrender.

"I feel so anxious," I say when she answers. "I am so full of fear."

She says, "I am praying for you. I am sending angels. This will be difficult. But you will see a humility from your husband that will heal your heart." I hang up my phone and nod my head.

"Pain can be the pathway to progress," I remind myself as I drive the short distance to the office. This 12-step mantra has never seemed more fitting. I take a deep breath, place a hand on my heart, and step out of my car.

When I settle onto my therapist's couch, I feel like I'm blindfolded, waiting for someone to whack me upside the head with a huge 2x4. I'm not sure if or when the blow is coming, when the pain will sear down my spine.

"You ready for this?" my therapist asks me, and continues, "I'm right here. It's going to be okay. I'm right here with you." I nod my head. I trust him.

My husband knocks on the door, and my job is to invite him into the room. I think this is intended to give me a sense of power, and I remind myself that I am here by choice. For a split second, I think of my bishop's firm counsel to never speak of Nate's affair again. The thought makes me laugh in the face of where we now sit, over two years down the road, and it's a relief to feel a split second of humor before the fear grips me again. I place my hand on my heart to honor the courage it takes to face hard things and heal. To honor all it has meant to come this far. Nobody could possibly know but Nate and me.

My voice is shaky and sounds far away as I say, "Come in." When Nate opens the door, I already feel worse. He avoids my gaze. His face is hard. My stomach sinks. He looks like a stranger. A lump forms in my throat, and ice settles in my chest. He moves toward his couch, taking short glances at me, and sits down gingerly, like he is afraid to do it wrong. Maybe he is scared, but his body language reads to me as anger, and my body tightens even more. My breath is shallow, my chest rising too quickly, my head fuzzy. I am cold, and I realize I'm shaking: my entire body is an uncontrollable tremor, a common trauma symptom for me in intense moments. My therapist offers me a blanket to wrap up in and a pillow to hug. He helps me take a deep breath, and I send my focus out of my spinning thoughts and into my breath and body.

God at my center... I breathe and feel the familiar warmth at the center of my chest. *I am not alone. God is right here with me. No matter what happens next, He's got my back. I can do this.*

Our therapist reminds us both of the ground rules: as the betrayed partner, I get to hold the remote control on this Disclosure. If I need to pause, we pause. If I need Nate to fast-forward through something I don't want to hear about, we fast-forward. If I need to rewind and ask more questions about anything, we rewind.

Okay. Deep breath. We begin.

My husband begins reading his printed story, which starts in early childhood. His voice is mechanical, and his words are so rushed that the sound of them startles me. My eyes search him, but his eyes are glued to the paper in front of him. His tension is so strong it fills the room, and I start to feel like someone is squeezing the back of my skull. There is a gnawing feeling inside me that something is wrong. This doesn't feel like the humility that Holly promised. This feels like a blank wall, like a robot talking. His face and voice are an emotional void.

I share his story here only with his permission and input, and our purpose in sharing is to help, not harm. Over the years, we've become acutely aware that Nate is not the only one in our community to have such experiences—experiences that through a decade of 12-step and mindfulness work seem almost universal to our culture. Our hope is that in sharing our story, in speaking aloud what so many work so hard to hide or forget, those who've suffered in silence and shame will have more understanding, empathy, tools, and compassion to heal.

Nate grew up as an only child in a quiet Idaho town, and he was welcomed as a true "Miracle Son." He grew up happily puddle-busting and riding the ditch banks on the family farm. As he recounts his earliest sexual memories, what began as natural body curiosity became a coping strategy by junior high. Masturbation becomes his compulsive escape from emotions that would never be talked about.

Church is a big deal in the family and brings a lot of pressure. Paste on a smile. Sit in the front pew at church with a perfectly pressed shirt and don't make a peep. Everything looks perfect on the outside. Important church titles and status. But the inside feels disconnected, confusing, and all alone. No words, no way to express. Crying is for wimps. He wants so badly to be the perfect son.

He doesn't even realize what he's doing until a church interview with his bishop. "Do you have a problem with masturbation?" The Bishop asks. "Uh-hhh…no," says Nate. He goes home and looks up the word in the dictionary.

Oh no… I had a feeling I shouldn't be doing that. This feels scary. He doesn't know what to do. According to the church, masturbation means unworthiness: a sin serious enough to keep him out of the temple, maybe even to restrict him from taking the sacrament at weekly worship services. *What would my parents think if they saw me decline the bread and water?*

Despite his fear, he goes back to the Bishop and confesses. He's just a young junior high kid when he first steps on the merry-go-round of regular confessions to Bishops, and he is counseled differently from their place of authority every time. To some, masturbation is no big deal, and he's encouraged not to be so hard on himself. To others, his behavior deems him unworthy to take the sacrament on Sundays, pray in church meetings, or enter the temple. He swings from feeling justified and defensive to feeling deeply shameful and unworthy. And there's nobody in his real life he can talk to about it.

As he gets older, he discovers MTV and the Sports Illustrated Swimsuit edition…the perfect companion to masturbation. Soon, real girls enter the picture, and a pattern emerges: Numb. Hide. Push the limit of kissing, touching forbidden places. Confess enough to get out of trouble, to be back in good graces with the church. Preserve the possibility to serve the mission… the mission is the motivation, the very public marker of success for a male Mormon teen and his parents. Nate understands implicitly: the mission is everything. So round and round the cycle goes, and each time he leaves the Bishop's office with the same hope: Move on, and hope that this time will be the last.

But it never is. And over time, it only seems to get worse, to progress to a deeper level of off-limits behavior. Whether the Bishop is soft and kind or harsh and punishing, it doesn't seem to matter. None of them has any idea how to actually help him understand why he feels so out of control or how to stop.

When Nate reflects, he considers that pushing things to church limits, sexually speaking, is his way of sticking it to the man, rebelling against the religious lines that threaten belonging and feel fake anyway. It seems like everyone knows what they're not supposed to be doing, but they're doing it anyway, behind closed doors. As long as the shirt is clean and pressed on Sunday, the ugly stuff can be swept under the rug. This appears to be obvious everywhere he looks.

Without knowing it, sexual behavior has become his emotional regulator. He learns to stuff feelings without even knowing he's doing it: Fear. Anger. Loneliness. Boredom. Embarrassment. He numbs them all. He learns he can just push the reset button and will never have to actually move through the discomfort, the potent cocktail of resentment, betrayal, and guilt so often churning inside. It's so much easier to just switch it off. Change the channel. Escape in the quiet of the bathroom.

He's never sure… *Do I belong? How do I connect?* So, he opts for a false connection. On TV. In magazines. With girls he hardly knows.

Up until this point, Nate's story is familiar, one he's already shared with me and one I sincerely empathize with. As I sit on the couch in our therapist's office, I'm on board. I'm okay. But then it takes a turn: unfamiliar high school and college experiences suddenly feel like new boulders falling on me. I was so sure I knew his story. Until I don't.

Wait. What? There is more? I hear him talking, but the words are lost as hot anger rises in my gut with the heat of fresh betrayal. After all the midnight confessions, the month-long marathons of wrestling through ongoing disclosures… *You were still hiding things from me?*

Slow down. I have questions… Slow down. What was that? What are you sliding past? Hoping I won't notice like the tip-toe words on the Sunday Night that started this two and a half years ago?

The terrain is changing, and I feel the earth shift beneath me. Every time I have a question, he squirms and sighs, his voice defensive and irritated. His face is so hard. I try to stay grounded, but my body starts to dissociate, and soon I am floating, strangely detached from the wreckage.

In the face of my questions, Nate defensively insists that these experiences were already "taken care of," that he was expressly told by church authorities that there was no need to bring them up again. But when I think of the two of us sitting face to face on our bed so many nights—tearful, passionate, crazy, traumatized—battling for our marriage with our lives, I couldn't care less what any authority had to say. At the end of the day, he was still hiding from me. I was stripping down my whole soul for him, and he was still lying to me.

And as his face goes tight and his short responses fill with contempt, there is a weight in the pit of my stomach, a calm, terrified knowing. It's not the words he is saying; it's the way he is saying them. The monster is still in there. After all the crocodile tears and good behavior and gold stars, it is *still* in there, untouched as freshly fallen snow: The hardness. The defiance. The stone-cold wall. The justified anger that runs like a river underneath his often-sunny Jekyll-and-Hyde exterior, but overflows when anything he says gets challenged.

Yes, it's still there, alive and well. I can see it in his eyes. Hard. Cold. Hating me. Making it my fault. I can feel it poking through the holes in his story, ignited by my audacity to question him.

Nothing has changed. No, nothing has changed at all… I can't believe it.

And somehow, in this primal moment, I shift. I stop watching him, and instead, I am watching me. I listen, I wonder, I observe from above. I imagine the angels that Holly has sent; they are pressing their hands against my back like she does when I'm resting in child's pose at yoga.

You are supported, I hear them whisper. *Just keep breathing. Just focus on your next breath.*

Two more years pass in his story. Our marriage. Then, college graduation.

"So, Nate, what are you going to do with your life?" everyone starts to ask.

Fear. Pressure. He can't say the words: "This is hard. I feel scared." And just like that, he's right back to his old comfort zone. Hides it. Stuffs it. Blames it on me. Blames it on people at work. Blames it on anybody available. Back to porn. Back to the Bishop. Back to the cycle. Getting married and being able to have sex were supposed to fix the problem. He can't believe he's here again.

Two years later, the baby comes. "Where is my attention?" he says. "Nobody appreciates me," he says.

Blames his feelings on me. Blames his feelings on the baby. Shuts off. Back to porn. Back to hiding. Shame. Anger. Resentment. Porn.

It's so unsettling for me to sit amidst stories I recognize, now interwoven into a landscape of his past I've known nothing about. My ears feel hot and far away. And the hardness and defiance in his face and voice. And the pinprick tension in the room as I squeeze my pillow. And then, his disclosure turns to his extramarital online affair, and my whole body tightens up.

I hear his mechanical voice begin to recount this paramount series of events, and an unexpected heat rises up my throat into my face. My heart pounds through my clutched pillow, and I suddenly have questions I didn't know I had, and I must know. I mean, I MUST know. I want words, the real words, not glossed-over bullshit words like "inappropriate relationship." I want to hear this defensive blank-faced robot-man who looks and sounds like my husband actually say the words he spoke to this woman. I want him to say out loud the words she would speak to him in their hundreds of texts and calls over the course of months. I want to hear each syllable. I want to see him say it.

And I want him to feel something, goddammit!

I ask for words, and he argues with me. I insist, and he looks with pleading eyes at the therapist. But I am resolute. The tension is palpable. Our therapist suggests we take a break. I walk down the hall, shake out my arms, and steady my shaky breath. I do full vinyasa breathing in the bathroom until I can feel my feet. And when I come back to the couch, I haven't changed my mind. Something inside me simply has to know.

As promised, our therapist backs me up. He gently guides Nate to share the ugly details. I watch my husband say the words he said to his mistress. I witness my heart break and my stomach twist with a strange detachment. I am dead inside.

So, this is what this feels like. Time floats like eternity.

I start to realize we have been at this for hours. Three hours? Four? A lifetime? I am exhausted. Depleted. Empty. I am floating above the room. I am watching the nightmare unfold, but I am no longer shaking. There is a strange calm inside of me.

I see a man who I understand is my husband talking, and it all appears in a way I've never seen things before. I suddenly recognize each subtle justification as it comes spilling out of his mouth, almost as though a great God of Truth has given an omnipotent highlighter with which I can point out each place where he flips into justified self-protection. How, so subtly, he plays the charismatic part of the good guy and pushes blame onto others—anyone, everyone, except for himself. So tricky, it's almost imperceptible underneath his "nice guy" mask of self-pity.

If you weren't well acquainted with addict behaviors, you might not even notice. I certainly hadn't. For over a decade, I was so intent on defending myself from his attacks that I couldn't step away from my *own* self-protection to see the game we were really playing. But now, in the terrible magic of this Disclosure, I can see what I could never see before: He is playing victim, playing martyr, all in a complex game to hide the truth. From me, yes…but really from himself.

I mean, the *real* problem is that nobody ever seems to see what a good guy he really is deep down, underneath this little—insignificant, really—problem, especially compared to so many other people… It's an underlying attitude that is so subtle he doesn't even know it's there. But in this moment, with angels whispering in my ears and holding my hands, I can see the disconnect as clear as day. It is written in his body, his face, his jaw. Even the hardness of his voice gives it away. Everything I have learned about healing in the past two and a half years clicks into place as I see the Truth unfold before my eyes.

He is not where I thought he was.

And neither am I. For the first time, the immutable fact sinks into my heart with a fully embodied knowing: *This is not about me at all.* The relationship, the addiction, the never-ending hole that I've never been able to fill… none of it has *anything* to do with me, and now I know it—it's inescapable in the narrative that has just painted an entirely new recovery landscape in our therapist's office.

It's not about me.

These are words I have pictured, tried to convince myself of, and recited in 12-step circles, but never truly believed. But this revelation doesn't free me the way I always thought it would. In fact, I have never felt more powerless. I have never felt that I was facing anything bigger. In this moment, I don't know what my life has been or what it will be. But as I hear him talk and I feel his energy, I know this with absolute surety: *This is not recovery…and there's nothing I can do to change it.*

I know this with a terrible calm that settles into the pit of my stomach and fills my insides with lead. After two and a half years of sobriety. After hundreds of hours in journals and 12-step meetings and sponsorship and blog posts. After thousands of dollars of therapy. After all this "recovery." We are still at Square One.

As we wind down, our therapist thanks us for our time and our courage. He shifts in his seat, looking taken aback, and shakes his head with raised eyebrows like he is trying to find the right words.

"Nate, I think it's time we focus on some regular individual sessions with you. I wasn't expecting the straight-up emotional vacuum we felt throughout this disclosure."

I think he is as surprised as I am.

"Clearly," he states, looking right into my husband's eyes, "we are not here simply to help Becky."

Marriage Prep Course
Curriculum Correction
Becky Moller, May 2014

*Marriage Prep is a notorious course at Brigham Young University
about preparing for successful marriages and families*

Why don't they tell you in Marriage Prep,
That your husband will fantasize about other women,
That you will never be enough to satisfy his appetite,
Then we wouldn't take it so hard when it happens.

Why don't they tell you in Marriage Prep,
That men have a deep, dark carnal side,
That supersedes everything good in life,
And drowns them in a lake of gluttonous lust.

Why don't they tell you in Marriage Prep,
That every fight you will ever have,
Will in some way be tied back to sex,
Not enough, not adventurous, not aggressive enough for him.

Why don't they tell you in Marriage Prep,
That you will just be an object for use
And he will turn to another object when he grows tired of you.
That you will play the role of hundreds of
Pornographic images over the years,
All the while thinking he is only making love to you.

Why don't they just out and say it in Marriage Prep,
That fidelity is impossible, and love is a lie.
That marriage is a sham, and will be the most
painful experience you will ever endure,
That your partner will hurt you more than you ever dreamed
you could survive.

And that you will end up a defeated shell of all the bright and
shiny you once were.
When all those men were chasing you.
Guess you picked the wrong one.
Or maybe they're all the same.

I wish they would have told me in Marriage Prep.

CHAPTER TWENTY-TWO

NEW ROCK BOTTOM

After Full Disclosure, I leave the office without a glance or word at my husband and drive straight to the Holiday Inn as the September sun is setting. I briefly call Holly, who is proud of me and encourages me to take care of myself. I check in with my parents, who mostly just want this all to be okay again. I meet my sister at a restaurant, who lovingly distracts me while I pick at the food on my plate. I am empty, hollow, dead inside. Hours pass, and I lie awake in a dark and quiet hotel room like I am in a torture chamber.

It is 3 a.m. I have not slept.

It is 4 a.m. I cannot fathom how I will ever sleep again. My brain is back to the movie reel, only now, a lifetime of new footage flickers across the screen of my obsessing mind. I call Holly and leave scores of surrenders on her voicemail. None of them eases my pain. I write dozens of pages in my journal. I open a book and try to read, but I cannot focus. My brain can't stop looping.

I lie in the dark, held captive by an army of useless interrogations: accusing me, accusing my husband, accusing God, accusing life.

To myself: *After all this time, how can you be married to a complete stranger?*

To Nate: *Who even are you? Who have you ever been? How can you live with yourself?!*

To God: *Is recovery even possible? Does any of this stuff actually work? For anyone?!?*

As my mind marinates in a whole new library of footage to add to my nightmares, I get the sinking feeling that I have been tricked, duped, and manipulated since the day I met Nate. That this whole relationship, from its very beginning, was a deception, a subtle misleading. It's not about what he did or didn't do with himself or whomever; it's about the fact that he was always hiding and portraying an incomplete picture, from the moment I met him. And that time after time in our marriage, he manipulated me to feel like I had done something wrong as his actions created a gulf between us. Time after time, he found a way to blame me instead of acknowledging his own deceit. Again and again, he chose to protect himself instead of protecting me or our kids. And now, each seemingly justified deception has somehow led one day, one month, one moment at a time to right here—where any chance of trust or connection feels utterly extinct.

I compulsively pore through memories of the months and years we dated. *Why did I choose him? I had so many options. Why in the hell did I choose* him? I cannot forgive myself for being so stupid. I hate him more than I ever have. I hate myself for choosing him. I google the clinical definition of a narcissist and add the fitting definition to my arsenal of justified rage against him.

Even though it feels like the night will never end, eventually tomorrow comes. I wear shades to hide my puffy eyes as I check out of the hotel with lead in my stomach. When I return home, I find Nate working in his office. I quietly ask him to leave for the weekend. He nods his head and disappears into our bedroom; I assume to collect his things. Maybe he will go to a friend's house. Maybe he will check into a hotel. I am not in charge, and I don't care where he stays, as long as it isn't here. I cannot imagine looking him in the face. Not today. Not for a long time. I will fix up the basement bedroom for when he returns.

I cannot get over how wrong I have been, from the moment I let him into my heart as a naïve nineteen-year-old college girl. *Who was I then? What was I looking for?* I see his playful teasing and our long talks on my apartment couches, and my heart aches and body yearns…

But I didn't really know him! I argue with my tender feelings. I didn't really know the first thing about him. Even after two years of dating, I never saw a hint of his dark, angry side. *How did I miss it? Why did I buy so easily into the outward show, the suit and tie, the big title at church?*

Maybe that was what I was after the whole time…just the right package with the right credentials. Maybe I was using him as much as he was using me. Maybe I got what I deserved. I am confused about myself as much as I am confused about him.

Did I even really love Nate? Do I even know what love is?

"I love that you once made me feel pretty." "I love that you once made me feel like I'm not alone." "I love that you once made me feel wanted." "I love that you once made me feel heard."

But in my raw, searching state, I see through my own mindsets: none of these self-centered emotions is actually love. Love is not taking. It's giving. Love is something deeper than the pleasant payoff I get when someone shows up the way I want them to, something I've started to recognize in the gentle, mindful ways I've been learning to meet myself. Love is saying: *I see you, not just the bright and shiny parts, but all of you. And there's room for you here.* Love is acknowledging the wholeness and beauty in a human soul with all its imperfections. Love is a witnessing that has no judgment, no measure to meet.

Have I given this kind of Love to Nate—ever? Have I given it to myself?

I am utterly humbled and empty-handed for answers—about myself, my recovery, his recovery.

We have put in so much time, so much effort, survived so many showdowns, had so many breakthroughs...and what has it added up to?

A sober narcissist. Branches that have been neatly trimmed but roots still untouched.

How will I ever trust myself again? I am terrified of myself. I always make the wrong decision. I am so broken. I am so blind. I am so full of ego. How much pride did I attach to his sobriety date? How secure did I feel as he checked the recovery boxes? Why do I buy into that stuff, again and again? What meaning has any of it held? What does it mean now? Why couldn't I see this before? Where do I even go from here?

Before my kids come home from school, I open a clean white screen in a fresh Google Doc. My first recovery journal, 500 pages plus, has been devoted to following all the rules, answering all the questions, completing all the assignments, trying so methodically to do everything right so that I can somehow pass this test. Now I sit facing the empty space on the screen, the undeniable fruits of all my futile efforts to control the outcome. I take a deep breath, and I type:

Recovery Journal Round 2
Friday, September 23rd

I surrender my marriage.
I surrender my love for Nate.
I surrender Nate's love for me.
I surrender my security and comfort.
I surrender my desire for romantic love.
I surrender my need to be wanted, desired, and cared for.
I surrender my financial stability.
I surrender my dreams for what my life would be.
I surrender my belief that if I can just keep Nate at my center, he won't go back to his addiction.
I give up.
I ask God to teach me what it feels like to have Him at my center.
I ask God to show me that His peace and love are the only things that can really fill me.
I ask God to teach me what love really looks like, feels like, acts like.
I ask God to take my broken heart and my broken life and to turn it into something beautiful, whatever that may look like.
I am letting go.
I feel peace.

This surrender carves a stillness inside me, and when the kids return from school, Nate and I are able to meet them as emotional grown-ups. We calmly explain that we're working through recovery stuff, and Dad will be staying with friends for a few days. He gives hugs and packs a duffel bag. I hunker down for the weekend with my children, and we do nothing but cuddle and care for ourselves with movies and simple meals.

With all my mindfulness practice, I am becoming acutely aware of my effect on my little ones: I can almost sense them calibrating to my nervous system, constantly looking to me to see if *I'm* okay, if *we're* okay, if *they're* okay. And I can see how my surrendered self creates a stabilizing energy from the inside out, a safety they most desperately need. I'm understanding more and more: the most important thing I can do for them is find this spiritual center within myself, moment to moment. They need this clarity from me even more than perfect circumstances.

As we watch Disney cartoons and I run my fingers through my oldest daughter's golden hair, I think back to our past rock bottom over two years ago and remember how often I would find my pillow covered with her hand-sketched pictures of encouragement and love. Madi's colored-pencil rainbows and stick-figure happy families often depicted Nate and me holding hands with hearts above our heads: "We love each other" in scrawled-out pencil letters.

I recognize now that these pictures were evidence that even without any direct knowledge of what was happening, her little seven-year-old mind was mapping our instability. She was trying to fix things, help me, heal me. She was taking on the burden of my pain, and she wasn't the only one. Our children were unconsciously campaigning for our reconciliation without explicitly understanding the dissolution. Their fear and anxiety were a natural response to the crisis energy that starkly disrupted their previously stable existence. The more I'm learning to understand the energy created by my own thoughts, beliefs, and emotions, the more I see the spill-over effect of my trauma onto my children. What a heavy burden for them to bear.

"Trauma that is not transformed will be transmitted," a statement I've heard dozens of times in my recovery studies, weighs heavily in my mind. Time and again, I've seen intergenerational patterns of addiction and abuse play out in dozens of stories in recovery circles. Kids are smart. They absorb the energy of what's going on, even if they don't know the details. We all do. Not to mention, fear and repression attract the very thing they're trying to avoid. As Carl Jung famously taught, "What you resist persists."

I can't hide what's here. And I don't want to pass this on to them. I did the best I could two years ago, but now I have so many more tools. I will do it differently this time. This time, I will do better for them.

When Nate returns to the house on Monday, he settles into the basement bedroom, the beginning of an in-house separation. That evening, I insist that we sit down at the kitchen table with our three oldest to directly address the uncertainty that hovers like fluttering moths around them.

"Thanks for sitting down with us. We want to talk to you about what's going on, and we want you to know that you can ask us anything, any time, and we will be honest with you. We know that life changed for all of us two years ago, and that it's been hard. We want you to know that you aren't crazy for noticing that." As I start to talk, my kids' eyes are wide and their breath shallow.

Nate begins to talk to them about addiction in general terms and all he is doing to recover from it. I talk to them about trauma and all I'm doing to heal from it. We talk about therapy and Twelve Steps and all the experts who are helping us—*the best in the business*, we assure them, and it's true. We normalize the fact that lots of people have experienced things like this and point out that the people helping us have helped hundreds of other people through similar things. They don't have to feel afraid or ashamed.

Their shoulders start to relax, and Nate and I make eye contact.

"So, the next best step for us is for me to move down to the basement for a while. It will give both me and Mom time and space to keep working on our own recovery so we can get stronger in the ways we each need to," Nate explains with calm confidence.

"Yeah, it's like the Zen empty cup story I've talked to you about before: when our cup is full, there's no room for God to pour the tea. All this recovery is teaching us how to rely on God and what it means to really trust Him, and sometimes that means we have to stop relying so much on each other. We know He can help us create something new, something healthier and better for our whole family, but it needs some time and distance." As I speak, our kids furrow their brows and nod their heads. This apparently makes sense to them.

As we close our family pow-wow, we try to create an open space for the ongoing questions they might have and put the responsibility for moving through the situation squarely on our own shoulders. I want to make sure that *we* are playing the role of emotional grown-ups, so our kids don't have to. They seem to leave with anxious butterflies put mainly to rest, happy to go back to life as normal with the mostly irrelevant detail of Dad living in the basement.

It feels like a new chapter, where Nate and I have similar growing up to do in our relationship with each other. But now, we have the tools to start showing up with more accountability and awareness. Our new rock bottom quiets to an introspective detachment, our disillusionment carrying a fertile emptiness. After all our recovery tricks and gold stars, there is nowhere left to turn but up.

PAIN
BECKY MOLLER, JANUARY 2024

I hate
that you will never know
what it is to feel this much pain.

I hate
that you will never know
how much it hurts to be
Rejected,
abandoned,
lied to,
and betrayed
by the person you
love and trust
most in the
world.

I'm trying to tell myself that I have never felt your pain either...
But then this little voice tells me that
You have never felt pain.
You have never held pain.

You just numb your way out of pain
by doing things that hurt others,
Mostly me.
You have never felt pain.
You have just hurt people.

And I hate you for this
as I sit here
drowning
in
pain.

CHAPTER TWENTY-THREE

EMBRACING MY INNER WARRIOR

I t's interesting to return to a state of trauma and experience the internal chaos with all the new tools I've gained. In the stillness of a new rock bottom, the clamoring voices in my head seem jarring and out of place. But instead of panicking and pushing away like I've done in the past, I start to hold them just as they are.

"What do you need?" I start asking.

"I need an advocate," they tell me.

So, with curiosity and respect, I make room to investigate. I find that they come from a warrior woman inside me who is finally seeing clearly, finally fed up with enabling bullshit. Under all their desperation is a powerful and feisty clarity: they know what they know, and they know what they need.

So, with their assistance, I write a letter: a straightforward smackdown of where I am, what I see, and what I need to move forward. It's a line in the sand aligned with my own inner guide, a clear delineation that claims my own position and allows Nate to choose his. It becomes my formal response to Full Disclosure, which I share with Nate in our therapist's office the next week.

> Thank you for sharing your Full Disclosure with me. These are the things I feel I need to express from that experience:
>
> Throughout the disclosure, I felt a sense of blame, self-pity, minimization, and justification in the way you told your story. I did not feel a sense of Humble, Honest, Accountable.

Throughout the disclosure, I felt a sense of defensiveness and irritation at my questions.

I felt an inability to recognize or admit emotions.

I feel particularly troubled about why you never shared your sexual past with me when we were dating. I feel in my gut that on some level, you knowingly manipulated me to believe you were someone you were not.

I feel troubled that many of the items in your disclosure were "half-disclosed" to me at the time they occurred. This pattern of half-disclosing the truth makes me feel extremely unsafe.

Your "half-truths" deeply damage any ability I have to trust that the confessions or gold-star behaviors intended to provide safety are anything more than manipulation attempts. This leaves me wondering how we will ever rebuild trust.

I feel that even this disclosure and the way you wrote it demonstrate your need to be seen as a "good guy" or a "poster child" in life. I feel a fundamental lack of acknowledging the reality of where your life has been and a continual practice of setting yourself apart as "the exception" or "the special one."

I have seen, in this disclosure and throughout our marriage, an inability to experience any negative emotions other than anger, self-pity, or blame. This is not something I am willing to accept in our marriage and family.

I feel like there is an inability to experience shame or true remorse for your actions. Rather, I have felt an attitude of "It wasn't that bad... it wasn't that big a deal...at least it didn't go THIS far like those other guys with real problems..." or, "Good thing I've got this figured out now."

In my heart, I believe you have not yet experienced a personal rock bottom of humiliation/humility that creates true change. I feel I experienced this two and a half years ago and am able to comment on and recognize this state. Without your own deeply personal shift, I don't think I can get myself to trust you.

I feel that this disclosure made manifest to me the lack of authentic emotional digging that has gone on for you personally about your recovery. You spend a lot of time reading about "the right way to recover" and are involved in helping others find this path. But what about your path?

When pressed with questions about your own heart, your own pain, I don't think you even know where to begin. What is this hole that you are trying to fill? Where did it come from? Why did you keep coming back to it? How can you just shut yourself off from any sense of morality and live in full justification? Why do you need so much attention? Why do you need so many gold stars? These are the types of questions I need you to answer if I am going to be able to trust that you are even capable of the self-honesty that will lead to recovery.

Ultimately, I feel that our marriage is at another Ground Zero. My prayer for Disclosure for myself was that this experience would be what God needed it to be for me, and that He would show me the Truth about where we've been and where we are. My prayer for you was that Disclosure would be whatever you needed it to be in your recovery.

I feel that this prayer was answered for both of us.

I am fully committed to putting in whatever work it takes to rebuild from Ground Zero. But please be aware that I am not the same frightened, co-dependent wife that hit rock bottom two and a half years ago. I have grown. I have changed. Today, I know who I am and what gives me value. Today, I understand that I have the right to choose the person I want to become and the types of relationships I want to be involved in. Today, I understand much more about what addict behaviors and manipulations look like. Today, I will trust my gut along with the insights of my sponsor and therapist.

Two years ago, I chose God, and I chose recovery. With or without you. Today, you get to make that same choice for yourself. I look forward to seeing your decision at work in our lives.

Boom: Drop the mic. The words on the paper quiet the voices in my head. I read them dispassionately to Nate at our therapist's office and drive home in my separate car, feeling neither victorious nor afraid. My stance is my stance, and Nate can do with it what he will. For the first time in our marriage, maybe even my life, I really don't care who is happy with me. I'm happy with myself.

This is a radical new energy for me, and now that I've let it out of its "good girl" cage, it's only growing. This Warrior Advocate sees through the bullshit, and she's calling me on all my games of playing nice to secure safety and approval. My people-pleasing has caused harm, it's undeniable, and seeing it isn't shameful. It's empowering.

As a follow-up to Disclosure, Nate and I have been assigned to watch *Helping Her Heal* by Dr. Doug Weiss, a renowned sexual addiction therapist. With the kids in bed, we sit side by side on our living room couch as the doctor describes with heart-wrenching accuracy the splintering fragmentation of security, identity, and shattering emotions that accompany a spouse's betrayal.

"You did this to her," he says, looking straight through the camera to all the offending spouses looking to fix their seemingly crazy partners. "She didn't ask for this. You did this to her."

Soon, it is one in the morning, long after we retreated to our separate rooms without a word after watching the workshop. I lie in bed, staring into the darkness, heart pounding, mind racing. Tears stream from my eyes as I try to understand the sensations whirring inside of me: relief, anger, clarity, rage, vindication. Something that's been missing is clicking into place, sparking permission to feel emotions I've long been afraid to admit are there—even to myself.

For so long, I've kept my focus glued to my own part, my own shortcomings, afraid to accuse. For so long, I've carried the shame of my pathetic unraveling. For so long, I've believed that this whole mess was really a reflection of me. But now I feel something new swelling within me; something strong, encouraged by Dr. Weiss's words. Another painful, excruciating revelation: *I've enabled it. I've enabled the blame. I've enabled the gaslighting. I've bought right into his narrative.*

And now, my feisty warrior rises from ashes in my belly like a colorful dragon, and I sit up in my bed, reliving the night this all started. The haphazard mention of an "inappropriate relationship," the confusion, the flying dishes, the screaming in the kitchen, my terrified child, the heart pounding in my ears and throat for endless hours, and finally, finally, in the blackness of 4 a.m. on our living room couches, the most crippling words of all:

"I haven't felt you loved me for three years."

Like I've learned to do in meditation, my mind's eye watches my face fall, my body slump. I still feel the reverberations of those words in my stomach. This was the moment, more than any other, that broke me.

But now, for the first time, the movie in my mind pauses, and it occurs to me to look over to the other couch. I rewind and watch my husband mutter the same words. I see the hard and defiant mask on his face, the mask I've come to know well. The same mask I saw just a week ago in Full Disclosure.

And I suddenly see with crystal clarity what I could never see before: his cowardice and desperation. The self-protective flailing of one who has backed himself into his own corner. The emotionally immature, gut reaction of a self-centered asshole who sidesteps the bullet to leave someone else, anyone else...even *his best friend...* in its path.

"I haven't felt you loved me in three years..." Suddenly, those words aren't damning. They're self-exposing, passive-aggressive, self-pitying. Suddenly, I see right through them.

This isn't about you at all. The man behind that mask has never had anything to do with you at all—ever.

Something inside of me knows this like I've never known it before. And now, I move, with power, with purpose, with valid anger. I fly out of my bed and down the stairs like a Chinese dragon with flames licking the night air around me. I flick the basement light on, stride down the hall, and open his door with one fell swoop. Words begin pouring out without my even waking him:

"Two and a half years ago, when you told me about your affair, it was like you ran me over with your car. I was completely blindsided. I knew you were distant, but I had no clue that something like that could ever be actually happening. And then, after you hit me and I'm down on the floor, bleeding out, in shock, you look straight at me, and you essentially say, 'And by the way...it's your fault.' Do you realize that? Do you realize that's what you did? You just backed over me and parked the damn car right on my chest. And you just left it there! For nearly three years, you've left it! That car has just been sitting on my chest, crushing me, and you haven't said a word about it! After all the work we've done, and the *sorries* you've made, you never once took *those* words back. You just let them sit there. For almost three years, those words have been ringing in my ears. How many times have you let me apologize for how broken and depressed I am? How many years of recovery have we been working...and yet, not once...not even once, have you said, 'This is my fault. I did this to you...' Never once. *Never!!*

"Since the moment you finally had the guts to tell me the truth, you have let me believe it was my fault. You have let me think I was crazy. You have let me carry the weight of trying to fix this and get myself normal enough that you won't leave me again. You have let me carry it all. The blame for what you did. The blame for where I am. And I have taken it. Well, no more. No more. What you did is not my fault. The craziness I feel is not my fault. I will not carry the blame anymore. And I will never feel safe with you until I see that you can carry the weight of what you've done and how it's affected not only me, but our whole family. I am done taking accountability for your choices. Your choices are yours to carry from here on out. And if you can't, well, that's fine, too. I will be okay either way. Whether we work out or we don't. I will be okay. But I won't carry this anymore."

My husband stares at me with shock in his sleep-deprived face as my trembling tirade comes to a close, and I whirl around, slam the door, and march back up the stairs. And then I collapse, somehow finding my way to the couch, huddled in a blanket, sobbing and shaking. My trauma tremors have gripped me again. I lie there shaking for a long time. My heart begins to slow down, my breath begins to deepen.

I focus on my inhale—2—3—4, exhale—2—3—4; I come back to my body, exhausted but triumphant. I have said what has needed to be said for well over two years. I have broken my subconscious ceiling, finally using my voice to violently reject the false belief that's kept me underwater for so long—no matter how sober my husband was, no matter how many 12-step meetings I attended, journal pages I wrote, or therapy sessions I went to.

For the first time, I finally believe that my husband's choices were not about me. I can feel the shift inside my very soul. Something has clicked, and my Warrior helped me do it. My valid anger has paved a pathway for change.

I am no longer a prisoner to anyone else's expectations or my own insatiable need to please. I am not defined by other people's opinions of me. I will no longer take responsibility for the happiness of others. I will not enable my husband to placate his own conscience by throwing me under the bus. I will no longer convince myself that there is anything noble in doing so. I will no longer accept the belief that there is something inherently wrong with me that makes me deserve to be mistreated or abandoned. That is a lie!

Even as my heart pounds, I know I will no longer take responsibility for what is not mine. With my husband or anyone else. I am becoming a grown-up, taking back my power. I am living in my Truth and trusting the light and the softness and the fire I feel inside me—it all has a place. It all belongs. I am trusting that my own soul knows the way to freedom. I will never again expect somebody else to be my defender. I am my own defender. With God at my back, there is nothing to fear. I have set free another piece of my soul.

My eyes drift closed, and the next thing I know, I hear soft footsteps up the stairs, and my husband is crouching down on the floor, looking up at me. His eyes are full and sincere. He is trying so hard. He is scared and unsure.

He clasps my hands and says, "Beck, I need to tell you something. How you feel *is* my fault. I made you feel this way. You didn't ask for this. You had no idea what you were getting into. You didn't ask to be married to an addict. This is my fault, and it always was. I was too afraid to admit that when I first told you. I said those words to you because they were the words I told myself. That was the only way I could justify what I was doing. I am so sorry. I am sorry for what I've done to you. I am so sorry for what I've done to us."

His mask is gone. The boy I fell in love with appears to be growing up right in front of me: humble, honest, accountable. Tears are streaming down his cheeks. Tears are streaming down my cheeks. It is the middle of the night, and I am so tired I cannot fully register what he is saying.

Do I believe it? Do I believe the words he is saying to me? I don't know yet. And ironically, I don't need to. There's something rooting deep inside me that is even more steadying than his heartfelt acknowledgment.

After two and a half years of sobriety, therapy, and Twelve Steps, this feels like a deeper surrender for me, the start of Nate's deeper recovery...and maybe, a real, new beginning for *us*.

I Don't Trust

Becky Moller, February 2023

I don't trust
Any holy music
That doesn't include
Some
Serious swearing.

Getting to know God
Is more a
Mud wrestle
Than a
Hallelujah!

PART THREE

LARGER
HORIZONS

The Spiritual Path
Becky Moller, September 2017

The Spiritual Path
In the End
Is nothing more than
These four words:

I   Might   Be   Wrong

CHAPTER TWENTY-FOUR

UNEXPECTED RUNOFF

Underneath a glacier lies a layer of earth called permafrost—ground that remains frozen for more than two consecutive years. When a glacier recedes and the ground warms, the ice in the permafrost melts, making the earth soft and unstable. It can slump, causing rock and landslides, floods, and coastal erosion. Anything that isn't solid is likely to be carried away in a massive run-off, clearing the landscape of anything nonessential. The water has changed its function: from a frozen excavator uprooting boulders to a cleansing agent clearing impurities. The seemingly permanent ice fixture softens into a purifying flow, uncovering a new and empty landscape.

Before Betrayal Trauma, I thought my lifelong stumbling block was going to be my body anxiety and disordered eating. *Above-and-beyond-all-reasonable-expectations* was the only place I felt comfortable, in weight and in life. Losing my period at age 18 put me safely in that sphere, and throughout my adult life, any tip toward a normal weight brought buzzing anxiety. This background static was so constant, I couldn't imagine life without it, and I didn't really want to: the anxiety kept me in check. It kept my ego safe. I was in bondage to my own fear, powerless to free myself from my own trap, because it *felt* safe. It made me feel like I was in control.

Until I wasn't. Betrayal Trauma interrupted the false illusion; it was the glacier that unearthed the heavy boulder of my compulsion. With so much beyond my control, betrayal forced me into a corner where I had no choice but to face my deepest fears: Failure. Not-enoughness. Powerlessness. Abandonment. Rock bottom.

Looking back, Full Disclosure feels like the point where all that frozen fear begins to melt, and I realize my core foundation is literally sinking out from under me. It's the lowest low point: the emptiest cup I've yet experienced. Because even with all my recovery knowledge, I'm still not in control. The harshness of this reality shocks me into stillness, and the runoff starts to wear my small self away at an accelerated pace. And I'm no longer resisting, no longer trying to hold things together into that safe, frozen shape.

After our post-Disclosure showdown, Nate and I settle into a calm and separate existence, barely communicating but very cordial as we logistically co-parent. Our recovery friends rally around us as we share and process in our respective groups each week. Many others have been where we are, and their hope, strength, and experience are a life raft for us both, individually. They are all rooting for us, and they know from their own lives that there are no shortcuts in these treacherous waters. These fellows intimately know the weight and complexity of what we're trying to do. We are emotionally differentiating from one another, and it's no small task.

At home, I grapple for a light in the dark, for some sort of rhythm in this new normal where my husband lives downstairs, and I carry ice chips in my chest each time I see him. The days pass like weeks. I've never been so broken, so powerless, so surrendered. After years of recovery work, the walls I've used in the past to shield myself have crumbled: I've no heart to research for more answers, find new books or podcasts, justify myself or my rightness in any way. I'm an open target: naked, vulnerable, and without energy or appetite for any more tricks to protect myself.

Two and a half years ago, sex was my daily escape from the pain and fear of our initial *Sunday Night*. Nate's body helped ease the tear in my soul. But now Nate is in the basement, and my soul is splayed open. It's time to face this pain, and I've got nothing: no plan of attack, no surge of I-can-fix-this determination, no metaphorical binkie to distract me. I just have space and time.

In some ways, it feels like a major step backwards into darkness and the quicksand of depression. Back into hopelessness and slow-motion survival. But something deep inside me knows there is progress in this emptiness. Something inside me has shifted, ripening within the words I wrote on the page that night in the hotel: "I surrender…"

Something inside of me has finally let go. I am no longer motivated by "trying to save the marriage," no longer unconsciously grasping for Nate's love or validation. No longer trying to get him to stay or to figure it out or to choose me. For the first time since that *Sunday Night*, I have truly let go of the outcome. I am living just in the Now and waiting for my next right step to emerge. I am empty and open and still.

I buy myself Snuggie pajamas, warm and soft. I wash and press my bedsheets, trying to make the idea of a room to myself appealing. The autumn evenings grow cold, and I find comfort in the warm blankets I pile on top of my comforter. I retreat into my inner world of journaling, reading, and 12-step work. These are the same outer motions that have moved me through the past two and a half years, but their inner quality feels different. Now, I am not trying to get somewhere. Now, I am fully present right where I am. This is what's here. So this must be exactly what I need. All I can think of every day is peace, and what I need to let go of to find it.

Who am I, God? What do you want for my life? Everything I thought I knew, I don't. Show me Your way. Show me how to live. Show me how to love.

One morning, as I pad routinely to the bathroom, I am shocked to find myself staring at bright red blood on my undergarments. It takes me a full minute to register that I am staring at a period. My first real period in eighteen years, between fertility drugs, nursing babies, and rigid calorie-counting.

I blink twice, taking it in. For almost the past two decades, a period meant danger to me: Body fat. Fear. Self-disgust. Panic.

But today, I stare at a red stain on snowy white fabric and feel a surprising calm begin to warm my very center. I breathe. I feel. I consider. *Hmmm… that's interesting.*

In my mind's eye, I see the sketched-out scenarios from my therapeutic Trauma Egg; the stories unconsciously linked to the suffering I've been so helplessly pinned under since my world blew up: I see the little girl striving in the classroom. I see the big sister wanting to take it all on and resenting the fact that she couldn't. I see the pimple-covered teenager, ashamed and yet fighting to find her place. I see the exhausted high-school senior melting down in the main office. And now, the nightmarish images of our therapist's office and Nate's robotic reading of his Full Disclosure. I lean in and allow myself to feel fully the powerlessness that's been percolating within me since that moment. It feels like bright white chains wrapping like boa constrictors around my chest, choking me. I gasp and sob and feel my feet.

I'm here. I'm right here. I deepen my breath. I can stay with this.

And as I do, words of deep knowing float up from somewhere deep within me, ringing in my ears: *None of this has anything to do with you at all.*

In a flash of insight, the illusions of the past twenty years combine with the circumstances of this very moment to flip a cosmic switch inside me. Puzzle pieces I was previously powerless over click into place, and I suddenly see the Truth I couldn't see for decades, clear as day.

I see the pointless futility of all the *doing*. I see how unproductive it's been to mold not only my appearance, but every aspect of my life into idealized boxes. My "perfection" hasn't protected me from anything at all! I believed that my thinness would protect me, would guarantee me belonging and acceptance, *but it didn't*. My husband had, in fact, betrayed me when I was at one of my lowest weights in our marriage. This fact is important!

And now the scarlet stain registers with almost laughable transparency: I have sacrificed, suffered, punished, and hated myself for no reason at all. I have put my eggs in a basket that has brought me to the very place I was running from all along. I have unconsciously created my deepest fear by running from it so desperately. It's so obvious I am almost laughing out loud as I sit on the toilet and stare at my underwear.

The time has come to pull my head out of fantasy and start living in reality. It's time to grow up.

And I do. In that very moment in my bathroom, gazing at the darkness of my own blood, the most surprising emotion slowly fills my being... I expect fear or self-disgust. I expect a firm resolve to begin calorie counting tomorrow. But as I simply watch and listen, I don't feel any of those old, familiar friends.

Instead, I see a vision of myself as a little girl under a Christmas tree, unwrapping a tall stack of presents and pushing them away in spoiled fashion. *"I don't want that gift! I want this one! I don't want to be 110 pounds! I want to be 100!"* I see myself stomp and huff and cross my arms, and with some humor, I know that this is exactly what I've been doing for the past twenty years.

And just look where it's gotten me.

And in my mind, God is face to face with me now, grabbing my cheeks, nose to nose, eyeball to eyeball. For the first time ever, He's got all my attention. *"Just want me…and see what I can do for you. Just want My way more than you want your way. I promise I will blow your mind."*

And just like that, I believe Him. Just like that, I let go. And it feels like a giddy bubble-pop in my belly.

All that drama, all that kicking and screaming for so long, when it was just that simple to step through that invisible wall. Waves of relief and soul-shaking gratitude rise from the pit of my stomach and flow up my ribs to overwhelm my open heart. A sob escapes my too-tightly-held throat. For the first time, I am willing to take Him on His terms.

Finally.

Finally, I am not afraid.

Finally, I want God more than I want anything else.

Finally, I am not resisting the body and the life He has given me.

Finally, I am open to His will instead of clinging to my own.

"Okay, God. I give up. Let's do it Your way."

Finally, my heart is changed, and I am ready.

Finally, I surrender.

After eighteen years of amenorrhea, the glacial runoff carries away a lifetime of striving and pain. My body reunites with my spirit, never again to be parted. To date of this publication, I've not missed a single menstrual cycle. Each monthly cycle is to me a reminder of this phenomenal healing, a sacred symbol of peace, relief, and gratitude. Each and every time it comes, I praise. The holy water flowing through me is a tangible sign that for today, my body, mind, and spirit are aligned with a will Higher than my own, that I am in the Flow of the life He has given me. And that is truly all I want.

Never again do I step on a scale nor count a single calorie, nor even feel a strong desire to; a change of heart is no less miraculous to me than the healing of the blind, the walking of the lame. The chains that bound me are simply gone, evaporated, and exposed as the illusion they always were. The carving out, creating unexpected new terrain: open, wild, and free.

BODY IMAGE
BECKY MOLLER, NOVEMBER 2016

I was never meant to be a sculpture of perfection
Streamlined for the showroom
Flawless lines to be admired.

I was always meant to be real,
Skinned knees and bloody elbows, bumps and lumps and bruises,
Battle-worn with scars and cellulite.
A holy vehicle to experience this life.

Soft-pillow tummy,
Small mountain of my shame.
Why am I so afraid of you?
You represent the parts of me that I can't control
And don't want to choose
But somehow still do.
The parts that others will call ugly
And when pointed out, will make them feel
A little more superior.

I'm so afraid that if I don't appear flawless
That I won't matter.
Why?
Because at times it's been true.
I shrunk with fear,
All my insides sucked out by my desperate clinging
To find success
And matter.
And suddenly I did,
In ways I never had before.
So when the fear sets in,
It is really asking quite a lot to tell me to let go
And be.
I can only do it when I feel
You
So close
That I cannot be
Confused about
Who
I Am.

CHAPTER TWENTY-FIVE
LETTING GO

In the weeks following Full Disclosure, Holly's yoga class becomes my mid-week spiritual staple, a refuge that feels like a necessity more than a luxury. My nine-year-old daughter Madi joins me, and we drive to the library each week to move and breathe, to feel and re-center and survive. Hardly a week passes that I'm not in tears during the final resting posture of Savasana, releasing powerful emotions or meandering through visions that redefine my conception of my true nature and my Higher Power.

Madi loves coming with me. As a dancer, she excels here, and not just at the postures. Even at nine years old, her soul runs like a ferocious river: powerful, deep, and expansive. Our weekly yoga pilgrimages become a holy oasis: we share our Savasanas on car rides home as Love reveals itself through each meditation. Together, we discover the embodied language of Spirit, and we're amazed at how much we can know, how much we can understand, and how much we can share, without words capable of capturing the knowledge. We are amazed at how different we can feel when nothing outside of us has changed. Even at nine years old, these are rememberings that the soul can grasp.

Without realizing it, I am showing my daughter how to heal; how to face pain and move through it. I'm showing her how to reach out and be seen; to show up for yourself and not care who sees you fall apart. How to look inward to find herself and look upward to find her next right step. How to put her heart and life and love and wholeness over all the other stuff. But when my pain fills me to the brim, there's no avoiding the overspill onto those I want to protect most.

One day, Holly pulls me aside after class. "Hey, I just wanted you to be aware…sometimes when you're in meditation, Madi is just lying there watching you with tears pouring down her cheeks."

My heart breaks. One of the hardest things I've had to hold, then and now, is my daughters' pain from all this mess. But I can't deny that this pain sits unavoidably juxtaposed to the glow of Divine Love that radiates like the sun between us each time we leave the library together. In some intangible, mystical way, my daughter and I are intertwined in the tendrils of both trauma and healing, connected by a cosmic web that cannot be escaped. Somehow, she carries it all with me, a sturdy buttress to my still often-unsteady soul. And as I gaze across to the passenger seat and we drive back home to uncertainty, I pray that God will help her bear the cost of all that I couldn't protect her from. That I can somehow give her the tools and strength and soul-level trust to allow life, however it presents itself, to serve her awakening, come what may.

This standing mother-daughter date becomes another safety net, weaving a thick cloth of divine insight one thread at a time into the new blank space of our undone life. Each week, the now-familiar postures release my fearfully stored emotions in an organic dance of healing. My grief bubbles up through hip openers, my rage releases as I reverse my Warrior, my pride unravels as I get more comfortable being upside-down. I wear my hair loose and hide behind it; it covers the tears that often overflow from my practice.

Yoga is another form of holy run-off, clearing clutter from my mind and body. Stepping onto my mat becomes a behavioral response: it taps into the parts of my subconscious, now fully engaged in the serious and unruly business of soul-shifting. The poses are simple and familiar, but the comprehensive effect is stunning, clearing space for divine connection that surpasses anything I've experienced in all my buttoned-up religiosity. And the whole dance is aimed to prepare a wide-open mental canvas for the grand finale: my meditative wanderings.

By now, Holly has guided me often enough that I've cracked the code for myself. No matter what her prompt is on any given day, I can find my way into my own profound encounters through a simple, reliable recipe guided by my own subconscious need.

Step One: Begin with a safe haven, a place that feels so home-like, it is written on the very cells of your body. Know this place so deeply that your mind, body, spirit can recreate it in your imagination simply with one conscious breath: you will know because with practice, such a place, such a breath, can activate the relaxation response in your brain with a magical immediacy that begins to feel like warm, sticky, honey-Love pouring over your head and down your shoulders.

My safe place almost always starts on the beach: the same beach in Door County, Wisconsin, that I've traveled to every summer for as long as I can remember. Soft sand covers my toes; a soft breeze kisses my cheek and whispers through the trees along the shoreline. Light sparkles on the ripples across the lake. This place carries the stillness of a dozen moonlit nights glowing across the water, the magic of a hundred minnows nibbling at my toes, the power of scores of thunderstorms rattling windowpanes, the presence and belonging of grandmas and grandpas, aunts and uncles laughing over decks of cards, cousins shrieking through wiffle-ball games in sprawled-out fields. Through every season of my life, this place remains the constant, unchanging reminder of who I really am; of all that is timeless, beyond me and within me.

Step Two: Invite a Higher Power into this space with you. For some people, this step takes open-minded creativity and intentional practice, but it was easy for me. I had been raised in a faith that nurtured my internal spiritual connection. Maybe I called it the Holy Ghost, but whatever you call it, I was well-versed in the goosebumpy thrill from head to toe that signified to me a connection to Something Greater Than Myself. This embodied signal was a spiritual language that translated, and it took on new meaning through my new tools.

Holly was a Mormon like me, and she often entwined a familiar Heavenly Father or resurrected Savior into her meditations: masculine beings with exalted bodies of flesh and blood, creating intimate and compassionate encounters that felt safe and familiar. But her intuitive flow also played new possibilities into my traditional perceptions: a Higher Power might approach as a beam of light, sometimes It would make Its way toward me as a gentle river, sometimes a steady tree or a light or ungraspable cloud. Many times, a Higher Power came in the form of a Heavenly Mother, opening my mind to the unique textures and love-tones of the Divine Feminine. The loving heavenly entities of Holly's meditations felt seamless to my upbringing but wider, boundless, and freer. Higher Power meditations put action and universal images to the Divine Beings I had learned about my whole life but never personally experienced. Each week, the Love I felt in this space overwhelmed me, one meditation at a time. More than anywhere else, my yoga mat has been the holy ground where I allowed myself to be undone, where my brain's been rewired, and my core beliefs have shifted in a cellular way.

* * *

...Today, I see my Higher Power coming towards me as a man dressed in white, through the clouds, a bright light emitting love, warmth, and peace. We have met on this beach again and again in meditation, while the corporeal me lies on my yoga mat in the library. These meditations have become the foundation of our new relationship, the safety I retreat to when the confusion and uncertainty is too much. Out there in my real life, I may not know what is real or right, what has been good or bad, but *this* feels like home. When I'm here with God, I seem to be traveling with the part of me that never left Him, that knows exactly who He is. It feels so easy. I trust It.

As He approaches, I move toward Him and He scoops me into His arms, our usual greeting. He is always so delighted to see me. He allows me to nestle into His embrace, gently rocking me back and forth like a mother rocks her child. Here I can rest. Here I am safe. I feel the tension ease out of my shoulders and chest, my heart-space melts open...there is no need for a guard. This is home.

He gently sets me down when I am ready, and I look up at Him and grin as we wiggle our toes in the sandy beach. There is never anything particular to do in these meditative spaces. There is no agenda. We just *are,* in perfect contentment, and He seems to delight in the tiniest things, like watching butterflies or feeling the ticklish imprint of bug's legs crawl across our skin.

His hand, sure and steady, envelops mine, and we begin to walk toward the lush foliage along the shore. With no sense of urgency, He pauses, and we stoop down to take a closer look at a sad and spindly little plant. Its leaves are dry and papery, black and burnt, scorched from too much heat.

Suddenly, it registers that we are looking at *me:* that this plant is a mystical symbol for my own unfolding soul. I resist the urge to look away and instead study the full extent of my withered self with morbid curiosity: the plant is wilted with ragged leaves, shriveled stem, and fallen petals. My stomach drops and I wonder: *Is it dead?*

My Higher Power seems to read my heart and, with great tenderness and purpose, He reaches towards the plant, guiding my hand to do the same. Before I realize what's happening, we grip the stem firmly, and with His steady hand around my shaking one, we jerk that plant right out of the ground from the roots up.

But now I stand, bereft, in shock, with the remnants of this dead plant that is me in my upturned hands, feeling the loss cold and hard in my stomach. Confusion blows through my shattered brain like the wind off the lake that sends wisps of my hair flying in all directions. I am stunned and unstable. My breath quickens and I start to panic. *This can't be right!*

But in my peripheral view, I realize He is not finished. In one swift motion, almost in stride with the pruning, He reaches down into the earth and His strong hands carefully place a new seed. I watch as He scoops dirt and pats it down with tenderness and care. Somehow, I understand that He is nurturing a new start: a fresh beginning of me.

Like magic, tiny green shoots start to curl up from the sandy soil, blooming whites and soft pinks, bringing color to the dark and dismal beach. A storm is brewing, but I am captive, transfixed by the ease with which new life blossoms under the care of His miraculous healing hands.

"Beautiful," I whisper, fingering the fragile petals in reverent awe.

But I am still too fearful to wonder for long. Grief from my gut tugs me back to the body I stand in, the metaphorical remnants of who I have been lying lifeless and broken in my hands. Sadness overwhelms my heart until it might burst open, ominous thunderclouds gathering in the sky that express all the rage and fear I feel inside.

"What am I supposed to do with this?" My words come out as an accusation more than a question, ripped from my throat towards the heavens as I lift the ragged carcass in my outstretched arms. He is gone, and I am alone at the beach, small and defiant.

A powerful breeze plunges from behind me and carries my words into the open and blustery sky. Now dead scratchy leaves are also blowing through the air, flying out of my hands, up towards the gloom, and out across the water. I panic, terrified, desperately grasping at the black shreds in the air. I am resisting, hard.

"No! No! I am not ready! I am not ready to lose these! Please… I'm not ready to let them go! I don't want them to just disappear like they don't even matter!" Tears stream down my face. I claw at the air. "This was me…it was who I am. This was my goodness. This was my pain, this was my suffering. This was…so much. This was…everything. If I let go…it's like it won't even matter. It's like it will be forgotten…maybe I'll get hurt again… Oh please, God… I'm not ready to let go yet…"

From behind, my Higher Power places a gentle, steadying hand on my back and watches the black ash scatter with me. His hand is so steadying and strong, like Holly's hand when I'm resting in child's pose on my yoga mat. *"You are supported."*

In His touch, there's no pressure, no judgment, no attempt to rescue me from my temper tantrum. He is with me in my sadness. He holds room for all my tears. He just waits, with perfect understanding and infinite patience.

"As long as it takes," He seems to say through His steady presence. And with so much space, my sobs eventually slow, and I grow quiet. I feel the breeze on my skin like a gentle kiss. As my breath slows and my heart relaxes, my view widens. I begin to see something besides obliteration in the dark specks of me floating farther and farther beyond my reach.

The remnants are disappearing into the thundering sky, absorbed into the heavy cloud cover. The sky will reform into clouds that will one day burst forth into life-giving rain. Those nourishing droplets will eventually reach this very beach and be the very thing that allows this new plant to grow, thrive, bloom, become. In a way, they will be reborn: something new, something useful.

In my mind's eye, I already envision fragments of the old papery leaves in the dirt around my new burgeoning blossoms, imbuing life and depth for this fragile, pink and white version of me to grow. The old pieces of me: my false belief systems, my coping strategies, my ego tricks, even my grief and my pain and my fear of being hurt again...they needed to be uprooted, I see that now. But oh, how it hurts to let them go! As the particles dissipate into the air, I recognize this surrender as the bravest thing I have ever done...

* * *

Letting go of the old me doesn't mean that my pain doesn't matter. It doesn't mean that what happened was okay or that I'm somehow giving it permission to happen again. Letting go means creating space for something new to grow. It means trusting the creative process of the Universe: from life to death, from destruction to rebirth, from pain to progress, from frozen glacier to empty, open terrain...with hope and trust of a vibrant landscape to come.

The remnants of my suffering are the magical ingredients that will allow me to thrive and grow into something more beautiful, stronger, softer, deeper...different. There is loss in letting go of the illusion of all I once was, but my sadness settles into a deep knowing, a willing acceptance. My heart expands and opens with gratitude and trust.

I can do this. I can let go, if I know this sacred passage wasn't wasted; that all I've been through wasn't for nothing.

I can do this. I can let the old me die. I can allow this new seed inside of me to blossom in His hands. I can stop wishing for my old life and start fully living my new one, wherever it may take me.

I can surrender.

MONKEY ON MY BACK
BECKY MOLLER, OCTOBER 2017

Fear is a Monkey on my back,
Jumping on my shoulders,
Crashing cymbals in my ears.
Telling me that
I am Unworthy,
Unlovable, Inadequate,
And sooner or later,
I will be abandoned!!

The pain of it crushes my soul,
Crumbles my spinal column.
My insides implode and I tremble under the weight.
So weak. So powerless.

Until I realize it's just a Monkey.
And I pull it gently from my shoulders
And into my lap.
Setting cymbals aside, cradling it in my arms.

"Hello, old friend," I say.
"You are trying to protect me again."

And I lovingly send it on its way,
Patting its rear end from behind
As it scampers off,
Cymbals crashing,
To return another day
And I am free
To see Truth and understand
What I need to change
Or surrender,
Without the drama.
The secret to growth seems to be
Learning
To make friends with the Monkey.

CHAPTER TWENTY-SIX

TRACING BACK

New awareness sometimes cuts through like a sharp gorge, but it's always connected to other meandering streams if you follow it far enough down the way. So, as I start to release my limiting perceptions, my mind eventually makes its way downstream to my sexuality, a tender thorn in my side that's festered since Nate's original *Sunday Night Disclosure*. Full Disclosure has only served to exacerbate this wound: leaving me alone in the welcome safety of my own bed, wondering nightly what God could possibly have been thinking when He created sex.

I spend hours of my time perusing old journals, both mine and Nate's, searching for answers, for some kind of sign of what was to come. Stupefied that I didn't sense the incessant coping sooner. I look for evidence of his acting-out episodes, of his decision to hide important information from me when we were dating. For evidence that he did truly love me...or that he didn't. For something that could help me make sense of where I now sit and where to go next. But the more I read, the less I know. None of it satisfies. Reading the voices of the ghosts we once were only leads me to more questions, more sadness, more illusions to surrender.

I bring all of these to my yoga mat, and as I make space in meditation, unexpected memories float to the surface, weaving a map to the secret location that holds my core beliefs.

First, I hear my mother's voice, clear as day, commenting on celebrity gossip. "How sad," she says, "that Mick Fleetwood could never be with Stevie Nicks. You know, that's the woman he really loved, but he was already married. The poor man was trapped."

I feel myself wince and my heart sting. *Hmmm…that's interesting.*

There's nothing special about this particular instance; I've overheard my mother break down similar scenarios throughout my life with off-handed, seemingly harmless social-consumerist remarks…*so why did this comment show up in my meditation? And why does it sting so bad?*

I lean in and recognize there's a hook here for me that feels bigger than this comment alone. It's the flippancy with which she talks about such affairs. There's an energy to it. It triggers my stomach and catches my breath. It springs tears behind my eyes. *Why?*

There's a voice now in my head, hands on hips, defiant, defensive, desperate, proving:

Her off-handed opinions always seem to imply that something's wrong with the wife! That the wife must be cold and distant. That there must be a reason for the man to go looking elsewhere. That if the man left, then there must be something wrong with her. And it's so…unfair!!!

And now I feel the shame creeping up the back of my neck, that old familiar darkness seeping into my skin and down into my soul.

Is that what she thinks about me?

Is that what I think about me? When Nate left, it meant there was something wrong with me? I must be cold and distant. Poor Nate was trapped in a bad marriage. Poor Nate will never be able to be with the one he really wants.

My inner voice so clearly mirrors my mother's unconscious belief systems, her unprocessed perceptions of safety, and I see how this voice has become my own through years of shame and fear. In the aftermath of Full Disclosure, with all the new awareness of the enormity of Nate's behaviors before I even entered the scene, *does it still have me in its grasp?*

Before I can answer, the meditation shifts and now I see my father, adoring my mother, spoiling her, catering to her. She is his queen on a pedestal. For as long as forever, he has only had eyes for her. I see the pages of their high school yearbooks, pages I perused for my whole childhood. I see a schoolmate's comment scrawled in pen: "Have a great summer. You are one lucky guy. Heidi is a great-looking girl."

Dad was the student body president and captain of the football team. Mom was the cheerleader. They were prom king and queen; the wholesome dreams high school was made of. I'd heard the story a hundred times: he fell for her at a junior high picnic and chased her for years before she finally agreed to be his girlfriend. He waited faithfully for her when she went to college far across the country for a full year. She was his world, his universe. What had she done to deserve such devotion? Just exist. That's how valuable she is. That's how much he loves her. That's what someone would do for such a "great-looking girl."

These are not memories I expect, and I'm caught off guard by the painful emotion that surfaces with them. I start to argue with myself: *My parents' love story is a cherished treasure to me. They are each other's one and only love. They are each other's everything. I love their story!*

But I cannot deny the knife in my heart and the tears that spring to my eyes. *Something is wrong with you!* Another voice screams in my head. *Your husband left you! What did you do to make him go? You aren't the stuff of pedestals and prom queens. It's so sad that your husband had to look elsewhere for what you lack. Now, everyone knows you're a cold bitch. I bet they weren't even surprised.*

In my mind, I'm suddenly sure that my family has discussed this: has shaken their heads at each other and raised their eyebrows. "She *is* a handful..." they shrug their shoulders. "What can you do? She's a lot. Should have seen that one coming."

My heart beats faster, and humiliated tears stream at the imagined story.

But now the meditation morphs again, and I see my older brother, the one I adore. He is my pedestal, the bright and shiny example I've looked up to and been pressed under my entire life. In the memory, he is newly married, and I am barely twenty. I've been in Europe for the summer semester, backpacking the continent—single, young, adventurous, and free.

I fly home for his wedding reception and cannot wait to see him. We meet for lunch, and I'm excited to hear about married life. I pull up a chair as we settle into our sandwiches, and quickly realize that all he can talk about, almost every word out of his mouth, is about sex. How great it is, how much he loves it. It's all he seems to be able to think about. His entire summary of his first month of marriage revolves around one thing: his unlimited access to his wife's naked body. I am shocked; intrigued. Surprised, to say the least.

This is helpful information. This is good to know. I had no idea that sex was going to be so important.

And now my meditative mind, clearly weaving a pattern, connecting unrelated dots I haven't considered in years, skips to the night before my wedding. It's my last night of virginity. I cannot even remember if I am nervous, although I must be—because I wake up the next morning with a mouth full of canker sores. My mom has always been open with me about sex education, so there's no need for a full "Birds & the Bees" discussion. She simply offers one piece of advice; one nugget of wisdom:

"Sex is a powerful thing, Becky. You will see. It's such a big deal to men. So it's important that you say yes as much as you can. If you say yes, it will keep them happy. And that's a lot of power, you know, because it's something they can only get from you. It keeps them close."

And now tears of awareness begin to stream down my face as these seemingly disjointed memories fill my mind: my mom's off-handed comments about Fleetwood Mac of all things. My parents' high school love story. My brother's take on his honeymoon marriage. My mom's wedding night advice. Separate stars creating the fuzzy constellation I've been using to navigate my sexuality for my entire adult life.

I lie on my mat, and I breathe. I breathe and I lie and I feel. Scenes flooding the movie screen of my mind, narratives overlapping, belief systems clicking into place. I see it all now.

I see how sex became a checklist. How sex became an obligation. How sex became a way to manage moods and settle situations. How sex became about proving my worth, desperately trying to keep Nate happy, and how confusing it was that all my yeses were never enough. They didn't bridge the gap. They didn't make him stay. And how it all led me to conclude, with the finality of indisputable fact, that it was my fault. I was not enough and never would be. I was cold and distant, and he was the victim. I hadn't kept him close enough.

That's where those beliefs had come from. Through best intentions and imperfect lenses, just like my own. I can trace them back now. I can see where they started. That's what I believed then. *But what do I believe now?*

Now that I can see, I get to choose. And so, I make a commitment to myself: I will not use sex as a way to manipulate or manage my husband. I will be free of timetables. I will not worry or track how long it has been between intimate encounters, and if I feel pressure or pouting from my husband, I will address it. I will not take responsibility for his God-hunger or emotional dysregulation. I will only connect when I can connect authentically. I will not use sex to solve our marriage problems. I will reject the belief that my husband's sexual appetite is my responsibility.

These old beliefs are ones I choose to let go of. These old beliefs have not served me nor kept me safe. I can forgive myself for my blindness. I can let go of the pain of the past.

But how do You want me to move forward, God? What does my sexuality mean to You? What does it mean to me?

As the icy water carries away the contaminated run-off, what will be left, solid and essential? What new landscape do I want to create?

What Do I Want?
Becky Moller, November 2022

I want to create,
To dance and play,
To see the world through magic spectacles
That make everything *beautiful*
And Divine.

I want to move through life
With poetry pouring out of me,
Savoring every last drop,
Without a worry

Of reward or applause.
I want to perform only for
My own firmament,
Of angels, Gods, and
Awakened Ones,

Letting Their Light
Flow through my
Tireless hands and
Willing Heart.

CHAPTER TWENTY-SEVEN

HAPPILY IN THE MOMENT, ONE DAY AT A TIME

Nate and I have been separated in our home for two months when we load up the minivan in mid-October for a Fall Break family trip. This excursion marks a slightly terrifying experiment—we've booked a cottage in the Redwoods for four days, and we'll be sharing a room and a bed for the first time in months. My guard is up. I am on high alert for narcissistic behaviors and skeptical that this whole thing may just be a disaster.

By mid-way through the 18-hour drive, most of me wants to climb back into my own bed, safe and alone. Nate is already irritated with the incessant squabbling from the back seats, and my body freaks out every time he sharply chides our little ones. I'm so afraid to crack any door open in my heart, fiercely intent to protect my kids and myself from his dark, manipulative side.

We're all relieved when we eventually arrive at our quirky VRBO cottage, complete with cobwebs and a wood-fired stove, damp and dark, nestled in the towering trees. There's a Jurassic world right outside our window and the smoky fragrance of burning logs inside. And despite myself, I begin to relax into a feeling of mystery and possibility. After all, I am fully armed with my 12-step and mindfulness tools: detach with love, hold boundaries, pause and breathe into my tight places—body and soul, reach out to my sponsor, read recovery literature, surrender.

And now that we're settled here, my husband is showing consistent recovery behavior: humble, honest, and accountable...and grateful to be together, too. He's been showing these behaviors for several weeks now—quietly, without fanfare this time. Since I stopped giving gold stars, he's stopped pandering for them.

My deeper surrender since Full Disclosure has shifted the energy I bring to our relationship. I'm no longer managing him because I no longer need him to choose me. I know it and so does he. It's slightly terrifying. Without the foregone conclusion of my determined grasping, neither one of us feels entirely sure—*What is going to happen?*

Without me to report to, he's been left to decide for himself what he really wants. His recovery is now his own. And although early recovery is a faltering toddler, sometimes tipping back into old coping modes of attack, resentment, defensiveness, and self-seeking, I can see that he's quicker to recognize and quicker to make amends. He's prioritizing his weekly therapy sessions and 12-step meetings, even shifting his schedule to make these happen with the steady determination of a grown-up acting from his own volition.

I observe all this with the ambivalence of a detached observer. Healthy boundaries have given me space to focus on my own stuff, instead of being constantly distracted by his, and for two months, I honestly haven't paid much attention to him. This is uncomfortable progress for both of us. We've never been more unplugged from each other, never more out of sync with our former ping-pong game of triggers and clinging, attacks and reactions, validation-seeking and resentment. We've never stood more on our own two feet as differentiated humans.

My attention is now fully on my *own* recovery: *What do I need to let go of to feel God at my center today?*

It's a tenuous honeymoon, and I'm still on shaky ground with myself, building trust one moment, one day at a time. I have to stay closely connected to my breath and body to keep my feet on the ground. I check in with myself dozens of times a day:

How am I doing? Can I feel my fingertips? My toes?
Is my heart open? What's at my center right now?

The idea of exposing myself to Nate on this family trip is enough to throw my shaky center off-balance. What if I slide right back into my codependent clinging? Parts of me are still so fragile and unsure: I see the delicate pink and white blossoms in my mind. I want to be so careful with them. I want them to grow. *Maybe it's too soon...*

But it's difficult not to feel a sense of magic when we spend our days walking in wet sand, barefoot on the beach, kids jumping white crests, feeling the rhythmic pull of the entire ocean. There's a sense of something solid in these ever-moving waves, in transition, in change. My life is in transition, too. Maybe there's something to trust in this constant pull, this ebb and flow. Maybe there's a way to find steadiness in what's moving, what's unexpected. It feels like a new sentiment I'm trying on for size.

And then, there are the trees, these towering and majestic giants. Walking under their canopy, I feel like I'm breathing in new air, new life. I'm floored by the sheer immensity of existence around me, the impossibility of stopping a Universe hell-bent on expansion, through darkness and light. My heart is expanding, too, and it's a sensation I'm coming to trust more than anything I've ever known.

As we hike along trails with our littles, my husband and I begin to talk lightly together, to laugh. We are cautious and careful with one another, like teenagers on a first date. We don't want to assume anything, to take a single thing for granted. This energy between us is precious and flimsy, like the thin and spindly starts of the dewy vines winding their way along the forest floor. Any heavy tread of careless boot might tear it to shreds. We're both mindful of each footstep, taking note to place things just so, fully aware of what the crunch feels like under our feet.

How does this feel? I keep asking myself.

Do I feel safe?

Does this feel right?

Do I want to say yes to this?

Breathing in this air is like inhaling hope for fresh beginnings. Each divinely crafted skyscraper reaches out in maternal protection, shielding me from too much rain or sun, helping me relax into the surety that something beyond comprehension in Mother Earth has always held me and always will. Dirt floor feels soft and solid under my shoes: each step, supported. Strong trunk behind my back, sturdy and steadying, nudging me to trust, to risk, to know.

I am surrounded by an army of ancient sentinels, every particle in the Universe conspiring to support me, to advance me toward my soul's deepest fruition. Like the giants around me, something in me wants to soar. Something in me is rooted deep, deep enough to reach for something more, more than I currently know. More than I can currently see. Here in these woods, I can feel it—deeper than the God of skin and bones who tests and tries and puts people in boxes of worthiness. This Divinity is flowing in every molecule of dewy air that I breathe. It's in the green moss that turns a rotting tree into a soft and brilliant carpet teeming with life. It's Life living through us. It's all that is and ever was, here in this forest, alive in my body. Waking up to Its own magic and freedom and splendor and unspeakable heights—through me. Through this sacred moment.

I get to choose. I am supported. I want to live, to open my heart wide as this sky and shock myself at my ability to love. And Nate is the beautiful human standing next to me, holding my hand.

This turning towards each other is not a magical momentary whim, not a rushed free-fall into romantic wishes, but a deliberate birthplace for hope and an intentional burial ground for fear. This Jurassic world is where I start to trust myself enough to realize: *I get to make this choice.*

I can choose to take this risk: to trust a Higher Power that I can't contain or comprehend. To step fully into a life with no guarantees. To trust *myself.*

I will know recovery behavior. I will feel when it is right and when it is not. I can let life move through me. I don't need to see the ending; I only need the next right step. One day at a time. And if it falls apart again, all of this will still be here, to hold me.

I am not who I was. I cannot be destroyed again, not the same way. Today, I am the trees and the wind and the ocean. I am the spacious sky and the joyful birds. I am Life itself.

I breathe in the Redwoods, and I look at Nate and without uttering a word, *I choose* to let my heart open again.

* * *

When we return home, we tentatively move Nate back into our bedroom. I'm happy to have his warmth beside me in bed and his friendship to soften my days. Our interactions feel safe and accountable. Things are going well, and within a few weeks, he tells me he's planned a fancy dinner date and wants me to clear my calendar.

But my heart races at his request, and part of me wants to run away. I've known this night was coming. In fact, I specifically asked for it: a formal new proposal with the jewelry to prove it.

"If we're going to officially decide to stay in this marriage," I had told him, "I need to know why it will be different this time. I need you to take time to answer all my written concerns from Full Disclosure—officially… and I need a new ring—I don't care how fancy. It doesn't need to be expensive. It just needs to be *real*. I need a new proposal. I just need a totally new rendition of the whole deal."

I must know I am getting to choose this time. I must know there is nothing off-limits to talk about. I must know that I've done everything I can to ensure that this relationship is safe.

As our date approaches, my mind remembers where we started on this journey. Two weeks in: *I need to forgive.* Four weeks in: *The time to grieve is passing.* Six weeks in: *Perhaps I need to be compelled to rely on Nate for guidance.* My bishop's early counsel: *Nothing good can come of discussing this further. I cannot detach from Nate during my process of recovery.* And the real kicker: *God is not leaving me. He is realigning me with His plan, re-establishing Nate as the head of our spiritual household.* Wow.

The juxtaposition of where we were and what it's actually taken to get us to where we are now stands in laughable contrast. And after three long years and a lifetime of unraveling, I'm afraid of making this decision real. The decision to stay. The decision to start again. The decision to say, "I'm in this for sure. Let's start over." The decision to give up the option of playing the "Well, then I guess I'm leaving!" card when things get hard.

My husband is nervous, too; I can feel it as we drive the hour to Salt Lake City. He pays for parking, and we walk down the frigid streets to where this all started a lifetime ago: the Japanese restaurant where he proposed, seventeen years past.

Who was I back then? Who was he? I try to capture those people in my mind, and my heart stings. *Those people are gone. Those people were idiots. I hate those people.* The old fearful narrative picks up like a broken record.

I take a pause and name it.

Hello, old friend—I see you. Let's just let you pass on by...

I settle into a soft cycle of deep breathing and bring myself back to the present moment.

It is fine, I am fine.

I am standing in a restaurant; I am waiting to be seated.

I am here, in the Now.

I close my eyes and try to feel the energy in my feet.

Here I am. I am safe.

I am grounded. Here we go.

They seat us in a private room, and like in other Asian restaurants, it's one where you take off your shoes and sit on the floor around the table. I feel grateful for the walls around us. Nate has big plans for the night, I can see. He opens his bag, and it is filled with notecards and envelopes, flowers, and a portable speaker.

Can I do this? I wonder. *Can I really do this, or am I going to fall apart and ruin everything with my crazy emotions?*

I take a breath and reach for courage.

I can do this. I am doing this.

We order extravagantly, and between each course, he presents an envelope labeled with my questions and concerns. This one reads, "Why this time will be different." Another, "Why I want to marry you." One reads, "Things I am learning about myself." The words he reads as he opens each envelope carry his heart. His voice is shaky and soft; light years from the robot I saw in our therapist's office three months earlier.

The moment starts to feel bigger than my body can contain. Our poor waitress awkwardly brings in food as tears stream from the corners of my eyes and I fight to choke back ugly sobs. And my husband is always right here, letting me be exactly where I am, clasping my hand, waiting patiently.

"As much time as it takes," his energy seems to say.

I feel the Light shining through him, the same Light I'm coming to know so well in myself. There's so much more room for it now, unclouded by the fear and justifications, grasping and lies. The work he's put in over the past months and years is paying its priceless dividends: his clear presence offers a precious safety that cannot be fabricated. His energy is humble, honest, accountable, and present. His eyes are clear and true. Like the boy I fell for all those years ago.

We don't talk much, just a few words about the incredible scallops are all the chit-chat I can muster. My heart is breaking and mending, molding and shifting in unintentional ways all at once. But we welcome the stillness as a friend, and it bathes us in its timeless, healing magic. I begin to consider Nate carefully, much more carefully than I did years ago in similar settings. I let my gaze take him in, head to toe, soul to soul, not with judgment but with curiosity.

Who are you, Nate? What's really in there? I want to know.

I take my time and feel the full agency of not being afraid of whatever path may lie ahead. Today, I'm not thinking about saying the right thing or if he thinks I'm pretty. Today I just want to be present enough to see *all* of him. Just like in Full Disclosure, my heart longs to know the Truth— whatever that may be. And with the dawn of awakening, another perfectly timed divine gift on this journey, I feel my eyes clear, and my vision expand.

I see Him, with a spacious freedom that carves out the deepest kind of embodied knowing. There He is—right in front of me—so much more than our sad story. So much bigger than his biggest mistakes. So much greater than his career or titles. There He is—a beautiful broken soul, just begging to be loved. He is Me. We are the same. And it's so exquisite.

And in this transcendent moment, I know, deep down, that I can only see all of him because I have learned to see all of me. I have faced my fears. I have faced my ugliness and my hidden scars. I have pieced together every moment I could uncover that hardened me with pain or shame or regret. I have seen the little girl crying underneath each one. I have held her and loved her and seen her golden and often misguided heart. I have known a Perfect One who has literally held her in His arms, who is capable of holding it all and turning even the darkest smudges magically to gold. I have felt this same One in me, somehow inexplicably the very deepest and truest expression of who and what I Am.

It is every Savasana on my mat, every 12-step meeting I have attended, every therapy-hangover I have endured, every journal page I have scribbled, every surrender phone call I have made, every conscious breath I have offered that has brought me to this moment. Each moment guiding my heart towards its deepest desire and most fervent longing: giving me new eyes to see through a new lens of deep and divine compassion, an untamed and intrepid trust.

And what do I see?

I see the little boy in the bathroom—alone, afraid, no words, no way. I see the incorrigible tease who won my heart—steady, persistent, easy laugh, listening ear. I see his assurance that it would all work out, that I would make the right decision in the end and choose him. I see myself finding comfort from my own confusion as I laid my head on his chest and felt his steady heartbeat.

"You see?" his twenty-two-year-old self would wink at me. "My heart always beats steady for you. My heart knows exactly what it wants."

I see how first and always, he was my friend. I see roommates barging through the door as we lie on separate couches, breaking down the universe for hours on end. I see them shake their heads and roll their eyes, "Again?!"

I see a whole year of dating and friendship when that's all there was… just talks…no touch. And when we got serious, I can still remember how it felt to work through something hard: a disagreement, a fear, an uncertainty about the future, real and raw and vulnerable. How every time, he patiently talked it through with me until my heart felt completely understood. Safe. Settled. Seen.

And in one earth-shattering moment, something in me knows with absolute clarity that it wasn't all a lie. He saw me. He saw the real me. Not just the bright and shiny that I did my best to put out to the world, to win the applause, to be approved of. He saw me for me—the good, the bad, and the ugly. He was the only one who really always had. He was my best friend. He wanted to know everything about me, peel off all my layers. Understand my heart. He always had.

He had no idea that he was an addict. He had no idea that he would break my heart. And neither did I.

I drop my gaze to my anxious hands fumbling in my lap, tears dripping on the tablecloth, and with a deep and shaky breath, I forgive the twenty-year-old us, so naïve, so trusting, so confident, so blind. I forgive them for being idiots—for not knowing what they had not yet learned. I sit cross-legged at our scallop-covered table and feel the full weight of their hopes and dreams and shattered expectations, and I simply and deeply allow it all to be.

I accept the grief. I accept the pain. I accept it all as a part of our story. This is us. And we are still here. Maybe there is beauty in that. Maybe we don't have to be ashamed of who we are.

And I realize that this is Love.

As I feel the sweet relief of this painful surrender flood my body, I realize there is one thing left to do—my culminating act of true bravery. I need to look straight into his eyes: a gesture I've avoided for three years, a response to the pain of having those trusted eyes betray me so deeply. For three years, I was afraid to look.

I have no idea who you are. You are a complete stranger to me.

I never knew whether I would see the addict's mask of hatred and blame, or the gentle and mischievous boy I fell in love with. And I didn't know which one had hurt me more; which one would be more painful to find gazing back at me.

But today, I need to know and I'm willing to see, so I gather my courage. *Do I know you today?*

I take a deep breath, let my gaze settle, and lose myself in pools of blue. I tune into my body to invite what it knows, letting the stories of the boy from days past fall away and focusing instead on the man sitting before me.

Who are you today, Nate? Who are we?

We are so different from the kids who made a promise here seventeen years ago. I see the wrinkles around his eyes, the weather of passing years. Today, I know exactly what those eyes have seen. I know exactly who he has been. I know exactly what he is capable of in his blindest moments. I know exactly how painful this mystery called marriage can be.

But I also know what recovery looks like and feels like. Today, I have boundaries that keep me safe. I know how to take accountability for myself, and I know I can ask for accountability from him. Today, I know the Higher Power that lives in me, that will never abandon me or leave me alone. Today, I can feel the ground underneath me, and I know I am supported. Today, I don't need to believe in a fairytale or rely on a prince to carry me off to a shiny castle. Today, I am capable of loving the human being before me. Today, I am capable of loving myself.

After all we have been through together, I know him more deeply than anyone else in this world. He is a human being, with strengths and weaknesses, just like me.

Is that enough? Can I accept him as he is? Can I accept myself?

In his eyes, I see the same sparkle from seventeen years ago, begging me, pleading with me, just like back then, *"Love me."*

It's the same childlike hope that broke down my original barriers, but there's also something deeper: a heaviness, an accountability, a wisdom. He is growing up, just like me.

"Love me even though you've seen my worst. Love me even though I am broken. Love me even though I've hurt you worse than anyone else ever has. Love me and I will promise you today. That's all I can promise. I will choose God today. I will choose you today." His eyes and his painstakingly planned cards and envelopes plead with me. I hear it in his words. I see it in his eyes. I feel it in his energy. I trust it in my gut.

I reach out and take his hand, and I decide: this is a promise I can believe. This is, in fact, the only promise I want. Just today. I will choose you today. I will choose God today. Isn't that all any of us can offer? And I decide to promise my today, too. I decide to say yes.

"Let's buy a new ring." We've got just the stone in mind: an aquamarine, symbolic of rebirth and trust; of transformation and letting go.

"Let's start over. Let's build something new. One day at a time. Humble. Honest. Accountable. Present. Broken together.

"Because, Nate—I want to know the real you, too—the good, the bad, the ugly—and I think I'm finally starting to. I want to know everything about you—peel off the layers and discover the mystery over the years ahead. I want to understand your heart. I want to share my life with you. I know it might hurt. But I'm willing to take the risk.

"Let's be best friends again."

A DIFFERENT KIND OF LOVE STORY
BECKY MOLLER, JANUARY 2017

So now we have a different kind of love story.
Cause now we have a deeper kind of love.
It may not seem impressive to the masses,
But I know it's a miracle, a gift straight from above.

So now our hearts have scars in secret places,
For now we know exactly where we've been.
And now we know each day's another present,
To live so we won't go back there again.

Now we see each other much more clearly,
And now we truly feel each other's pain.
Now we share the winding road, without the expectations,
We are grateful for the sunshine, and we accept the rain.

Can words express the meaning of this journey?
Who knew that life could bring us so much good,
Wrapped in heartbreak, suffering, betrayal,
This life has brought a depth that smoother roads just never could.

So I'm speechless at the gratitude I feel now,
That every day we both decide to choose,
To fall in love and feel the joy and newness,
Of loving when we've everything to lose.

CHAPTER TWENTY-EIGHT

CLEARING MY SIDE
OF THE STREET

Finally, marriage, family, life, and heck—self-actualization—are thriving. Nate and I are so grateful to be together, not even *back* together but *reborn* together—building something new and entirely our own. Each day feels like a true gift from God, with some unspeakable gift to discover, and I cannot wait to uncover Her next surprise. Instead of falling to pieces at the crumbling ground, we've turned our glaciated mess into a slip and slide, throwing ourselves to the whim of the melting run-off, arms and hearts wide open to the adventure. *Wheeeeeeee!!!* Life is suddenly a wild game of upward and outward expansion, as real and strong in its momentum as our downward trajectory has been. We are on fire.

On our flight back to Utah from our Wisconsin Christmas, I officially start writing a memoir—a purpose I've been feeling in my bones for a long while now—maybe even from the earliest weeks of rock bottom, when poems poured out of me at four in the morning. We've traversed so much darkness, and it's finally beginning to feel useful. In fact, it feels like the most useful knowledge I've ever acquired—academic endeavors included. There's something in me that's calling to put it all into words; to somehow organize it into a container that can be shared, and the New Year offers the inspiration I need to actually start. Even as I open a fresh new Google Doc on my computer on our long flight home, my fingers are itching, and my stomach is full of butterflies.

This feels different than the hundreds of journaling pages I've filled. This feels like something more important. Even if it just gives clarity to my own story, my own healing—something in me simply must write it down. And so, I do, reserving months of Sunday afternoons for the challenging and healing endeavor of writing a book about trauma; of capturing this miraculous healing into digestible shape. As I make my way through, I recognize that even just taking the time to process this way makes me more useful to my fellows in recovery.

And Nate and I are now heavily involved in our 12-step community. He runs the website, I write the Foundation's anonymous recovery blog, and we also volunteer our time at weekly Executive Board meetings. We serve in our weekly groups and sponsor people as they make their way through the worst. We are in love with recovery life and surrounded by a Dream Team of recovery role models, friends, and supporters.

We need much less therapy, which leaves more in our bank account, though we both agree the thousands of dollars we've invested in therapy were money well spent. Even so, it feels empowering to know that we now have the tools to sustain our forward motion with less-frequent support. Our nightly check-ins are flooded with new and connecting insights about ourselves, life, healing, and the Divine. Our intimate life is finding new, optimal alignment with lightness and ease—no tracking, agenda, or pressure. Our emotional closeness, gratitude for each other, and passion for living translate sexually in all the best ways.

But with all this happy expansion, there is an undeniably sticky spot in our weekly routine. Church is a landmine of triggers. The more clearly my personal life falls into alignment, the more bitterness I feel about the ways this structure failed me. Each Sunday, I find myself frustrated that so much of the rhetoric is words that our lives have proven untrue. Equations that didn't add up. Unconscious egoic narratives of chosenness and rightness that sucked me in for decades before recovery showed me a healthier way.

There's no way around it. I am spinning again in Betrayal Trauma, only this time with my religion. My healing has opened Pandora's box, and I can't go back to an operating system that has proven unhelpful, unhealthy, and utterly egoic. Week after week, I see right through it. The more 12-step stories

I hear from traumatized wives and addicted husbands, the more I see the trickle-down harm of so many religious mindsets, and it makes me furious.

None of these principles points people towards the inner freedom I now know is possible. They're sending people on the same wild goose chase for perfection and perceived safety that Nate and I have spent the past three years recovering from. Somebody's got to say something! Somebody's got to stand up for the people whose stories don't fit the box.

Every time I catch a glimpse of my bishop, it feels impossible not to throw daggers. Whenever he addresses the congregation, my heart closes. It's hard to forget his damaging words in the aftermath of Nate's disclosures. *"Don't tell anyone about what has happened. Keep this between you and him. Just think how hard it must have been for him to tell you."*

It's hard to forget his chastisements towards me after my Sunday School trauma reaction. *"You've got to drop this, or it will ruin your marriage. Your problem is you're focusing too much on yourself. You've got to rebuild with your husband instead of rebuilding yourself."* I can't imagine more ignorant counsel to a traumatized woman.

Where would we be today if I had listened to him? And to think how he talked to me with such authority... I fume inside when he approaches. All along, I realize that bitterness is not the wolf I want to feed. But I am in bondage to the heart wall that protects me from the abandonment and rejection I feel from his arrogance and his office.

In time, my 12-step work gently reminds me: "If I am disturbed, there is something wrong with *me*."[6] So, I bring my gnawing irritation at my bishop to Steps 8–9 of the Twelve Steps, an invitation to make amends. I ask myself:

What wrongs inside of me need to be made right in this situation?

Bitterness. A closed heart. Feeling unsafe and unseen. Judgment. Arrogance.

How do I bring these into alignment, for the Greater Good? How do I clean my side of the street?

I sit stumped with these questions for several weeks until one day in meditation, a surprising awareness lands in my heart: I've been searching for

---

6 Alcoholics Anonymous Big Book (4th ed.) (2002). Alcoholics Anonymous World Services.

answers to how to make amends to my bishop, but in truth, I transgressed against *my Self* that day. I allowed my need for approval to silence my voice. I chose conformity over authenticity. I valued my place in the power structure over my personal integrity. And in some ways, I still do. Every single Sunday.

I am accountable for my own resentment. With this clarifying 12-step mantra, I suddenly know my next right step: I will write a letter. Not to apologize to my church leader, but to make amends to *myself.*

So, I prayerfully sit down and write, expressing from my deepest soul what has longed to be heard in this setting: The pain of this journey. The shock of having my faith structure fail me when I needed it most. What I wish my bishop had known years ago when I stepped into his office, only to be encouraged in directions that led me further from actual healing. The betrayal of being misguided by trusted authorities.

And as I start to give this bitter part of me a voice, I find she has more valuable things to say than I realized. She wants to talk about more than just my bishop, more than just the ways our few confrontations were harmful. She wants to be an advocate for Nate, too. She wants to voice what she wishes every bishop had known along the way, the dozens of bishops that Nate met with over two decades. Bishops who had no understanding of what was really happening, nor how to help, but still counseled from a place of authority, only leading Nate deeper into the trap. She writes about healing and accountability, about compassion and understanding, about the humility to say "I don't know" and the strength in referring people to trained specialists who do.

She writes about trauma and what it takes to heal from it. She even writes about patriarchy: the inherent unsafety of an exclusively male priesthood leadership, putting unfaithful husbands and betrayed wives under the jurisdiction of untrained men making judgment calls and giving counsel they have no business giving—all in the name of God. She writes about forgiveness and gratitude and growth. She ends by sincerely thanking the Bishop for what she honestly can: the obvious love and respect he feels for his own wife.

When the letter is finished, I review it with good-humored surprise: Whenever I let God be in charge, I always end up somewhere different from where I thought I was going. The letter is good and true, kind and compassionate, straightforward and informative. The bitter part of me has calmed down, and I can sense it in the open and relaxed space of my body. After all, there's no need to make noise when you clearly have an advocate. My Self is finally standing up for her...for me.

Without delay, I make an appointment, and soon I am sitting down across a wide desk, staring at my bishop's face. I have not sat here since our last painful encounter. I offer a silent prayer for compassion, I take a deep breath, I surrender the outcome, and I begin to read. As my voice floats into the Bishop's office, a familiar wash of healing emotions flows over me. With each carefully chosen word, I feel the strength of showing up for myself. I feel the calm grounding of the Divine within me. I feel clarity of purpose: my bishop's reaction is irrelevant. I am doing this for me.

As I finish the letter, with the ease and fluency that can only come from a Power greater than my own, I am filled to the brim with a deep love and appreciation for the man sitting across the desk from me, the same man I haven't been able to stomach for the past three years. I see him with fresh eyes, a veil lifted. He wants to be good, just like me. He is doing the best he can, just like me. He is willing to meet with me and generously offers his time and talents to serve me and others. What a blessing. What a Grace.

My bishop listens to my words without argument, and in the end, he allows them to be just as they are. He thanks me for sharing. I leave his office with a genuine hug, with gratitude in my heart, with a spring in my step. I have spoken my truth. I have made amends...to my Self. I have risked disapproving the authority figure in order to be right with me, to be right with God. And magically, forgiveness has come, another gift from heaven, without a battle, without a fight. Another heart-wall cleared from this magical melting run-off. Another miracle. I am beginning to expect them now.

This Practice was a win: a clear next step, taking me closer to expansion and freedom. But it's only one bite of the elephant. My wrestle with the church overall is not so cut-and-dried. So, what do I do with it?

What serves my awakening? What serves my family? What is my next right step?

ALL THAT I AM
BECKY MOLLER, OCTOBER 2023

Stepping into
All that I Am
Is so damn satisfying.

A percolating that wants to
Spill up over my shoulders
Explode out of my chest
And pierce the entire Universe,

Painting the sky with color and Light,
Inspiring the whole world to look up in wonder
And see for themselves…

God is everywhere!

Please forgive me
If I bowl you over on the way.
This Spirit-drug running through my veins
Has me high as a kite

And I've quite forgotten myself.

CHAPTER TWENTY-NINE

EXPANDING LOVE

I am lying on my yoga mat on my 36th birthday, feeling the weight of this milestone with my new aquamarine ring on my finger. It feels like a monumental relief to be past the treacherous days when our marriage was hanging in the balance. But still, it hits hard as I survey the empty expanse of my new horizon, the soft and malleable landscape that's replaced the former crisis.

It's been a hard day. Ever since trauma, my birthdays always seem to be hard, enticing me back to the haunting illusions of everything I thought my life was supposed to be. The wistful fear that my life is a failure and I am a disappointment hangs low like a haze. Even though I am happy, even though I am actively healing and so is my husband, even though trauma is mostly behind me and I even teach and write about it now...something about my birthday opens the trauma folder and the darkness sucks me under.

Even with all my progress, I am still clearing space, still in want of the magical run-off that carries off chunks of ego identity that have always kept me shallowly safe, but never truly served me. My birthday gift to myself is coming to yoga tonight, and I gratefully move and breathe and settle into the divine wanderings of my Savasana.

* * *

...I begin again on the Door County beach, the wind in my hair, the soft sand a pillow for my weary soul. I take a deep breath and feel tension ease from my shoulders and chest. I am safe. I can lay my burdens down.

As I slowly allow myself to melt into this familiar rest, I realize that I am resting into a lap. I look up to see my Higher Power. His loving eyes look straight into mine as He brushes my hair back from my cheek and softly strokes my head. Peace settles into my heart-space, and I allow Him to hold me. I am so glad He is here.

I gently realize He is holding a baby and prop myself up to gaze at the little one in His arms. She is a perfect, tiny bundle in a soft blanket, pink hands reaching up to grasp His finger in innocent trust. As I gaze with delight into her squinty face, I realize that I am looking at me. My breath halts in my throat and my heart pulls away, just a fraction, at the strangeness of seeing myself this way. Such a small resistance one might not even notice. But deep down, something registers: I am afraid of this tiny person in front of me.

Hmmm...that's interesting.

Slowly, as if inspired by the tension in my chest, apparitions of my former self appear across the beach in front of me, and I watch as the future of this tiny bundle unfolds: phantom visions of the girl I have been... I see myself writing feverishly and spinning math problems at the grade-school desk, spitting venomous words at a younger sister from a jealous fearful heart; reciting theatrical lines with unabashed gusto as Mom looks on with approval and peers giggle and point; cleaning the kitchen until it sparkles, awaiting her gold star, straight bangs low across her pimpled forehead.

Now she appears as a teenager, acne and braces and uncertainty in every movement, standing on the edge of the crowd, afraid to laugh...*is it the right time to laugh now?* Hiding in the back of the classroom, erasing correct answers to keep everyone happy and unthreatened. Now marching across the stage, receiving awards, certificates, honors, applause. Keep going, this is how you're making them love you.

Now spinning frenetically, moving faster, everything in fast-forward now, belting the song onstage, bowing to applause, laughing with friends, watching the lightning in the sky, breaking the boy's heart, driving in the car down country roads that go nowhere, anywhere, everywhere but home, singing at the top of my lungs. And now I am pounding each foot on a road and pounding with each step into my brain: *You are fat! You are fat! You are fat! And no one will ever love you.* And I am trying to be what the boy deserves, and I am falling for the first time, and I am saying good-bye, and my heart is breaking, and I am shocked at the pain of it.

And now I am in college, endless parade of boys, flings, dates, friends, fun. Now crying in my room, huddled in a ball, afraid to eat, afraid to fail, afraid to disappoint. Now Nate, a marriage, a honeymoon, and babies, and spinning, spinning, spinning, from cleaning to carpools, to laundry, to school time, to the never-ending treadmill and pressure of sex, to playgroups, to rocking and nuzzling each precious one, so in love with them that my heart might break, and I am running, running, running, always running to the next moment, to the next achievement, to the next one who needs me, so desperate, always clinging, clinging, clinging to something in the Universe to tell me that it is enough! That I matter! That I am good!

Trying so hard, moving so fast, spinning so lost...

And in all the swirling chaos, I suddenly see the absolute futility of all the doing and striving in the ghostly phantoms of my past. And I deeply feel the pain and emptiness and desperation that comes with all of it. And I know, with perfect surety in my gut, that none of it, not a single bit of it at all, is *me*.

The depth of the knowing sinks into my cells, fading the phantoms until I'm standing in stillness on the emptied beach. Slowly, I turn to my Higher Power, defeated and confused, and ask, "But if all of that is just an illusion, then who am I?"

His face softens into a smile of knowing anticipation, like He's been waiting my whole life for me to ask Him this question. He shifts his stance until we're face to face and looks so deeply into my eyes that I may drown in His gaze. Slowly, He reaches out and places His hand on my heart. I slowly follow, reaching my hand to His chest, and together we breathe, staring into each other's eyes, heart to heart, soul to soul, frozen in no-time. A warm tingle fills my body as the entire Universe explodes in my chest, the magic of His message coursing through my veins, telling me in no uncertain terms... THIS is who I am. I am Him. He is me. We are one. We are the same.

Who I am has nothing at all to do with the antics of the little self behind me. All the spinning, the hustling, the striving, the tricks, the gold stars, and the painful failures. The apparitions of my little story have evaporated into the air, and yet I am still here, heart beating, eyes drinking, breathing in the Universe embodied in front of me. Steady and sure, beneath all the doing, this inexpressible Love has always been here. It is who I have always been. A tangible presence: a conscious awareness, wide and free as the open sky. The essence of Love itself.

And now we are standing apart, gazing down at the baby again, only now I am holding my infant self in my own arms. With new eyes, I search this innocent, tiny me as if for the very first time, my heart exploding with compassion for her. I cover her forehead with kisses, and tears gather in the corner of my eyes. She is so, so *valuable*. I press my cheek against the soft down of her hair and my heart feels so much. I drink in her tiny face, and I see her limitless potential.

And yet my heart weighs heavy. I cannot save her from the shadows on the shore. I cannot take away all her doing, her striving, her tricks, all her desperation and her struggling... I cannot save her from it. In my heart, I know she needs all of that to find what she's always searched for: to discover who she really is. I want to protect her from the pain, from the struggle, but I know I can't. It's the struggle that she came for. It's why she's here. Pain will be so much of her pathway to peace and progress.

The holograph visions again swirl and sway in the mists beyond the beach, but I feel no shame anymore. I feel no judgment. I am no longer afraid of them. I am no longer afraid of her.

I forgive her. I understand her. I kiss her head and thank her for enduring the cost of what I now understand. For bringing me to this very moment...

The shadow of clock-time hovers and the yoga instructor beckons softly. I begin to feel a deep sadness. I am sad because I know that when I wake up, I will forget again. I will get up off my yoga mat, I will get in my car and drive home, and I will slide back into phantom tricks of doing and performing and striving. I will lose the magic. The Universe swirling inside of me will fade. I can't keep it with me always...not like this.

I am tired of being human. I just want Him. I just want Home. For now. For always.

...eventually I realize He is gone. But I am still on the beach, for one more minute, alone and holding my infant self. I take a deep breath and relax into acceptance, letting go of resistance, releasing fear. I am willing to stay here, on this lonely beach, missing Him, another day, another year...

I am willing to accept what is. I am willing to find ways to find Him through the mess. I am willing to be this little bundle who will feel so much and make so many desperate mistakes.

Happy Birthday, Becky. You don't have to be ashamed of yourself. You don't have to be afraid of your life. You don't have to fear that you haven't done enough, and you don't matter. You are not a disappointment. You didn't come to save the world. You came to discover your Self. You know who You are. And so do I. Love, God.

* * *

It is this kind of spirituality that I long to feel in my faith community, the kind of gritty, embodied cellular knowing that nobody can take away from you once you've found it in yourself. A few months later, my next religious step appears before me, right on cue for my soul's healing path.

There's been a change in ward leadership, and I've been invited to meet with our newly assigned Bishop. He invites me to the task of leading singing time with the Primary—a twenty-minute weekly stint for children ages 3–12 and their teachers. My job is to teach a set curriculum of songs, and I consider the request with hesitation, feeling fraudulent and unsure.

Since Rock Bottom, I've been hiding in the backs of chapels and behind pianos, staying securely out of the public eye during Sunday services. I don't even know if I can fit my new off-script perspective into my former box. What's more, my past life was littered with notable church responsibilities, and I'm scared of getting sucked back into a system that fed my ego its addictive diet of validation and self-righteous superiority. Stepping back in toward church titles and up-front positions—even one as minor as Primary chorister—feels like entertaining the version of me I trust the least: the one who got cheated on while she was out dutifully serving.

But when I share all these concerns and the history behind them with my new bishop, I am met with deep listening, curiosity, understanding, and respect. Behind my reluctance, I start to feel a spark of curiosity. The words of Thich Nhat Hanh fill my mind, words that have kept me going on the days I most wanted to hurl my shoe at the pulpit. "We must encourage others... to go back to their traditions and rediscover the jewels that are there... If a Sangha (faith community) is having difficulties, the way to transform it is to begin by transforming yourself…any Sangha is better than a non-Sangha. Without a Sangha, you will be lost."[7]

For the past few years, I've taken these words to heart, searching for jewels at church. Some Sundays, I find them. Some Sundays, I don't. This new role in Primary would invite me to offer my own. So, with the full encouragement of my bishop, I decide to step in, sensing the possibility for something special: *How can I bring the beautiful fruits of mindfulness into my own community? How might it add to the jewels that are already here?*

My heart pounds on my first Sunday morning in Primary as I face two dozen children in ruffly dresses and skiwampus neckties. I won't pretend to be anywhere but where I am (religiously), and I feel exposed in front of the masses—albeit young ones. But as the weeks go by, I feel less shaky in front of both the children and the adult teachers, losing my self-consciousness and finding my rhythm. Despite the inner voices that still sometimes whisper I don't belong, I'm able to stand and speak to the Primary from my heart.

I find there are bridges of common ground I can build on: bridges of Love, peace, goodness, honesty, community, the beauty and Truth in the life of Jesus Christ. I want so badly to make sure they are receiving messages of unconditional love and belonging, not shame or control. I spend the moments as they fill the room, calming my breath and searching their eyes and faces. *God, help me to help them feel You. Help me be a tool in Your hands today.*

During the week, I peruse Primary song lyrics, and I delight to discover universal truths folded into their simple rhymes. Everything Jesus says now has a nuanced, mystical meaning to me that leads back to the deepest definition of who we all truly are: *I am a Child of God*—but what does that truly mean and how can we feel it here and now? My short teaching times offer playful and off-script explorations into these and other rich concepts that are typically skimmed over, like Love and what it means and how we experience it in our hearts and bodies.

I weave subtle ways to incorporate breath and simple movement into my methods. I long to give these little ones what yoga has given me—that vital spiritual connection available only through the body. I know for myself that when you look deeply enough, you will find the Love the scriptures talk about

---

7 Hanh, N. (2015). *Living Buddha, Living Christ*. Riverhead Books. Pages 68, 90, 196.

as your deepest Self, and only then does it become a part of you. Only then does Love become more than a doctrine, but a way of being.

Soon, each week becomes a magical spiritual adventure as open minds and wiggly bodies eagerly embrace both me and the messages I share. We turn out the lights and gather to sing around the imagined warmth of fake fires, reflecting on the warming sensations of how Love feels in our chest. We stand up through booming choruses, and when we're restless, we shake out our arms together, learning we can use our bodies to shift and release our beautiful, big energy when needed. We balance in a tree posture and experience the difference it makes in our balance when we have a clear, steady focus point, like the Savior. One week, I even take them all on a guided meditation through butterfly-filled meadows into Jesus's lap. When I do, teachers and students alike are astounded, tears streaming down their cheeks. They have never experienced anything like this. They are hungry for this mystical connection inside. Just like me.

Nothing I offer in Primary is typical or scripted from Pinterest or church manuals. It comes straight from my heart, from what I've learned from my mentors, from my own wonderings and discoveries, and it is welcomed in this childlike space. And before I know it, I look forward to being at church every week, passionately pouring out all that I love most dearly about the God I've come to know. In return, I feel this love reflected back at me in big, innocent eyes and unpretentious hearts—from children and teachers alike. My daily thoughts swirl with ideas about how to next introduce my little ones to God. I carefully fine-tune my message to only what feels True and what my heart most longs to share:

God is right here, inside You. Love is everywhere, and there is nothing you could ever do to not deserve it. Can you feel it? Can you feel it in your own heart? In your own wiggly body?

My spiritual practice is to see how completely present I can be with them. When it's not my turn to teach, I look into their eyes and faces.

What do you need today?

I check my inner body radar—their energy will tell me. I try to make eye contact and send a secret message that is just between the two of us:

"I love you exactly as you are. You are so special."

I believe in my heart that this secret message between us matters. That even though I am not speaking a word out loud, they can feel my heart, and it makes a difference. I want each and every one of them to leave that room feeling loved and seen.

Over time, these sweet and trusting faces soften my tired arguments and accusations. Each time I enter our noisy classroom and wink at my chubby and adoring fans, another piece of my heart heals. Unbeknownst to them, these little ones are taking my hand and tiptoeing me back to a place in the community I had shut out in my abandonment. We belong to each other in this world we've created—a magical world where we sing and dance and celebrate our sacred connection to the Divine...and only what really matters counts.

More and more, I find myself sitting through full church services without the urge to scream. I listen to a speaker and search for their heart rather than their flawed arguments. When someone says something ignorant, I close my eyes, envision my own devoted face ten years earlier, and whisper with hand on heart, *"Ahhh, yes. I remember what it was to be so sure. They're just like me."*

And slowly, I dare to believe that I *do* have something to offer. That there is still room for me here. That maybe I am needed after all. I feel less broken. And eventually, one summer Sunday, I sit in the stillness of a sacrament service and a sense of supreme gratitude, even awe, washes over me unexpectedly, like a Divine cloudburst I didn't see coming.

How lucky am I?

How lucky am I to be a part of a faith community? How lucky am I to be able to sit in these pews, filled with people who are all here because we want to be good, the best way we know how? How lucky am I to have the opportunity to serve and be served, to share in people's lives and families, and have them share in mine? How lucky to have this structure to help hold my family in rituals and traditions that provide a spiritual framework for our lives?

How lucky am I?

This church is not the end—no, no, this church is not the end at all. It's a bumpy, broken vehicle, one that may serve me at times and harm me at other times. But no matter its flaws, its imperfections, its blind spots, or its history, it's been a part of me since the time I was the ruffle-dressed blonde singing simple songs in Primary. It has been part of my great unfolding, has been so much a part of *me*, and today, as I look around and see the faces of so many people who've touched my life in one way or another, I will bow to her in reverence. I will hold her place sacred, no matter how I flow in or out of her bounds as we navigate each new season, no matter where I end up as our lifelong river runs its course.

The funny thing about the river is, you can't control where she'll choose to cut her path. When the glacier makes its way, you can't control the canyons it carves out. Better to surrender to them and give yourself wholly to the new landscape with wonder and willingness.

But falling in love with new terrain doesn't mean you have to castigate the old. Stepping into the wilderness doesn't have to make you an outsider. So, the church and I, we don't have to be enemies. Here or there, in or out, we don't have to build a case against each other, defend or prove a thing. In fact, that is and will be the very essence of our lifelong relationship, of our shared journey toward the salvation we both long for.

My true spiritual work unfolds in the invisible walls of my own soul. No matter where my path takes me, or how this community comes to view me, I can choose to hold it with Love. My journey is between me and my Beloved, and my *heart* is my masterpiece: open, soft, pliable, tender…in spite of everything.

Found at Sea

Becky Moller, November 2018

I am floating on the ocean of consciousness
Not sure where I am headed.
The months and years behind me were easier to mark,
I could sense my progress as I neared the buoys that marked
uncharted waters.
As I floated closer, I felt secure, still knowing where I was
In relation to where I'd been.

But the weeks have turned to months and years and
without even noticing,
Caught in the depth of the presence that carries me,
I have floated far beyond the buoys that marked my path.
They are but dots in the distance.
Don't bother me much. I just sense where they were
And that somehow
I am not there anymore.

Now I sit, getting more comfortable bobbing on the ups
and downs of daily life,
Carried on a vastness much greater than before.
The water is a deeper blue, a richer hue,
But I'm not exactly sure where I am.
Awareness and breath, the anchor to my soul.
Surrender
Returning me again and again to Center.

When I lift my eyes to the horizon, all I see
Is open sky and bobbing waves.
No buoys. No markers. No lines to keep me safely harbored in.
This is a new way to travel.
Where am I going?
There is no way to measure.
Now I rely on the compass within my heart
Instead of the posts set up by
The people, the suits, the pedestals.
I am growing quite comfortable with uncertainty,
Quite curious with pain,
And I trust that this anchor inside will lead me,
One wave at a time, to You.
After all, it has gotten me this
Far.

CHAPTER THIRTY

CATCHING WAVES

A glacier represents water in its solid form and lowest potential energy level. When frozen, water molecules have slowed enough that their attractions arrange them into fixed positions with tight, restricted vibration, a stuckness that hovered in my own mind-body-spirit through the years of my greatest pain. Like ice molecules, everything inside me was trembling to maintain a sense of control. To stay there, clinging forever, would have trapped me in my lowest potential.

As water melts, its potential energy increases. Molecules that were formerly bound in a hexagonal structure find the freedom to move and bend, creating a flow capable of even carving canyons. Such warming occurred in my own soul as I learned to surrender, to allow my experiences and emotions to move through me and alter my formerly fixed beliefs, identities, and perceptions.

In such a flow, all water eventually makes its way to the ocean, where banks recede and the bottom drops out. In such a vastness of space, unprecedented potential builds into massive waves, a conduit for pure energy. Water molecules in an ocean wave mostly bob up and down in an orbital pattern: their primary role is to allow a greater (or Higher) power to pass through them without restricting its flow. As each molecule plays its part, ocean waves can travel thousands of miles and reach swells over 100 feet tall. If nothing were to get in their way, these waves would never end, circling the planet in an endless and abundant flow of life-giving energy.[8]

Could I learn to become part of a wave like that?

Time passes, and before I know it, Nate and I are another year past our reconciliation, another year of growing and healing, the layers still peeling back. We're more like our annual drive to Wisconsin now: Triggers like foothills for both of us, still there but less steep, less treacherous. The ground feels more stable now, with long stretches like smooth and steady plains. We have more bandwidth to devote to other areas of life. It's been over four years now since *Sunday Night Disclosure*, and we're rolling in the steady rhythm of our New Normal.

Our young family keeps growing, and so does our grocery bill. Our oldest is fourteen, and baby Tyson is three. We have graduated from the seemingly endless stage of sleep-disrupted nights, diaper bags, and baby-proofing. We're gliding into a sweet spot where our parenting directives go mostly unchallenged, and at the same time, everyone can get themselves buckled in and out of their car seats. It feels like a golden era.

Nate's web development firm is running on all cylinders. He's a successful entrepreneur, a goal he's always dreamed of, and he's never been more consistently manifesting his best self. Recovery has brought a thriving accountability to every part of his life: He's never had more clients, never been more organized and efficient, and never had more friends—many of whom are part of our 12-step family.

I'm still chipping away at my Betrayal Trauma manuscript, teaching daily group exercise classes at UVU, and coordinating the extramural aerobics program at BYU. I'm finally back into a stable flow, and I've no inclination to make waves. That's why it was so odd when I step out of my car in the BYU parking lot before my class and feel a distinct impression as clear as a voice:

This position has run its course. You're going to leave it soon…to make room for recovery work. I note the feeling with surprised curiosity. *That's weird. Why would I ever leave my position at BYU? It's perfect for me.*

---

8 For molecular structure of ice:
   https://ourwinterworld.org/snow-science/ice-water-and-molecules/
   For molecular movement of ocean waves:
   https://oceangeneration.org/the-motion-of-the-ocean-explained-waves-and-tides/

Still, my mind is open, and my heart is willing. As our marriage has stabilized, our commitment to the Twelve Steps has only grown deeper. We feel so lucky to have survived the iceberg, and there's a deep satisfaction in helping others find their way. Our lives are filled with weekly group meetings, recovery blogs and sponsorship, early morning Board meetings to help plan events and develop long-term strategy, including Nate building a whole new website for the foundation.

Applying myself in this executive capacity has felt like a dangerous experiment, like picking up a part of myself I've tried to bury. The problem is the part of me I might call my Boss-Ass Bitch self, the part who creates and plans and sees the vision and makes it happen with laser-focused efficiency. Since rock bottom, she's become my sworn enemy: synonymous with ego striving, abandonment, and rigid control. At Nate's rock bottom, I was serving as the Young Women's president at church, and it's hard not to feel in some way that his actions were a direct response to this part of myself. And it's not just this low point with Nate that scares me. So many of the striving visions on the beach feel tainted by this part of myself.

I can see that it's one thing to release the fear of who I am in meditative visions on my Door County beach. It's another thing to trust myself in real life. But Nate sits by my side each Tuesday morning at the Foundation table, so I cautiously step in, careful not to lose myself in the fun of new creation.

My latest adventure is planning a Women's Retreat: the first Women's Retreat the Foundation has ever offered. It's been a whirlwind of lists and deadlines, details and agendas, and after all the backstage planning, I find myself on a cool spring day, welcoming a room full of beautiful, courageous, recently betrayed women from across the country. The trauma runs high, an almost palpable presence in the air. We'll spend three days together in this sacred space: sharing, learning, moving, and meditating. Logistically, I'm pretty much running the show. My stress is tight in my chest, but I'm so grateful to be here with the soul sisters and mentors who've created this event with me—including my own sponsor Holly.

As we move through the weekend, I watch them all shine, and I find myself in awe of their gifts and talents. I watch how the women flock to them, hungry for their energy, their attention, their perspective, their love, their Light. I've done the heavy lifting behind the scenes, but now that we're here, I begin to feel I have nothing of value to offer. Each of them has their unique place, their unique gift to give to this experience, and the only thing I seem to add is a reminder of the time and the schedule. They are bright and shiny, and I am organized and invisible. A growing sense of inadequacy festers within. By the time I retreat to my bunk on the first night, my gut is a tight ball of anxiety, and tears spring to my eyes in the welcome darkness. I can feel the tailspin coming, the old demon voices circling.

You are not enough. Nobody likes you—it's who you are. You're Type-A. You're uptight. You're bossy. You're plain. You can't change that. Nobody could love someone like you.

And now the synapses are clicking, and I'm sinking into scenes from my trauma egg. *My older brother is the bright and shiny. I am invisible. It's fine. It's just the way it is. I don't matter. I don't matter. I don't matter.*

I am supposed to help guide traumatized women through a healing weekend, but I am unraveling into my own trauma. I see it but am powerless to stop it. I pray, I surrender, I breathe, and I try to sleep.

The next morning, I'm gathered enough to lead the women through morning exercise. Teaching fitness is an embodied outlet that is almost second nature to me from my decade-plus of university experience. This is a part I know I can play. So, as we meet outside in the crisp morning air of the awakening mountains, my shaky mental state doesn't deter me from throwing my whole self into jumps, squats, kicks, and burpees. My intention is to break us down, empty our minds, and create a physical state conducive to spiritual surrender. And I do, me included.

So, I'm raw and open when I hand the baton to Holly, who instructs us to lay out our mats for yoga. Letting strong and capable Holly guide me through a morning yoga practice after emptying myself so completely is medicine to my soul. I breathe and fold and move and allow myself to be held by the softness of her voice and the strength of her Presence. My mind is quiet. I've come back to the moment. I sit in butterfly pose and relish the morning sun on my back. I hear Holly's wise and steadying voice in my ears. Her Light is so bright and so big. *I cannot compete with her Light. I do not matter. I cannot make a difference.* The self-deprecating voice in my head is fighting to get back online.

Hello, old friend. I see you.

I take a deep breath and let the comparing voices pass, gently bringing my focus back down into my body. I follow my exhale all the way down my throat and into my deep belly, and I feel the aliveness in my feet. And now I am not thinking about Holly's voice. I am not comparing myself to her or any of the other gifted women at this Retreat. Now, I am not thinking at all.

Instead, I am completely engrossed in the warmth and power of the Light that is shining on my back. It is the morning sun, and it seems to permeate my soul, seeping through my skin, almost consuming me in flames. It feels, in this moment, like this Light is actually cutting through my flesh and pouring through me, like a prism that splays rainbow shapes across the walls.

And somehow I know that God is speaking and I feel what He is saying: a knowing that arises from deep within me, an awareness that floats up from the space within and warms me with its Truth: This Light I see in Holly, in others, this Light I admire so much that I long to capture it and squeeze it to my chest and keep it for myself, this Light that I keep trying to attach to people and pedestals. This Light does not belong to any one of us. It is His. And there is enough and more to shine through all of us.

"Don't worry," He seems to be saying. *"You will get your turn. After all, love, it can't be your turn all the time. Just be. Let go. And try to trust Me. I promise, I know just how I want to use you."*

His message washes through every cell of my body, and I open my eyes with new awareness. I recognize how we are nestled in these mountains: their strength and stability reaching around us to hold us safe. And suddenly I see it: my own Earthiness, my structured, organized, background strength—my Boss-Ass Bitch self. And I realize that this very moment, in all its wonder, has been manifested through this part of me that I am so afraid of, that I want to push away, hate, and hide. It is the part that handily picked a date and booked a venue, that created an agenda and scheduled speakers. It's the part that set up information on the website, sent out email campaigns, created a budget, and designed schedules. These people are here because the Earth in me planned and prepared and created the foundation to bring all of us together. Just like the Earth underneath me supports me in this very moment. Often unseen. Rarely acknowledged. But always silently carrying the burden of holding it all up.

And as I sit in butterfly position with Light flooding through me, I realize I have been told a thousand times that this part of me is bad. Annoying. Unlovable. Ugly. Too much. Unfeminine. I have hated this part of me—have hidden it, avoided it, denied it was there, shoved it down, and stomped on it. I have blamed it for Nate's betrayal and banished it from my life.

And yet, this is the part of me that makes so much possible, the ring of stones that creates the space and boundaries for Holly's Light and Fire, and how I love to watch her burn. Like Earth elements, our gifts are interconnected; incomplete without the other. Like it or not, this sturdy grounded energy is so much of how the Light shines through me.

Will I surrender to it? Can I forgive myself for being who I am? Can I allow another's Light to shine without it threatening my own? Can I allow my Light to shine without fearing it will threaten others?

Can I trust God when He tells me, *"Don't worry. You will get your turn again. For now, just bask in all the Light that's shining…everywhere. And know it's a part of you, too. Because it's all Me. We are One. We are the same. Let yourself be a part of a much bigger picture. Because I have so much fun painting with Light. And I have so many breathtaking Prisms."*

This instant at the Women's Retreat becomes a pivotal awakening: a small crack in the coffin where I'd buried my Boss-Ass Bitch self four years ago. And as our entire 12-step board basks in the clear success of the Women's Retreat, I can't deny her usefulness—at least in small doses, for a good cause. I also can't deny how stepping into this uncomfortable space is serving my own healing, creating win-wins: I'm able to help those whom I serve, and the opportunity itself is pushing me to face my edges.

Over the coming weeks and months, I start to notice how many strengths I have chosen to lay down, how many skills I have buried. I make inventory and see so many distinct moments from my life when I chose to make myself smaller for fear of rejection. Changing answers on tests. Happily sitting in the back seat because big brother was going to take the front—or else. Dropping twenty pounds in two months to be liked better by boys. I've learned to appear small enough to be appealing: in weight, intelligence, tone of voice, even creative output. So many small self-betrayals because of my want for love and belonging. So many strengths that lie dormant and unusable because of my unwillingness to appear threatening or unfeminine: so much Light I wouldn't touch because I wanted people to like me.

God, I offer myself to Thee…to build with and do with me as Thou wilt.[9] The 3rd Step Prayer from AA has been my morning prayer for the past four years: It's helped me release my traumas, my fears, my self-defeating behaviors, my limiting beliefs, my ego identities.

Relieve me of the bondage of self…that I may better do Thy will.[10] But what would it look like to surrender my *strengths* to God? What would it look like to offer *all* of me to the Divine—to use every quality, every strength, every weakness, as the Universe sees fit—without regard for how it's perceived? Without fear for what others will think? Without protecting myself from rejection, humiliation, or judgment?

With some trepidation, on a typical afternoon in the quiet of my own bedroom, I surrender my whole self to God through a simple 7th step prayer with heartfelt intention. It's a tiny, seemingly insignificant moment, but it creates a tangible shift inside me that carries into the subsequent trajectory of my life. Within weeks, I begin to feel like a surfer catching the swell of Divine Waves I couldn't dream were coming.

First, I feel the undeniable tug to share my Betrayal Trauma Memoir manuscript with my daughters' dance studio director, Nesha. At first, I argue with myself. Nesha has long been someone I pedestalize and admire. But sharing my manuscript with someone I respect so much and know so little seems utterly out of the blue. We're barely associates—what am I supposed to do, knock on her door and say I've written a book about trauma, and I feel like she's supposed to read it? *That's crazy!*

But the urge is so strong that within a few weeks, that's exactly what I do. Nesha answers the door with surprise and receives me graciously. Even as I stumble through my words and offer a Reader's Digest of all that brought me to her door, I can feel that I am safe. She's not judging. She's open, curious, and even grateful as she accepts the thick spiral-bound manuscript.

Within a day or two, I receive a phone call from Nesha in distress, trying to make sense of what appears to be her own trauma tailspin. The timing of

---

9 3rd Step Prayer, Alcoholics Anonymous. www.aa.org

10 3rd Step Prayer, Alcoholics Anonymous. www.aa.org

my visit couldn't have been better: the very day she began reading, she found herself in a meltdown she would never have had words for otherwise. I walk through the trauma response with Nesha just like I've done for my fellows in recovery, and a beautiful new relationship is born.

Soon after, I find myself sitting across the table from our beloved 12-step founders, a couple who are like parents to Nate and me. They've invited us to dinner at a lovely restaurant. I figure it's a gesture of gratitude for the many volunteer hours we offer, but before the check comes, they ask me if I will be their new Executive Director. I'm dumbfounded.

Nate sits next to me, and I instinctively reach for his hand. I feel my heart swell up into my throat: the fear—it's clawing at me. *What would this mean? I don't even know how to be an Executive Director! Do I really want to open this coffin—do I really want to invite Boss-Ass Bitch back into the driver's seat in my everyday life? What if she runs me over? What if she runs Nate back into his addiction? What if I can't keep her under control? What if I lose all the stillness I've gained in this holy healing—and I can never find it again? And what about my book?*

Nate and I go home to think about it. It's not just my internal world that I'm worried about. *What about my job as Aerobics Coordinator at BYU?*

I know I won't have the bandwidth to do both positions well, and I struggle inside myself to choose. But in my gut, I remember the premonition in the parking lot, and I marvel that here I am in the exact moment it was preparing me for. Within days, the founders offer a salary that exactly matches what I'll be leaving at BYU, and before I can even notify BYU of my decision to step away, my boss surprisingly informs me that they've absorbed my Coordinator position into one of their existing departments, and I will no longer be needed. *Wow.*

The Wave is strong and steady, the bottom dropping out, and the direction clear. Although I feel like I'm being tossed into open water, I trust the flow too much to turn back now. Nate is nervous about how this new work will impact my time and our connection, but he's loving and supportive. So, with eyes wide open and heart reaching for courage, I choose, with my whole soul.

Yes. I will let this part of me back out into the world. Yes. I will trust my Higher Power and my Self to work with her more skillfully. Yes. I will trust the Wave that's so clearly flowing through my life and whisking me up on its unexpected current. As scared as I feel, something inside of me knows it's my next right step.

Yes, I will keep showing up to serve a Greater Good, still healing, still expanding.

A Crystal Chandelier
Becky Moller, May 2017

This world
A giant chandelier

Each one of us,
A hand-cut crystal
Carefully crafted to refract
His light in its
Own unique array
Of colors, patterns, beauty.

Wow!
Look around and
Open your eyes
To the magnificent
Spectacle
Of God's Light
Everywhere,

Shining through a million
Different crystals,
Each One perfectly
Designed to manifest
All that He is
In as many miraculous
Ways.

CHAPTER THIRTY-ONE

UNPRECEDENTED FLOW

T hus begins three magical years of creation, collaboration, laughter, tears, fundraising, retreats, conferences, Philly cheesesteak business lunches, and my first real experience in authorship. It's on-the-job learning, and I repeatedly find myself in places I never dreamed I'd be: speaking at the world's largest Conference for sexual addiction awareness, long-range planning with our beloved non-profit guru at his gorgeous cabin in Bear Lake, helping to manage and train facilitators for over fifty weekly group meetings, reaching thousands of people in addiction and trauma recovery from all over the world.

Although I may have been hesitant to start, I quickly succumb to the vision that fuels me: to get the crucial tools for healing to more people. It's possible, I can feel it in my bones. The internet is the vehicle, and all we need to do is build a structure that will guide people back to their own hearts and embodied practice. This is the Source that carries the holy medicine—and it's right within them! This is the purpose that wakes me in the middle of the night, just itching with new ideas to start working on.

Nate and I carry this dream together—his web design skills are the perfect companion to my content creation, and the non-profit board lets us run unrestrained. Together, we build an online curriculum to work the Twelve Steps, and for the first time ever, the Foundation has a consistent source of revenue to fund its mission. All cylinders are rolling in late 2019 when I begin work on an important new project: a flagship manual for the Foundation, its own addition to the body of 12-step literature we've inherited from AA, SA, and S-Anon.

The task of the manual is overwhelming, to say the least. Writing weekly blog posts for the past three years is a far cry from the painstaking work of embodying an entire approach to recovery. Writing the manual becomes an exacting endeavor and forces me to intricately study every facet of this mysterious whirlwind called healing I've been engaged in over the past seven years. I collect dozens of stories from 12-steppers, write original content from my own understanding and observations, and piece together what shows through as the essential elements of healing, framed neatly around our Foundation's four recovery pillars.

When I finally finish the initial draft, our founder introduces me to an editor who's generously volunteered her help in the final stages before publication. I am grateful for the additional perspective and feedback on what has been a solo undertaking.

But Lynda enters the scene like a tornado—powerful, direct, brilliant, and maybe a little terrifying. I'm expecting her to point out a few grammatical errors—she questions the premise of the entire book, hitting head-on at issues that we, the Foundation, have never even considered. When I reach out for clarification, the founders keep reminding me that *we* are the experts on recovery. Lynda isn't. We can all appreciate her good intentions, but this is more than any of us expected.

But soon, Lynda and I are neck-deep in Google Docs comment threads that I can't pull myself out of. Every comment she makes lights me up—*Who is she to talk to me like that?!...* And yet I can't put them down because I recognize their value. Her perspective forces me to face the underlying assumptions I missed before—all the ways I've built the narrative to fit into the discourse community rather than *add* to it. Lynda and I don't always arrive at a point of exact agreement, but without fail, her voice changes my view and clarifies my perspective. The result is a manual that is much stronger, more honest, and original than before.

For close to two months, Lynda and I exist in our own universe—both of us expanding through the stimulating interplay of ideas and experiences that have deeply shaped our life journey, evenly matched in ways that heal and empower my soul. There's a Flow between us like nothing I've ever experienced, like a Divine download dumping over my head, and I can scarcely pull myself out from the flood enough to breathe.

As summer heats up, we gasp our way across the finish line with a supreme thrill of accomplishment and a tentative satisfaction that our final product holds up to scrutiny, rings true to the experience, and is being delivered through a literary format and rhetorical framework that honors its intention …and, most of all, that God was so clearly in all of it.

So, it's a shock to deliver the new and improved manuscript to the founders and be met with stark rejection, an immovable line in the sand, and a trusting, almost familial relationship that seems to have shifted overnight.

I have never before been anything but a "yes-woman" in this space. But then again, I've never invested so much to clarify my own convictions. I know exactly why I'm taking the position I am, and I cannot get myself to just back down. In the face of an unprecedented stalemate, we put the project on hold, and I spend my summer praying, grieving, compromising, and trying to understand my next right step, professionally.

No matter that I'm the one who created every word of that manual, that I spent days and weeks and months scrutinizing and challenging every aspect of our recovery model, and they've barely even picked up the manuscript. No matter. Don't matter. I don't matter. I don't matter. I don't matter. I guess I'm supposed to just get in the back seat again.

The voices that swirl in my head lead back to traces of old traumas, and I see again the unwanted patterns I keep repeating in my life. But by now I understand the wisdom in valid anger: it can motivate me to do the hard things I would otherwise avoid or talk myself out of. Valid anger has been a powerful, even necessary, vehicle for change.

So I hold my pain with compassion, and I wonder: *How can I change this self-defeating pattern? How can I honor the foundation and also honor my own integrity? What inside me needs to shift to bring this situation into better alignment?*

Part of me wishes everything could go back to the way it was, that I could be the founders' golden child again. But another part of me doesn't. Something inside me has already shifted…enchanted by the magic of creating something truly powerful with Lynda…the magic of being my whole Boss-Ass Bitch self, of arm-wrestling ideas until they settle into clarity, of not being afraid to ask tough questions or point out inconsistencies, of not playing small or being carefully "nice." Something incredible happened in our joint commitment to getting as close as we could to the Truth, no matter whose feelings were hurt.

And after such power and freedom, something inside me can't go back to simply propping up people whom I've conceded are more important than I am. And I can feel it all the way down to my bones that this is more than a job outcome for me. This is a soul outcome. This is the next conditioned pattern life is inviting me to release, the next level of free range for Waves that might want to use me in their Flow. And it's going to ask me to do more hard things.

So, on my way to another dissonant meeting with the founders on an early fall afternoon, part of me knows what I need to do—even before the baby fawn jumps in front of my car. The fawn simply makes the message unmistakable, jumping right in front of my car out of nowhere as I pull up to the lodge. After I slam the brakes, she stops by the side of the road and turns to look at me, utterly unafraid. She holds my gaze for a forever moment before she bounds away, disappearing into the fields at the foot of the rusty mountains.

My heart thunders in my chest from the abrupt interruption, like a lightning bolt that the Universe doesn't want me to miss. I sit in my car, just down the road from the lodge, my fingers fumbling to look up the totem meaning of baby deer. As I quickly scan through the search engine findings, I'm drawn to an entry from quornesha.com, a source I've never seen before. From the very first line, the words I read feel like a blatant act of Grace, each paragraph a personalized letter sent just to me to make my path forward unmistakable.

The fawn deer, it says, appears to symbolize the end of a chapter and the dawn of new beginnings: financially, emotionally, spiritually, creatively. With each sentence, I feel so seen: the reading repeatedly mentions the importance of silence and meditation, a key element of the teachings I feel called to bring forward. I feel encouraged: the reading invites me to trust in my own unique "genius," allowing my Light to shine freely with no thought for how it will be received by others. I feel called out: the reading challenges me to release my negative feelings, stop living my life to please others, mature my vision and values, and step forward unapologetically into my own abilities, trusting in the angels and guides. After all, only I have the power to know who I am and what I'm here for, a power that I should never have given to anyone else. In other words, in so many ways unique to this exact moment, it's time to grow up.

I can't believe it. The Universe has placed a crystal ball right in my lap. *I am supported.*

When I step out of my minivan and approach the inevitable conflict behind the familiar lodge door, I no longer feel dread in my stomach. Instead, I feel strangely bursting with joy, so full I might explode. Everything I see, the trees, the mountains, and the endless blue sky, feels new and alive and fresh and miraculous. This may be an ending of work and relationship and community, but it's also a new beginning. I am stepping into the unknown, and I feel so clearly guided that I don't even think to look back.

Instead, within the week, Nate and I return to this sacred Lodge where we've met for five years on the Foundation Board and where I've gathered for the past seven years for my weekly 12-step meeting. This time, our arms are full of boxes: all the pamphlets, books, and materials we've been storing at our house for three years.

"I can't be your Executive Director anymore," I tell the founders, our dear friends and mentors, my voice shaky but firm. Their eyes are sad but knowing: We all felt this moment was coming. I give hugs. I thank them for all they taught me and all the opportunities they gave me to grow. I give them the manual: my baby, my labor of love, and my first sustained flash of insight—and I entrust it to their care even as it rips my heart out. I know it was given for their purpose and meant for their community. I surrender its outcome as I leave it in their outstretched arms.

And I walk out the door, Nate by my side, into a new version of me. *It is all as it should be.*

GOOD MORNING, NEW LIFE
BECKY MOLLER, OCTOBER 2020

New horizon,
It is lovely to see you,
Sparkling with sunlit diamonds,
Unfamiliar but *undeniably intriguing*
New landscape taking shape.

I choose to welcome you
With open heart and trusting arms.
And practice the precarious art of
Riding waves much bigger than me.
Letting them gently lift and carry me
Higher than I could ever propel myself.

I let go of the urge to constrict and tighten
Against the fear of where I might land
Or how much it may hurt.

Instead, I practice
Loving the sensation
Of Something Greater
Moving through me.
I close my eyes, quiet my mind,
And trust the momentum in my soul.
No more safekeeping my security.
I step toward a more intrepid life.

Where will it lead me?
Not important.
Who will it make me?
Yours.
Lead on, Dreamgiver.

CHAPTER THIRTY-TWO
Good Morning, New Life

I am sitting on a second-story deck, overlooking stretches of sand that spread to the misty expanse of the Pacific Ocean. It is Fall Break, and our family is staying at a quaint, cobblestoned VRBO on Newport Peninsula. My kids are down at the beach with Nate, playing in the surf across the half-mile of sand between us. I'm enjoying the rays of the sun and a rare moment of solitude.

So much has happened in the last few weeks to widen my borders, and even though it's scary, I'm trying in every moment to be that wave molecule that simply holds its center and allows a Power greater than itself to move through unobstructed. I'm finding the ride exhilarating to be sure, but painful, too. Surrendering to the open expanse of unprecedented potential means I have no idea where I will end up. It appears that letting go of outcomes and attachments doesn't ever become easy. I'm learning that there is no greater act of faith.

So here I sit, overlooking the endless horizon, knowing there is more for me to give, more for me to offer, and it's already taking shape. Remember Nesha—my daughters' dance studio director? Over the past three years, we've become more than close spiritual friends through my Betrayal Trauma manuscript. Two years ago, she asked me to write her annual Fireside, a two-hour performance that weaves together dance and narration to explore spiritual concepts, and I've been writing these scripts for her ever since. Nesha's been dropping hints lately about an idea she's had on the back burner for a decade: Lifehouse Body & Soul, a place she's envisioned for women to come heal body image, perfectionism, and disordered eating, the primary traumas

Nesha's been dealing with for a lifetime. At the time, I was fully committed to the Foundation and shrugged off her invitations as pie-in-the-sky dreams.

But when Nesha heard about the dissonance with the Foundation over the summer, she carefully mentioned, "I think we could really build something together, you and me. I'm ready whenever you are." So, with the clarity of a clear totem behind me, I knew from almost the moment Nate and I drove away from the Lodge empty-handed that building something beautiful with Nesha was going to be my next right step.

After all, the vision that fueled me didn't belong to the Foundation. The framework I'd begun piecing together for almost a decade belonged to the Universe, and it was bigger than addiction or betrayal trauma, body image or perfectionism, for that matter. It was a puzzle of healing that applied to the whole human race, and I knew it could benefit any person who stepped in with an open and willing heart. With trust and presence and a heart open to an uncharted path, maybe I can get it to them after all.

So, I sit on this oceanfront deck with the October sun warm on my face and the breeze cool on my skin. I breathe deep until I feel it tingle all the way down to my toes. My fingertips light up and my heart-space warms, and it feels like coming home. This breath is the ever-relevant tool that has sustained me in every possible circumstance: the unchangeable thread that anchors me to my truest Self as life keeps changing.

I will never go back to the same moment. I will never step in the same river. Everything keeps rearranging: my work life, my recovery community, my view of healing, my family relationships, even my conception of God. What felt like solid ground for so many years now feels like sand slipping through my fingers. I am not quite sure where I stand or how I got here. This kind of uncertainty once felt traumatizing, but today I sit overlooking the ocean and feel as many possibilities as the infinite expanse before me.

Evolution.

Evolution is the beautiful word that keeps floating up like a hopeful glimmer. It relates to more than just my professional life. Evolution applies to every aspect of who I am in this moment. It's the freedom to step away from the 12-step world and the addiction model to move toward something that's more compassionate, hopeful, and universal. It's not shying away from the tough questions that can't be reconciled religiously. It's allowing the present moment to dictate what serves me and my family now, and releasing the illusion that safety somehow equates to staying in the same place.

As grief and hope intertwine inside of me, I can sense that the stability we've created over the past seven years isn't the destination after all, but the springboard to even more. And that maybe it's time to stop looking for destinations altogether. Because the truth is, I can't guarantee that I won't get hurt again. I can't guarantee that I'll be safe, and I now realize that this is what I've been trying to do for my entire life. With overachieving. With my weight. With marriage. With religion.

Safety can't be guaranteed by perfectly arranging the world around me. It can only be secured inside: by knowing myself fully, loving myself fiercely, and continually deepening my connection to the wholeness within me that's capable of handling whatever comes with wisdom and ease.

I see myself at the end of my first 12-step meeting in the lodge, professing: "I'm coming back, and I'll be here to stay. I'm in this for the long haul." As soon as I felt the goodness there, I had already decided: *I'm never leaving this place. I will give my whole life to it. I will stay with this forever. I will be immovable.*

I see myself as a college student, enthralled by the spirit I felt at BYU and the goodness the church had brought into my life. *I'm never leaving this place. I will give my whole life to it. I will stay with this forever. I will be immovable.*

I see myself in my wedding dress, gazing across an altar to Nate, anticipating the eternity before us, bound by covenants, friendship, and love. *I'm never leaving this man. I will give my whole life to him. I will stay with him forever. I will be immovable.*

It suddenly seems so interesting that I've been taught to call it a "faith crisis" when people ask questions or have experiences that challenge their accepted belief system. This terminology seems to presuppose two things: One, that faith is directly and even exclusively tied to religious doctrine or membership. Two, that evolution equates to a crisis. But as I stand up and close my eyes to feel the ocean breeze in my hair, I know that neither of these notions could be further from the truth.

As I once again face the unknown, faith to me has become my absolute trust in a Greater Good, in Something Higher moving in and through everything that exists. It's the embodied belief that allows us to plant seeds in the ground, to bid the sun farewell each night without losing our minds for fear of never-ending darkness. Faith to me is not something to "profess" and has nothing to do with accepting historical stories as fact or fiction.

Instead, it's an organic unfolding that happens quite naturally as we observe the present moment: the Way It Is. As we pay attention, we learn for ourselves that the dead of winter eventually gives way to blooming spring, that the sun does indeed rise again in the morning. When we open ourselves to learn from *all* our experiences, we come to trust that life is indeed *for* us. The entire Universe, an intelligence that is constantly conspiring in favor of our expansion. *This* is faith. And it seems to blossom most as we step into the darkness.

Again and again, from parents to church to marriage to 12-step, I've laid my life at the feet of an institution and sacrificed my all, believing that my total commitment would be my protection, would rescue me. Again and again, life keeps expanding me by sailing me out of the safe harbor—by exposing the holes in my own blind trust when it all falls apart.

Nobody is coming to rescue me. It's up to me to find my path.

How could greater awareness and accountability be failure? It's not.

Changing perspective may well be inconvenient, but I can see now it's actually the very definition of progress. Asking God to transform me without touching my religious or recovery perceptions would be like skydiving with a blindfold on: all of the terror with none of the expanded view. New experience equates to new insights—how could it be any other way?

It's so odd to define success as refusing to think critically, and even stranger to wave flags in defense of the Truth. Truth needs no defense and fears no question. Truth begs us to ask, investigate, and challenge, for that is the only way to excavate that which is ultimately indestructible: beyond notion, concept, or doctrine. And that alone is Truth. Truth always, inevitably, comes out in the wash, because It simply Is. I know this in my bones, from my own lived experience, and it's an unapologetic knowing that won't be silenced.

Courageously facing the ways our current beliefs aren't adding up is no crisis. It's an expansion.

I'm finally getting the message: *I Am* my only true home. *I Am* my only true safety. *I Am* the Self that unfolds in the present moment to guide my life with intuitive wisdom. *I Am* God within me. And I'm blocking my access to

It by clinging to the illusions of safety outside of myself. As seagulls squawk above me, I feel the sensation of floating untethered in space, and for the first time ever, I do not feel afraid.

What happens now?

What happens when life isn't framed around what I'm running away from? What happens when I'm not trying to control and prevent? What happens when I peel back the fear and ask my heart *what it actually wants?*

The bigness of the question calls me back to my breath and the Universe clears the clutter of my conditioning into the salty sea air. *What does my heart most long for? What does Life want from me?*

And I feel my deepest knowing, strong, steady, and clear. If I could give the world one thing, it would be *this*. This awareness of who they really are. This awakening to the vastness that's right here, underneath all the noise. *This is the medicine the world needs—I feel it in my bones.*

I can help them find it.

My heart is on fire, leaping out of my chest, urging me recklessly forward. Something in me is dying to create, to zoom out the lens and bring the same tools that have served me so well in recovery to an infinitely wider focus. These tools aren't addiction and trauma tools. They're human tools. Everybody needs them   because they land us all in the same place: the emptied, essential Self. The same Self I feel right now, exploding from my heart-space above the beach.

I am ready for more. I am ready for a new chapter. I am ready to evolve. I am ready to trust in abundance instead of fear. I am ready for life beyond Betrayal Trauma.

Yes, after all the all-consuming energy of it… *I am ready for life beyond Betrayal Trauma!*

I drop my journal and stand on the rooftop deck above the Newport Beach boardwalk, throw my arms wide and shout into the air, *"I AM NOT BETRAYAL TRAUMA!"*

I scamper down the stairs from the upper deck and out onto the stretches of sand, careless of who sees or hears me in my giddy joy. I feel each tiny grain scratch and stick between my toes. Pleasant or unpleasant, it's all part of the magic that's here in front of me, and something inside me wants to experience it all.

But what if I'm wrong? What if Nate goes back out there and we end up right back where we started? Isn't it better to stay put in the Twelve Steps where we know we've been safe? To stay in the nest that somebody else built? To follow their rules and hold onto their labels and trust in their guarantee?

For a brief moment, the fear claws back up into my throat. It catches my breath and my stomach feels cold. I place my hand there and breathe: *It's okay, I see you.*

It's the part of me that wants to be the good girl, that knows how to secure the gold star and play by the rules and ride in the back seat resentfully. She's scared. It makes sense. I'm stepping outside the logical lines of the structures that have promised safety. It's so tempting to hand my trust back to their outside authority and hope they'll rescue me: for with all that trust, goes all the responsibility. It's so much easier to let someone else carry it.

I hear all her arguments, breathe softness to where she's tightening my belly, and assure her that I'm here and I'm listening. There is room for her, too.

But as I walk through the sand and the ocean gets louder, the ceaseless hushing of each wave relaxes my belly and my fear. The rhythmic hush calls to me and the blue horizon stretches as far as my eyes can see: no beginning and no end in sight. The waves crash against the shoreline, powerful, wild, and each one remarkably new.

I can see my children tumbling in them now, and my heart opens as I watch them laugh, giggle, jump, splash. Sometimes, they crawl out from a powerful surge that's toppled them upside down, spitting and coughing, pulling shells and seaweed from their upturned hair. Sometimes they bob and float in the gentle rise and fall of a swell that is kind and tender. But always, always, their shrieks of delight draw them back for more.

"One more, Mom! Just one more!! Please!"

"Did you see that, Mom? Did you see it? Did you see me jump there? Did you see how I got flipped upside down by that one?!"

They can't get enough. Pleasant or unpleasant, rise or fall, gentle or punishing, scrapes and all. They are yearning to taste it; to ride the waves, to *live,* damn it. And finally, *finally,* I'm ready to pull off my modest cover-up, don my first-ever bikini, and jump in—imperfect, uncovered, and unafraid.

OCEAN
BECKY MOLLER, OCTOBER 2020

God is Breathing,
The entire Universe in constant process,
Of Inhales and Exhales,
Outward flow of manifestation
Inward return to rest
And insight.
Beauty, Power, and God
In both.

All tiny passengers
Riding waves that lift us off our feet,
Then suck us back into our Selves,
Sometimes tossing us into rocks
Along the way.
The trick is learning to move
with the Flow.

Ride momentum
with Grace and Trust,
And allow the inward pull to bring us back
To Home,
To Center,
To Self,
To You.

Don't get stuck in the churning confusion
Of water that topples too close together,
Losing its rhythm,
Not knowing which way is up or down,
Push or pull,
No flow, no presence,
Just chaos, anxiety, bubbling and spitting,
Going nowhere.
In its rush it has forgotten
Where its Power comes from.

Life is a deep breath.
Let patience have its perfect work,
And wait for the waves,
Knowing
There is always
Enough
Time for both
The exhale and
The inhale.

Trust that
One can't exist
Without the other.

CHAPTER THIRTY-THREE

GOD AT MY CENTER

I am outside on my deck, sitting cross-legged on my mat, hands palm up, hoping to receive. The wind tickles traces of hair across my face. I feel the sun peeking over the tops of the trees, beaming light over my knees, warm and comforting. My spine is straight, but my head is fuzzy, and my heart is closed.

Lifehouse Body & Soul, our fledgling mindfulness and wellness studio, is taking shape, and the momentum of it is all-consuming. Each morning, I guide our small start-up class through workouts, yoga, and guided meditation driven by breath, and designed to release energy and emotion. Holly and Nesha are by my side, supporting me in the weight of creation and helping to facilitate our weekly mindfulness classes. Our unique curriculum takes shape as I sit in the rust-colored chair in the corner of my bedroom and channel the healing bridges I've discovered through the separate worlds of 12-step, trauma recovery, and embodied mindfulness.

Most afternoons, I pull out my laptop and ponder: *How did I get from there to here? How have I witnessed others get from there to here? If I had to break down the essence of healing as I've come to understand it to the tiniest steps of acceptance, awareness, and behaviors, so clear that anyone could follow...what would that look like?* One week, one topic at a time, this lived-experience roadmap becomes my signature year-round program, a compassionate and embodied way of expanding through life.

Each week, I feel confident we are offering something uncommonly transformative as I see the fruits in the participants that show up from all walks of life. Gratitude is a beaming fullness that I carry in my chest, which sits right alongside the gripping terror in my stomach, and it all comes with the momentum of a Wave beginning to break. Even with so much assurance that I've found my path, it's still a leap of faith to step into all this new journey requires. Courage in the face of self-doubt, countless hours of focused labor, and new pressures on my work-life balance are just a few.

On days like today, it all feels overwhelming, and I feel far away, removed. There's so much to do, so many people to help, so many burdens to lift—never-ending projects to move my work forward and the next class to teach and the grocery shopping and laundry to fold and messes to tidy and always, always, always, someone needing me. Every second of every day, at work and home, can feel consumed by need. "Feed me! Help me! Show me! Inspire me! Fill me!"

I am Mom. I am wife. I am teacher. I am mentor. I am boss, graphic designer, marketer, accountant. I am partner, planner, manifester. I am fellow. I am friend.

Sometimes, it feels so heavy, and then I remind myself once again—I'm not the Higher Power. I cannot fill the hole. I cannot quench the God-hunger. It's not my job to fix the world. It's my job to awaken to the presence of God that's within me. I can put down the psychological burden and trust.

So today, I sit on my mat, with the morning sun filtering through the trees. I practice asanas, move my body, and try to find Stillness before the day starts and the drowning begins.

Where are you, Love? I wonder. I stand myself up and lean against the rail, letting the breeze carry my words more quickly to the open sky.

Where are you, Peace? Why can't I find you? What do I need to do?

I mentally flip through lists and resolves—maybe when I finish this project, maybe if I write more often in my journal, maybe when our kids are older…the breeze settles and I pause and allow my eyes to gently close. My breath becomes a glacier gliding over my cluttered mind. My heart expands and my mind clears. Each inhale, a sheet of ice freezing out all the unsettled debris, clearing space that seemed impossible just seconds earlier. Each exhale, a release of all the notions between myself and the Now.

Tectonic plates collide through the muck of ego identities and expectations, and my perspective begins to shift. I am not irreplaceable. I am not the only one holding this up—at work or at home. When I feel overwhelmed, I can ask for help. When I feel resentful, I'm responsible for saying no. This isn't a test. It's a playground. *What parts of my internal landscape need to be reshaped here? What do I need to let go of right now to feel peace?* My exhale becomes an excavation of the fears and beliefs that make things so heavy and tight.

For one magical moment, it is just Me. No breeze. No thoughts. No words. No lists. Just breath and peace and Oneness, and stillness so spacious, I suddenly *know*. Silly me. How could I forget again? I cannot grasp for God in the trees or clouds. Peace is as elusive as the breeze when I try to pin It down in my lists and tasks. I cannot capture Magic and keep It on my shelf. That just isn't how this works. The Divine works in me like It does in the Universe itself—through *expansion*. When It's here, I feel the extension in every cell of my body. I know it like I know my own reflection in the mirror.

Ahh, there you are, Love. You are right where You have always been. Where you always are. I don't need to go looking for You, in the world and the busy and the lists and the titles and the grasping and the stuff. You are safely tucked where You will always be… Here… Now…right at the very center of Me. You have been here, waiting underneath my tricks, all along. And each day, each beautiful or ugly or painful or glorious day, is my sacred opportunity to peel back the cloudy haze and be still enough to find You again.

Don't You worry. I will keep on coming.

I let my clinging resolves float away on the next gust of air and watch them disappear in the no-thing that stretches to space above, an endless horizon, the open sky a reflection of the same vastness I feel within my own soul.

NOTE TO SELF
BECKY MOLLER, JANUARY 2024

When in struggle,
Trust.

Your Highest Self is
Waiting
To bring you back to
Alignment
and

She knows
Just how to do it.
Just because you can't feel the

F - L - O - W

Doesn't mean it's
Not there.

CHAPTER THIRTY-FOUR

WHOLENESS

Healing is wholeness. This much I've learned. The more I surrender to the Waves, the less confined I am by the smallness of my personality and abilities. The more I know my Self as no-thing, the more I Am Everything. Through this Practice and my work, I see myself at times become an open, empty space for That which serves. What is needful changes moment to moment, and my abilities adapt to meet what's here.

At times, I am Earth: establishing schedules, systems, and structures to hold our growing mindfulness community on a journey of self-discovery. I build web pages, design emails, train and manage instructors, welcome participants, and create and edit our course materials.

Other times, I am Fire: advocating for the overlooked and unseen, teaching with passion and Presence, holding a frequency that warms the room and ignites hearts to inspired action.

Then, I am Water: able to flow with flexible solutions, pivoting to catch the current as it shifts direction, surrendering timelines and outcomes, holding it all lightly, playing with it as a magical, mysterious Game.

And then amazingly, I am Air: lost in the clouds of new creation for days and weeks on end when the Flow is strong and Something Beautiful wants to be born into being.

In Presence, I am a portal to All that exists: the once-frozen molecule that's learning to simply surrender itself to a much greater Power moving freely on Its way. It's not my Wave I'm riding. The more I know this, the less I get in the way. With God at my center, I am enough, and the right people always seem to appear to fill the gaps. In the end, none of this work has much of anything to do with me. It's only when I forget this crucial fact that things feel heavy and hard.

And each day, it's all a Practice—for me as much as anyone, housed at long last under my own name and brand: Undone Academy at beckymoller.com.

The consistent magic in this work, whether in embodiment classes, mindfulness groups, or one-on-one mentoring, comes from constantly guiding things back to Presence, through the body. No matter what specific lens we might explore week to week, everything in my method speaks to the same essence: the Divine connection that's right here, ever-present, and always available. My job is simply to hold that space and gently offer the embodied cues to help my students become more present, conscious, and aware of themselves.

Nowadays, I don't even know what to call the Universal Divine that flows with so much free range inside me. I rarely think of my Higher Power as a Being these days...so often It's simply the expansive sensation of spaciousness...an undefinable warmth that feels like Love, connecting me to every living thing, making life so unspeakably beautiful that I want to weep at the miraculous fact that I'm here living it. This indefinable essence is what God is to me now: in me and around me, the essence of everything I see.

It's always simple questions that bring people back to the Real, that help us peel back the layers of small self that obscure the Vast One. And through embodied Practice, it's easier to get there. When I lead a class, I drop into my own body, connect with my own breath, and guide my students to do the same. Once the breath is deep and steady, we might make the mind like an open sky, allowing thoughts and stories to float through like clouds. The words I speak spill over spontaneously from the unfolding Presence that fills the room. My phrases come out slow and intentional. I don't want to get in the way; I'm simply giving shape to the energy and images that flood my mind-body-spirit. They emanate from the Presence we've built here together. We might work with a specific memory, a specific situation, a self-defeating behavior, or a Part we want to understand better. We watch for an attached narrative and observe it in a detached space of loving curiosity. Trailing from each narrative, an emotion may arise. I might ask,

See if you can let the narrative float by and fix your attention on the felt-sense of the emotion it brings with it.

Where do you feel the emotion in your body? Can you locate it?

What is the quality of it? Its texture? Temperature?

Is it sharp or soft?

Does it pulsate and grow?

Is it moving around or staying still in one place?

Watch how it starts to fade as the narrative passes.

Notice how the intensity of the emotion simply dissolves when you remove the story that feeds it.

Can you feel the power of bringing mindfulness to these waves of experience?

The comfort and perspective in impermanence?

Imagine yourself as the wide-open sky. Everything we think and feel is just passing weather.

But we...we are the vast spaciousness with the capacity to hold it.

Whatever you're moving through today...whatever it is...there is room for this, too.

Intuitively, I'm teaching the very tools that brought me to this moment; the tools I've deepened through a dozen trainings, the tools I still practice daily. The Undone, Awakening Framework I've developed is a visual description of how I move through life and how I work with my clients.

The medicine is the set of simple practices that uncover Its Source, a prescription that never fails when there's no ego or agenda in it. The tools come from within, connecting people to their own power and authority instead of mine or anyone else's. Every time I witness another's awakening to this Light within themselves, my life fills with meaning. And embodied Practice isn't the only place it's happening—running retreats, training teachers, individual mentoring, leading multiple groups each week—our space has expanded for both men and women.

It turns out that men need this awakening as desperately as we women do, and we're in it together.

I've learned so much as I've sat with men struggling to share emotions and experiences they've never put to words. It's a foreign language for so many to feel their feet and sense their own inner body aliveness. It's an emotional intelligence that most have never tapped into—have never known existed.

THE UNDONE, AWAKENING FRAMEWORK
"Conscious Awareness—driven by compassionate curiosity."

There's never been a safe space like Undone Academy for the majority, with tangible tools to explore their inner world and acknowledge that they do, in fact, feel things other than anger, sex drive, irritation, or "fine."

In Utah, the shared female traumas of never-enoughness around appearance and self-sacrifice seem to reflect in similar ways for our masculine counterparts. For men, it's typically: not successful enough, not rich enough, often not righteous enough, and almost always, not enough sex. The longer I listen, the more they teach me, and the more my focus is drawn toward the wounds underneath the coping.

What I once defined as culturally rampant sexual addiction now appears fundamentally different to me: what I might call collective trauma. By now I've heard hundreds of stories of early male sexual experiences, and I regularly witness the reverberating waves of shame that still grip grown men in the retelling of these memories. For most, this shame is attached to entirely normal developmental behaviors.

The trauma, or soul-separation, seemed to occur the moment they awakened to the inescapable reality that they are, indeed, a sexual being, and had no way to integrate that fact into their definition of "goodness," into a healthy self-concept. If what we resist persists, it's no wonder we see so many Utah Mormons identify and behave as sex addicts. If the disowned parts of ourselves become open outlets just waiting for someone to plug into, it's no wonder so many struggle with compulsive thoughts and behaviors. If healing equals wholeness, rigid, fear-based morality never gives us a chance.

This kind of setup creates a soul-level split. We can't belong to ourselves and also belong to our caregivers and community...or even and especially, our conception of God. We can't authentically own our emotions and experience and still be safely seen, even by ourselves. So, people, especially children, will cut off or repress parts of themselves because they must in order to survive. And when this happens, we lose the wholeness of the Self. We start to operate in the world through games, hiding, coping, manipulating, escaping, and addiction.

Sexually and otherwise, this split often manifests as a painful pendulum: repression on one end, fixation on the other. We might spend decades on either end of the cycle, but both are laced with shame and justification, as well as a desperate insistence from something inside of us that we're just trying to get our needs met. And this part of us is exactly right. This part of us knows that in some fundamental way, we have lost our wholeness.

This is the adaptive pattern for all of us in trauma, and sexuality is no different than any other wound or coping strategy. But it's not more or kinkier sex that will solve the problem. Just like it's not another beer, it's not being prettier, or sexier, or more perfect. What solves the problem is becoming aware of the wound underneath the pain, underneath the fixation, and owning it as our own. Allowing ourselves to meet it with love and compassion, to feel and know that pain and that wounded part of ourselves. It's bringing it to the Higher Self we all carry within us, whose qualities of love, clarity, courage, compassion, and curiosity intuitively know how to bring it to safety and integrate it as part of us with perfect alignment. I know this from my own experience, and my training has only deepened that conviction.

Healing is wholeness. It's as simple as that.

I've never once met with a student or sponsee or seen an instance in myself or Nate where this fundamental Truth hasn't lined up and pointed people to greater freedom. It makes me wonder at all the unnecessary suffering we create, men and women alike, simply by our fundamental misunderstanding of what it is to be human.

And what is it to be human? Flawed, limited, and in desperate want of belonging. And yet, a conduit for the infinite, a never-again-to-be-duplicated manifestation of the Divine. All of it. The more I feel and face my own humanity, the more sacred I hold the same in others. I can only love another to the limits of my ability to love myself.

This is so much the purpose of this book and the Undone programs: to speak to the deepest and fullest level of this humanity, to expand our capacity to love, to free our shadows, right our wrongs, and reclaim ALL parts of ourselves. Each is beautiful. Each belongs. Each can be wisely integrated into the whole. And as much as I love my work with others, the people I want this freedom for most profoundly are the people within the walls of my own home.

"Daily Living is the Spiritual Practice" is the Eckhart Tolle quote that hangs on our wall, and rightly so. Nothing is more important to me than how we show up for each other—because who we are in the privacy of our own home points us closest to what's Real. We can only teach what we are, and nobody sees this more transparently than our partners and children.

I love each of my five children with all the fierce passion of a mother-bear heart, and it hasn't been easy to watch them wounded through both Nate's and my humanity. But it's also been amazing to witness them being shaped by our healing. They've been swimming in gritty, unpretentious water since most of them were too young to remember anything else.

It's carved out the kind of strength and inner knowing that bubbled out of my 16-year-old Madi's mouth as we walked home after a typical Sunday. With sincerity, I had asked my girls if it was possible for them to be open at church after observing them spend another church meeting entirely checked out on their phones. They had bristled at the question and lengthened their strides. I had to jog to keep up, their long legs now inches past mine.

"Girls, slow down… I'm not trying to criticize or shame you… I'm asking you a sincere question. Can you pause for a moment? I really want to know… do you think it's possible for you to open your heart at church?"

For a moment, I thought they would stalk off ahead of me in silence, but suddenly I saw Madi's face soften, her eyes begin to shine, the red blush around her nose and lips the indicator of her honest engagement. She took a deep breath and tried to put her heart into words.

"No, Mom, it's not… I know this has been a safe place for you, I know you care about the community, I know you don't want to be ostracized from the neighborhood. I know you have a lot of years behind you, which makes this an okay place for you to be, even with all the stuff you disagree with. But it's not like that for us. It's *not* a safe place for us. I don't ever feel safe here. I don't ever feel seen here. I don't feel like there's ever a question asked that doesn't already assume it knows the answer. My experience, my perspective… it doesn't matter here. There's already a "right answer" they're trying to get me to say, and if mine doesn't match, then I'm wrong and they're right. And that doesn't feel safe for me. So, we come for an hour because you make us, and because it's better than coming for two. And yes, I can be quiet, but I really can't be open. Because it's all the same conversation, Mom. There's nothing for me here. So, I'll put in my time, but that's all I can do."

Her voice was strong but shaky, full of conviction and passion…and pain. Her pain surprised me. It also made sense, and it mattered to me, even as I felt my body respond—my stomach tightening and my chest restricting in defensive anxiety. Yes, critical thinking makes things complicated, but I will never again ask my kids or myself to back away from asking questions about what isn't adding up in our lived experience.

In some ways, they are so much stronger than I've ever been. They have so much less attachment to the way they're perceived, so much less need to be approved of than I had at their age or maybe even now. Even though they're mine, they're made from a sturdier mettle. And I would never dream of standing in the way of their own unique and messy evolution. They are my everything, and as they grow into young adults, my main practice is to step back, one moment at a time, and use my energy to consistently communicate: *I love you. I trust that you can move through this. I trust that you've got everything you need to figure this out. I know You're in there.*

And I do.

Nate is my life partner in every sense of the word. As we both continue to evolve, I get to taste the sweetness of watching him reclaim himself in deeper and deeper ways. I witness him struggle in the deep, fight to stay in the moment, in the body, when it's so much easier to check out, to browse ESPN, or discharge his anger and insecurities at me or the kids. He is still fully committed to sobriety, although both of our perspectives around sexual addiction and acting out have changed dramatically. Sobriety today means being aware of and accountable for our own self-protective coping, the narratives we choose to indulge in, and how fully we allow ourselves to be seen.

Regular visits with our therapist are still an important tool in his toolkit, and in our joint sessions, I've had the humbling opportunity to witness Nate awaken to the traumas that were always underneath the addiction: the real wounds that always needed healing. For the first time ever, I see vulnerability overflow from the armored heart that guarded itself through decades of pushing away and numbing.

Through Internal Family Systems therapy, he is introduced to his Fear-of-Abandonment Part, and we both witness his Shameful Part surface. It thinks it's protecting him through its harsh and rigid expectations, criticism, and self-rejection, so unforgiving of his mistakes and so afraid his son will follow in his footsteps. I watch this Part have an entire conversation with our therapist, so desperate to protect his son from his own self, so filled with self-hatred and distrust. I watch Nate struggle to talk this Part down, to coax it into believing that it could, somehow, let go.

Over weeks and months, I behold these sacred moments with tears often streaming down my face. What I used to see as narcissistic traits or addict behaviors I now recognize as the same emotionally immature coping strategies I see at times in the vulnerable and fearful parts of all of us, myself included. Our therapist helps Nate meet each part with compassion, with tenderness, with gratitude for its effort in so desperately trying to protect him. And when she invites his Higher Self into the space, my heart bursts as I witness the obvious shift in body, mind, and spirit. With simple acknowledgement and the gentlest invitation, I feel the fearful clinging parts inside of my husband begin to surrender. To release their frenzied grip on the steering wheel. To let Something Higher drive. I am witnessing Nate wake up to his True Self, and my love for him grows like never before.

Finally, after all those years of *addiction* recovery, Nate's *trauma* is finally getting its due.

Adrienne Rich writes in *On Lies, Secrets, and Silence*: "An honorable, human relationship—that is, one in which two people have the right to use the word 'love'—is a process, delicate, often terrifying to both persons involved, a process of refining the truths they can tell each other. It is important to do this because it breaks down human self-delusion and isolation. It is important to do this because in doing so we do justice to our own complexity. It is important to do this because we can count on so few people to go that hard way with us."

Nate and I are certainly on that hard way, a journey which continues to be delicate and terrifying at times, and for which I'm eternally grateful. So much of who I am and the work I feel called to has come from the impetus of *us*—*our* story. And while I mostly teach straightforward principles and practices, there are times it serves to share the deeper well from which this journey came. This book is perhaps the most significant example.

I am humbled and, in some ways, awestruck that Nate has never seemed to resent me in this purpose. Never wished either one of us to step back and hide when it was clear that sharing could serve someone in need. Nate, my partner, my sweetheart, has stood by me and honored me as my own separate person with my own growth experiences to own and share as I feel called. He has held sacred all that's come from our journey together and been my greatest cheerleader with each step forward in my work. He may not feel called to write his own book, but he's the first to share in a group meeting or a one-on-one interaction. No need to hide, defend, or feel ashamed. We are, both of us, an ongoing work in progress. Humans on a journey; undone, unafraid. His courage to stand in his light and truth has, in so many ways, strengthened my own.

Healing is wholeness, this much I've learned. No parts left out. Each aspect of Self, a gift. Darkness and Light, each has a purpose and a place. Each is asking us to set a place at the table, to pull up a chair, to listen and honor. Each is asking to play its part as we make our way through life. I can only recognize this in others because I've come to know it so well in myself.

And this is my lifelong work, in my personal life as well as at Undone Academy: healing and wholeness, mindfulness and meaning. Week after week, we help our students ground into Love, until they know It with their entire bodies. Over time, we gently guide them to uncover the parts of themselves they've abandoned, helping them identify the beliefs they've mistakenly internalized.

So often, people can't feel these parts, can't connect to these beliefs in any deep way until they're in their bodies: through yoga, through breath, even just through Presence. And suddenly, there it is, a waterfall of emotion. A rainstorm of insight. A deep knowing of what was broken, and how it needs to be healed. Again and again, I watch it happen, and I'm amazed every time. They're just like me; their path, so much like mine. We're all so much the same.

Healing is wholeness. Everything you are looking for is already right here within you, exactly as you are in this very moment.

What you're running from might be your very invitation to something deeper: a life with greater purpose, love, freedom, and joy. I see it in my work only because I've known it in my bones. We're all the same, really: connected by the Namaste that binds us irrevocably together. The same Light. The same longings. The same ego waiting in the wings, loudest in moments of greatest distress and success. The same gentle sensations that swim inside us, waving flags to remind us who we really are, and that Something inside us knows the way back. The same terror in leaving the comfort of certainty. The same despairing free fall in the face of lost illusions. The same wrestle in learning to trust. The same eventual arrival that gently informs us there is nothing, after all, to forgive.

In my work, I see so many people who come for healing, blinded by stories, armored with identities, both bad and good, both right and wrong. I see it in them because I know it in myself. We're lost in our narratives, entrenched in our victimhood, trapped behind shells of self-protection that keep us looking everywhere but within ourselves for answers. The seed only cracks when we're willing to let go and finally see: our story is everyone's story. It's mine and it's yours, no matter the shameful or shocking details. And they're all pointing to the same thing: the One Truth of Who We Are, and a million pathways to get there.

One moment at a time, your own mind-body-spirit is the only compass that can reliably light your unique way. Anyone who tells you differently is selling you something.

WATCHING YOU HEAL
BECKY MOLLER, JANUARY 2024

Watching you heal
Is like witnessing the sun warm the
Glistening ice on a
Solitary branch.

Patient Light
Softens the rigid glare,
Melts away the brittle shell,
Uncovers what's always
Been

Real, Raw,
And
Unalterably
Connected
Underneath.

It's miraculous
To see the
you
that's been
Trying so hard,
So long,
to survive

Finally
Let go
And *allow* your
Heart
To melt
Open.

Ta-Da!!!
It's *You* in there.

EPILOGUE

I am on an airplane from Wisconsin to Utah on New Year's Day, almost nine years now from Rock Bottom. My kids are old enough that our seats are scattered, and I somehow wind up sitting alone. I don't mind—more time to catch up on work. I've spent the past seven days savoring my family and the sharp contrast of darkness and light in the Wisconsin north woods, where we hunker down in cabins to welcome the New Year. I've been using the plane time to download the insights gathered from this sacred pause, and I've noted my official New Year intentions before diving into weekly emails:

- Create more space for writing, creativity
- Trust the Flow and honor what is present: Don't try to force things, trust the timing and energy of what is arising. Know that it is all that is needed in the moment and that it all fits into a bigger picture that's being orchestrated by God/Universe/Love
- Finish and publish my Betrayal Trauma Manuscript

My Betrayal Trauma Manuscript still feels like a precious jewel I keep putting on the back burner. Since I stepped into administrative roles way back with the Foundation, there's always been two dozen more urgent tasks to keep up with. And besides, I've had no idea what to do with the project. Before I started Body and Soul, I blindly sent the manuscript to a handful of editors and publishers I'd found on Google with little to no response. So many won't touch poetry, and I am utterly unconnected. I have no idea how to break into the publishing world.

I'm happily typing away when my seatmate leans over.

"I see you're writing about abundance. Can I ask what you do for a living?" she inquires behind her paper mask. She's young, maybe late-twenties, and I've hardly noticed her aside from the occasional coughs that she points towards the window. I'm not usually one for small talk with strangers, but she seems genuinely interested, and I love talking about my work.

"I run a Mindfulness program," I share. "It's kind of like 12-step, but it incorporates mindfulness principles and practices and embodiment—like fitness and yoga. It's kind of hard to explain."

It's immediately apparent that I'm speaking her language, and we are quickly engrossed in deep conversation, our similar stories unfolding with the ease of long-time friendship. Marissa grew up in Wisconsin but lives out west now, just like me, and just happens to be a poet, author, editor, and publisher in the spiritual self-help genre. Before our flight lands, Marissa has tentatively offered to become the editor of my Betrayal Trauma manuscript.

"Call me when you get home," she says. "I'll need you to send over what you've got and see if it's something we can work with. I'll work up a proposal, and we'll figure out what feels right. Sound good?"

I can't believe it. I float through Denver airport toward our connecting flight.

I cannot freaking believe it. Moments after putting that intention out into the Universe. From behind a mask, as far from anything I could control as the waves on the Pacific Ocean itself. Marissa, the exact person I've been looking for these past six years: a poet and editor with recovery experience, with spiritual insight and perspective, and with flexible time and open-minded perspective, has fallen straight out of the sky and landed in my lap.

Finally…after all this time and all the Flow I've followed that's taken me away from it: my baby, my memoir, my tender labor of love, is ready to be born, and I've somehow stumbled upon the perfect midwife.

* * *

A 13th-century Sufi poet named Hafiz channeled some of the most beautiful spiritual poems ever written. Whenever I forget who God is, I pick up Hafiz and my whole soul remembers.

The story of Hafiz is as epic as his ecstatic poetry. A young peasant, Hafiz, works in a bakery and spots a woman of such breathtaking beauty that for weeks and months, his only thought is of her. She consumes all his desire, even though his plain appearance and low social position would seem to prevent any romantic relationship between them. Poems and songs pour from his passionate heart, professing an undying desire for her beauty. Soon, all the townspeople are repeating his lyrics and ballads.

In lovesick desperation, Hafiz dedicates himself to a miraculous feat. A 40-day vigil at the tomb of a local saint will supposedly earn any man his heart's desire, requiring such superhuman willpower and pure intention that God Himself must reward it. Night after night, Hafiz leaves the bakery and sits at the tomb without food or sleep, sustained only by longing for his beloved.

On the final night of his vigil, the glorious angel Gabriel appears to Hafiz, just as promised. "My child, what is your heart's desire?"

But in the Presence of Divinity, Hafiz is suddenly speechless, completely overwhelmed in a flood of Love and Light. He forgets every earthly desire as every cell in his body awakens with remembrance of the true Beloved. With absolute clarity, Hafiz proclaims, "I want *God*!"

Hafiz's poetry is a true manifestation of this most fervent desire, his hundreds of passionate love poems a still-vibrant portal to the Universal Beloved. His verses have passed through generations and still provide a reliable map to the Infinite, still relevant, centuries later.[11]

It is all just a Love Game, he teases. *It is all a fantastical trick of the Magi… you are the Sun in drag…don't you see? You are God in disguise.*[12]

Hafiz was just a simple baker, with no great position, appearance, wealth, or strength. When he chose God above all else, when he decided to follow Love, he had no idea where that choice would take him. He had no way of knowing that his pure desire and passionate words would impact millions of people for centuries. His lovesick soul thought it was securing a wife. What it found was the entire Universe.

When life becomes a Love Game, you never know what will happen. You might just catch a Wave you never knew was coming, but here's the catch. It will probably want to take you in a totally different direction from where you thought you were going. Only *you* can decide: do I let go and trust the Flow or do I grip tighter and paddle more desperately against the current?[13]

---

11 Hafiz (1999). *The Gift.* Translated by Daniel Ladinsky. Penguin. Pages 11–12.
12 Hafiz (1999). *The Gift.* Translated by Daniel Ladinsky. Penguin. Page 252.
13 Hafiz (1999). *The Gift.* Translated by Daniel Ladinsky. Penguin. Pages 11–12.

Betrayal and trauma were once massive, unwelcome detours on my pathway to perfection: glaciers that turned my world upside down. At rock bottom, I thought what I needed was to get back on track. But what I got was a *new* track: a carving out I didn't know I needed, muck up to my elbows I didn't know I'd accumulated, and a new horizon I had no idea I was hungry for—much bigger than betrayal or anything else that came before. What I found was as wide and inconceivable as the Ocean itself: a reclamation of my whole Self, more able to embrace all I now recognize in the other. One in a great human family. Everything and no-thing, all at once.

Trauma is part of every life and the impetus of most spiritual transformations. It touches every crevice of our identity and every person on the planet. Being human means being traumatized. We can't wake from our illusions without feeling disillusioned.

So, how to befriend this inevitable experience as part of the Love Game?

You've got to be skeptical enough to notice who's selling you safety that isn't adding up—and brave enough to start asking why.

You've got to be open-minded enough to welcome the shitshows with the same enthusiasm as the picture-perfect postcards.

Be a student of life and expect that She's sharing Her secrets in every moment—*pay attention!*

Stop taking selfies and looking for yourself in the images. Start closing your eyes and knowing your Self as the humming energy inside.

You've got to believe that the exact right Love Note will show up at the exact right time to help you find your next right step, all along the way. Look for them everywhere—in sunsets, in people, in totems, in timing. You will one day look back and recognize a magical trail leading you to where you now stand. You would never have found your way without it. *Be grateful.*

You'll discover that every single part of yourself is useful and purposeful. Each has a deep and intuitive intelligence and is worthy of your love, acknowledgement, and gratitude. You'll find the Universe inside your loved ones as wide and mysterious as the Universe inside of you, and you'll more easily recognize the privilege to evolve alongside another for a lifetime, creating something utterly unique that could only ever belong to the two of you; maybe even a marriage of thriving adventure, despite the inevitable muck.

Heck—you might even find yourself flying through the air and have the exact person for whom you've been waiting for over six years fall right into your lap. Embrace the breadcrumbs that beckon you forward and allow the path to evolve as it will; few endings ever turn out the exact way we started.

Our *trauma* is so often the tool that carves us out, that forces us to craft the embodied map from fear to freedom, that backs us into the corner where we've nowhere else to look for refuge but *right here*. And here It Is: the stillness, peace, magic, rest. The Light of Awareness. The Essential Self.

When the Light moves through us, we make the world a better place, no matter how big or small our place in it. We literally become a conduit for the Divine...*we are God* moving in the world. No matter how public or private, in these sacred moments, we're doing the most important thing anyone could ever do. We're living our purpose, and every cell in our body knows it.

Love is the turning point. Love is the magic ingredient—not as an idea or proclamation—but as an embodied longing that can't be contained. Love as expansive as the Universe inside you, Love so big it might explode from your fingertips and toes. Love that spreads its arms wide, forgets everything else, and exclaims, "I want *God!*" Love that spends the rest of its life writing love songs—whether anyone will ever read them or not.

Because each and every one of us has a purpose, a place, a gift to give the world that nobody else can offer. And not in spite of who we are and where we've been...but *because* of it.

You don't know where your Wave will take you. You can't always choose what your purpose will be. You will only know that you feel it in your bones when Something is urging you forward, when the Voice won't stop whispering in your ear:

That is the Wave you don't want to let pass you by. *That* is the life you don't want to miss.

It's a game of letting go, again and again, of surrendering to the mystery, of embracing the nothingness of who you are so Everything can flow through you.

Trauma, mindfulness, embodiment, healing, relationships, career, life itself—it's all really a Love Game. Come, roll up your sleeves, and play with me.

AFTERWORD
by Nesha Woodhouse

Before 2019, I didn't know Becky well, yet I had always felt a connection—she was a parent who really understood what Lifehouse Performing Arts Academy, my dance studio in Salem, Utah, was about. I could sense we were on a similar wavelength, even though we had only had brief conversations. Early that spring, Becky knocked on my door. Her daughter was a dance friend of my youngest child, and they were having a playdate. She held a manuscript in her hands and asked if I had a minute to talk. We visited for five minutes, and she shared briefly that the manuscript was the beginnings of her story and journey of healing over the last five years through betrayal trauma. She expressed respect for my busy schedule and said there was no expectation of a timeline, and to read it whenever I had the time.

Little did Becky know that the night before her visit, I had been on the floor of my bedroom, curled in the fetal position, crying uncontrollably, feeling like a crazy person, wanting desperately to escape from my body, my brain, and the overwhelming negative emotions flooding my system.

The worst part: I wasn't having this intense experience because of something truly catastrophic that logically warranted such a drastic response. Nope, all that had happened was my husband sharing concern that I had gained weight over the last three years and that he was struggling with being attracted to me. The more he tried to lay out his case in his logical, matter-of-fact way, the crazier and more out of control I felt. My emotional response was met by my husband's confusion alongside my own personal shame. Yep, I was a mess; something inside of me was broken.

I started reading Becky's book that evening, thinking I was going to help her: She had seemingly come to me for guidance as some sort of mentor. Instead, I found myself devouring its pages, finding language, understanding, and insight I had been looking for my entire life. I started to connect the dots; I found compassion for myself and my ridiculous behavior the night before.

Memories resurface and suddenly, reading Becky's book, I am flooded with pain—pain I have buried and ignored for years. Becky's manuscript and friendship give me hope that I can be with it. And, in fact, I have to be with it to heal it. I have to stop trying to control it and allow it to show me the deepest parts of myself. I realize that I have unrecognized, unhealed trauma. These experiences weren't logically a big deal, and yet the stories and belief systems they had created had been subconsciously controlling me for years. I start to recognize this as *my* pain and realize that it is my job to do the inner work to transform and heal it.

I tearfully called Becky the next day to tell her of my trauma meltdown. That conversation started a beautiful and important friendship, and I knew something else at that moment: Becky was the person I had been waiting for to carry out a vision I'd had five years earlier: Lifehouse Body & Soul, a place where people moved their bodies not to achieve a better physique, but to create a body and soul connection inside themselves.

Lifehouse Body & Soul (2021-2025) was formed on the shoulders of Becky's willingness, work ethic, love of people, and her own light. As we started discussing the vision for this program, Becky, through her own experience, recognized that the path to waking up and healing was really the same regardless of what your story and trauma have been. What was created and its impact has been a healing balm for my own soul, a source of sacred connection and a joyful endeavor.

As I finished Becky's completed manuscript, *Undone, Unafraid*, I was flooded with deep gratitude and awe as I considered this full circle moment of the original rough draft that started our beautiful friendship. This book feels sacred on so many levels. I marvel and bow to the courage and strength of Becky to do the hardest work there is—the true inner work of undoing, unraveling, and healing in a raw, real, go-for-the-throat sort of way. No excuses, no justifications, no coping strategies—just the relentless pursuit of truth and freedom.

She is a pioneer. She paid a great price for her transformation—the willingness to go to the deepest places of pain within her soul. Her willingness to thoughtfully create this book, her courage to share all of the beautiful, messy details, has transformed my life. The discoveries she has made on her journey will go forth and help so many others find their own unraveling—their own healing path to freedom and to God. I love you forever, my dear soul sister, and consider you and this work one of my life's greatest blessings.

And to you, dear reader, whether you're just beginning your inner journey, are in the messy middle, or far along the path of transformation, the most important work we do in this life is the work we do inside of ourselves. The biggest indicator of our quality of life is not the status of our bank accounts, the prestige of our position, the circumstances of our lives—it is the awakened state of our own heart—the alignment of our soul: mind, body, and spirit. It is the deep and abiding connection to ourselves, to others, and to a Higher Power. May the contents of this book give you the inspiration and courage to start your own process of discovery, waking up, healing, and awareness. May you feel the desire to do this inner work more than you want anything else; for, it is the greatest gift you will ever give yourself.

Your awakened heart is the greatest gift you can give the world. —Nesha Woodhouse

Author's Note

This work is the fruition of the past ten years of my life. It's been my baby, and I most gratefully acknowledge the sacrifices of my husband, Nate, and my five brave and beautiful children, who have supported me with so much grace along the way. My story is their story, and I am so grateful for their courage and willingness to be seen as we are—bumps and all. I cannot adequately express the love and gratitude I feel for each one of them.

We offer our story with the intent that in it, you may see yourself and find hope. No matter what darkness you may be facing, there is a way out. You are not alone. You are not dependent upon anyone or anything outside of yourself to be okay. You're not doomed to suffer and endure. You can thrive, expand, and grow. You can *be still and know*, even when doing so defies all logic. There really is a peace that passeth all understanding, and you'll find it within yourself.

No matter your age or circumstances, it is never too late to create a life you truly love and live it with passion. You are here for a reason. You have a gift to give the world that only you can give.

Every experience and trait you have—including the ugly ones—qualifies you uniquely for your purpose and is meant to serve the world in meaningful ways. Your desire for more is neither superficial nor selfish. In fact, your full and deep healing will serve the Greater Good more than any other single thing you could do with your time. Dedicate yourself to it, and your life will be transformed in ways you could not possibly imagine.

If my story resonates with you, please know that a similar awakening can be yours. There's nothing special about me that is not also in you. All that is required is a willing heart and a dedicated decision to show up and do the work.

When life changes, it's easy to feel lost, without community or structure. Generally speaking, we humans don't thrive on our own. Most of us need people, consistency, and practices to stay aligned and moving in a positive direction.

If you're looking for a framework to deeply heal unresolved traumas, practical tools to improve behaviors and relationships, and also the spiritual space to find your own authentic path, this is what my work is all about, and I would truly love to hear from you. You can find me at www.beckymoller.com.

This has become my catchall for the mindfulness-based, trauma-informed resources I've created, including individual mentoring, free webinars, live retreats, and my signature online program, Undone Academy: A Mindful Framework for Healing Almost Anything. Through this platform, you can plug into a supportive community and universal practices for healing and growth, no matter where you live.

If you're ready for progress, these tools can help you find your Self. You're worth every effort.

Don't settle for survival. Decide to thrive.

Learn more at https://beckymoller.com.

www.beckymoller.com

Further Resources

Since January 2021, Becky Moller has been building original resources to support others on their own journey of trauma healing and spiritual awakening. We'd love to help you clear space, rebuild, and eventually find your own Wave.

Available Resources

www.beckymoller.com & Undone Academy
https://www.beckymoller.com, becky@beckymoller.com

Available Resources Include:
- Undone Academy: A Mindful Framework for Healing Almost Anything (year-round curriculum, weekly group meetings, embodied practice)
- Individual Mentoring (one-to-one sessions with Becky)
- Masterclasses and DIY Courses
- Women's Retreats (typically held in spring)
- Couple's Retreats (typically held in fall)
- Silent Retreats (typically held in January)

Free Meditations and Mindful Living Tips released weekly on our YouTube channel: Becky Moller on YouTube
https://www.youtube.com/channel/UC8wzQA5FDVaTYUPox_NACSA

We'd love to see you at an upcoming Retreat or online with our next launch of Undone Academy. Individual Mentoring is reserved for those participating in our programs, as space is limited. When you're ready, come find us and take your journey to the next level.

www.beckymoller.com

About the Author

BECKY MOLLER is a spiritual seeker, writer, and mindfulness teacher who lives in Spanish Fork, Utah, with her husband, five children, and three cats. With a BA in English Education, Minors in Music and Marriage, Family & Human Development from Brigham Young University, and a 2-year certification as a Mindfulness and Meditation Teacher, she now offers fellow spiritual seekers a collection of comprehensive mindfulness programs that operate year-round as a structure to hold a lifelong journey of awakening through beckymoller.com online, with live options locally in Spanish Fork. You can also find her on YouTube at beckymoller or on Instagram @undoneacademy.

REVIEWS

"If you have ever felt betrayed, you know the deep prison of darkness, shame, rage, and hurt that it evokes. In this raw and beautifully written memoir, Becky Moller offers a pathway out of this darkness, one that brings healing to our hearts and reclaims the luminosity of our spirit."
—**Tara Brach,** Ph.D., spiritual teacher, psychologist and author of *Radical Compassion* and *Radical Acceptance*

"It is a rare privilege to be invited so deeply into another's soul, which Becky does with a beautiful vulnerability. This heartfelt book is clearly a labor of love, vulnerable and exposing in a way that both excavated parts of my own soul and set it at ease, mirroring and reflecting so much of my own inner angst and struggle, trial, and triumph. This memoir is a beautiful blend of emotion, authenticity, and encouragement, which will be a mirror both welcome and uncomfortable; a portal to growth, serving as an un-earthing of previously unexamined shadow, while also filled with beautiful, emotionally moving encouragements to continue on and find the magic in it all. Chills filled me every inch for countless portions of my reading."
—**Alaina Jo,** LCSW, www.resolutiontherapyutah.com

"Becky shares her shock, pain, confusion, and traumatic experiences following the discovery of sexual betrayal in her marriage in an honest way that mirrors the experiences of those who are betrayed in their primary relationships. What makes this book different from others is how it highlights and describes the spiritual impact of trauma, along with practices in communities of faith that sometimes (sadly) only add to the primary trauma. Becky bravely shares her spiritual experiences that contributed to the initial pain of betrayal, and then goes on to share her journey of what she found to be a more healthy and whole spiritual life. Post-traumatic growth, self-love, open-hearted spiritual experiences, and real resilience are possible and are the often-unexpected outcomes after betrayal. If you've been betrayed, you will see yourself in Becky's story. And you'll be encouraged."

—**Barbara Steffens,** PhD, Board Certified Coach, retired professional counselor, Founding president of APSATS (Association for Partners of Sex Addicts Trauma Specialists), Board member emeritus, Co-Author of *Your Sexually Addicted Spouse: How Partners Can Cope and Heal* (Steffens & Means, 2009; 2021)

"Moller's story is vulnerable and raw, but she tells it with great courage and authenticity. Her honesty reveals the complexities of dealing with betrayal trauma, but through her deeply personal journey, a reader can see both her resilience and witness her path towards healing. Moller's compelling narrative offers solace, validation, and empathy for the human experience, holding space for both herself and for her audience."

—**Melissa Davis,** esteemed English professor, critical thinker, and avid reader

"This book unfolds with honesty and self-awareness. It's beautiful and self-reflective to follow the un-doing and re-building of a life, to see it change from fragmented awareness to full, embodied presence. A journey worth reading."

—**Ashley Mae Hoiland,** Artist, mother, and author of *One Hundred Birds Taught Me to Fly*

"Becky's book is a must-read for anyone who's ever had the rug pulled out from under them and feels angry, hurt, confused, and/or completely lost. It's a roadmap to maneuvering through heartbreak with clarity, love, and compassion. Full of the kind of questions to ask ourselves when we feel like we're drowning in grief that can serve not only as a life preserver but a springboard to unimaginable heights."

—**Brielle Wollenzien,** mother of a beautiful human struggling with drug addiction, mixed-faith marriage navigator

"Becky's book is a guide for anyone who is navigating trauma in their lives. Her story provides a template for confronting the narratives that keep us from moving forward through the pain of trauma. I highly recommend this book!"
—**John Wollenzien,** faith transitioner

"*Undone, Unafraid* wrecked me in the best way. It's not just a story about betrayal—it's about what it means to lose everything you thought was safe and still choose to love, still choose to trust. Becky's words are sacred. I found pieces of myself in her grief and her fire."
—**Max Acalde,** spiritual seeker, Death & Rebirth Guide

"This book is a powerful testament to the resilience of the human spirit. Through the lens of betrayal trauma, Becky takes us on a raw and honest journey of awakening. She gives language to the healing and transformation I witness in my clients as a Marriage and Family therapist. After reading, I have a deeper sense of clarity and renewed commitment to mind-body-spirit integration in my own life."
—**Ali Springer,** MFT, pineviewtherapyclinic.com

"A breathtaking journey through the terrain of pain, courage, and the quiet magic of rising again. This book is for anyone who has shattered, grieved, and dared to gather their pieces with trembling hands. It doesn't offer perfection—it offers truth. A luminous reminder that healing is not linear, and resilience is not loud. It is steady, sacred, and beautifully human."
—**Robyn Maria,** Author of *From Surviving to Creating: A Journey to Abundance* and Founder of Unboxed Hearts: A Charity for Foster Children

"This book feels sacred on so many levels. I marvel and bow to the courage and strength of Becky to do the hardest work there is—the true inner work of undoing, unraveling, and healing in a raw, real, go-for-the-throat sort of way. No excuses, no justifications, no coping strategies—just the relentless pursuit of truth and freedom.
"She is a pioneer. She paid a great price for her transformation—the willingness to go to the deepest places of pain within her soul. Her willingness to

thoughtfully create this book, her courage to share all of the beautiful, messy details, has transformed my life. The discoveries she has made on her journey will go forth and help so many others find their own unraveling—their own healing path to freedom and to God. I love you forever, my dear soul sister, and consider you and this work one of my life's greatest blessings.

"And to you, dear reader, whether you're just beginning your inner journey, are in the messy middle, or far along the path of transformation, the most important work we do in this life is the work we do inside of ourselves. The biggest indicator of our quality of life is not the status of our bank accounts, the prestige of our position, the circumstances of our lives—it is the awakened state of our own heart—the alignment of our soul: mind, body, and spirit. It is the deep and abiding connection to ourselves, to others, and to a Higher Power. May the contents of this book give you the inspiration and courage to start your own process of discovery, waking up, healing, and awareness. May you feel the desire to do this inner work more than you want anything else; for, it is the greatest gift you will ever give yourself.

"Your awakened heart is the greatest gift you can give the world."

—**Nesha Woodhouse,** Truth-seeker, Co-founder of Lifehouse Body & Soul, Owner of Lifehouse Performing Arts Academy

www.ingramcontent.com/pod-product-compliance
Lightning Source LLC
Chambersburg PA
CBHW021212130626
46554CB00004B/1189